John Obadiah Justamond, Philip Dormer Chesterfield, Matthew Maty

Miscellaneous Works of the Late Philip Dormer Stanhope - Earl of Chesterfield

Vol. 2

John Obadiah Justamond, Philip Dormer Chesterfield, Matthew Maty

Miscellaneous Works of the Late Philip Dormer Stanhope - Earl of Chesterfield
Vol. 2

ISBN/EAN: 9783744715706

Printed in Europe, USA, Canada, Australia, Japan

Cover: Foto ©Thomas Meinert / pixelio.de

More available books at **www.hansebooks.com**

I.

FOG'S *JOURNAL*[*].

SATURDAY, Jan. 17, 1736. N° 376.

I AM not of the opinion of those who think that our anceſtors were in every reſpect wiſer than we, and who reject every new invention as chimerical, and brand it with the name of project. On the contrary, I am perſuaded, that moſt things are ſtill capable of improvement; for which reaſon I always give a fair and impartial hearing to all new propoſals, and have often, in the courſe of my life, found great advantage by ſo doing.

I very early took Mr. Ward's Drop, notwithſtanding the great diſcouragement it met with, in its infancy, from an honorable author, eminent for his political ſagacity, who aſſerted it to be liquid Popery and

[*] This was one of the weekly publications againſt ſir R. Walpole's adminiſtration. It was firſt intitled Miſt's Journal. I ſuſpect, that lord Cheſterfield had, ſeveral times before, lent his hand to the writers of this witty paper; but I have no authority to aſſert it. This, and the two following eſſays, were generally allowed to be his.

Jacobitiſm. I reaped great benefit from it, and recommended it to ſo many of my friends, that I queſtion whether the author of that great ſpecific is more obliged to any one man in the kingdom than myſelf, excepting one.

I have likewiſe, as well as my brother Caleb *, great hopes of public advantage, ariſing from the ſkill and diſcoveries of that ingenious operator, Dr. Taylor; notwithſtanding the late objections of Mrs. Oſborne †, and her moſt ſubtle diſtinctions between the eye politic, and the eye natural.

Some inventions have been improved ages after their firſt diſcovery, and extended to uſes ſo obvious, and ſo nearly reſembling thoſe for which they were at firſt intended, that it is ſurprizing how they could have ſo long eſcaped the ſagacity of mankind. For inſtance, printing, though uſed but within theſe few centuries, has in reality been invented thouſands of years; and it is aſtoniſhing, that it never occurred to thoſe, who firſt ſtampt images and inſcriptions upon metals, to ſtamp likewiſe their thoughts upon wax, barks of trees, or whatever elſe they wrote upon.

This example ſhould hinder one from thinking any thing brought to its *ne plus ultra* of perfection, when ſo plain an improvement lay for many ages undiſcovered.

* The Craftſman, in which lord Bolingbroke was principally engaged, went under the name of Caleb D'Anvers eſq.

† The ſignature to one of the miniſterial papers being F. Oſborne eſq; (who was the eldeſt and graveſt of their writers), his antagoniſts made an old woman of the author, and nick-named him Mother Oſborne, under which title he figures in the ſecond book of the Dunciad.

The

The ſcheme I am now going to offer to the public is of this nature, ſo very plain, obvious, and of ſuch evident emolument, that I am convinced my readers will both be ſurprized and concerned, that it did not occur to every body, and that it was not put in practice many years ago.

I took the firſt hint of it from an account a friend of mine gave me of what he himſelf had ſeen practiſed with ſucceſs at a foreign court; but I have extended it conſiderably, and I flatter myſelf, that it will, upon the ſtricteſt examination, appear to be the moſt practicable and uſeful, and, at this time, neceſſary project that has, it may be, ever been ſubmitted to the public.

My friend, having reſided ſome time at a very conſiderable court in Germany, had there contracted an intimacy with a German prince, whoſe dominions and revenues were as ſmall as his birth was great and illuſtrious; there are ſome few ſuch in the auguſt Germanic body. This prince made him promiſe, that whenever he ſhould return to England, he would take him in his way, and make him a viſit in his principality. Accordingly, ſome time afterwards, about two years ago, he waited upon his ſerene highneſs; who, being apprized a little beforehand of his arrival, reſolved to receive him with all poſſible marks of honor and diſtinction.

My friend was not a little ſurprized, to find himſelf conducted to the palace through a lane of ſoldiers reſting their firelocks, and the drums beating a march. His highneſs, who obſerved his ſurprize, and who, by the way, was a wag, after the first compliments usual upon such occasions, spoke very gravely to him thus:

"I do not wonder, that you, who are well informed of the narrowness both of my territories "and my fortune, should be astonished at the number of my standing forces; but I must acquaint "you, that the present critical situation of my affairs would not allow me to remain defenceless, "while all my neighbours were arming around me. "There is not a prince near me, that has not made "an augmentation in his forces, some of four, some "of eight, and some even of twelve men; so that "you must be sensible that it would have been consistent neither with my honor nor safety, not to "have increased mine. I have therefore augmented "my army up to forty effective men, from but "eight and twenty that they were before; but, in "order not to overburden my subjects with taxes, "nor oppress them by the quartering and insolence "of my troops, as well as to remove the least suspicion of my designing any thing against their liberties; to tell you the plain truth, my men are "of wax, and exercise by clock-work. You easily "perceive," added he smiling, "that, if I were in "any real danger, my forty men of wax are just as "good a security to me, as if they were of the very "best flesh and blood in Christendom: as for dignity and show, they answer those purposes full as "well; and in the mean time they cost me so little, "that our dinner will be much the better for it."

My friend respectfully signified to him his sincere approbation of his wise and prudent measures, and assured affured me that he had never in his life feen finer bodies of men, better-fized, nor more warlike countenances.

The ingenious contrivance of this wife and warlike potentate ftruck me immediately, as a hint that might be greatly improved to the public advantage, and without any one inconvenience, at leaft that occurred to me. I have turned it every way in my thoughts with the utmoft care, and fhall now prefent it to my readers, willing however to receive any further lights and affiftance from thofe who are more fkilled in military matters than I am.

I afk but two *poftulata*, which I think cannot be denied me; and then my propofal demonftrates its own utility.

Firft, That for thefe laft five and twenty years, our land forces have been of no ufe whatfoever, nor even employed, notwithftanding the almoft uninterrupted difturbances that have been in Europe, in which our interefts have been as nearly concerned as ever they are likely to be for thefe five and twenty years to come.

Secondly, That our prefent army is a very great expence to the nation, and has raifed jealoufies and difcontents in the minds of many of his majefty's fubjects.

I therefore humbly propofe, that, from and after the 25th day of March next, 1736, the prefent numerous and expenfive army be totally difbanded, the commiffion officers excepted; and that proper perfons be authorized to contract with Mrs. Salmon, for raifing the fame number of men in the beft of wax.

That the said persons be likewise authorized to treat with that ingenious mechanic, Myn Heer Von Pinchbeck, for the clock-work necessary for the said number of land-forces.

It appears from my first *postulatum*, that this future army will be, to all intents and purposes, as useful as ever our present one has been; and how much more beneficial it will be is what I now beg leave to shew.

The curious are often at great trouble and expence to make imitations of things, which things are to be had easier, cheaper, and in greater perfection themselves. Thus infinite pains have been taken of late, but alas in vain, to bring up our present army to the nicety and perfection of a waxen one: it has proved impossible to get such numbers of men, all of the same height, the same make, with their own hair, timing exactly together the several motions of their exercise, and, above all, with a certain military fierceness, that is not natural to British countenances: even some very considerable officers have been cashiered, for wanting SOME OF THE PROPERTIES OF WAX.

By my scheme, all these inconveniencies will be entirely removed; the men will be all of the same size, and, if thought necessary, of the same features and complexion: the requisite degree of fierceness may be given them, by the proper application of whiskers, scars, and such like indications of courage, according to the tastes of their respective officers; and their exercise will, by the skill and care of Myn Heer Von Pinchbeck, be in the highest German

taste,

taste, and may possibly arrive at the *one motion*, that great *desideratum* in our discipline. The whole, thus ordered, must certainly furnish a more delightful spectacle than any hitherto exhibited, to such as are curious of reviews and military exercitations.

I am here aware that the grave Mrs. Osborne will seriously object, that this army, not being alive, cannot be useful; and that the more lively and ingenious Mr. Walsingham * may possibly insinuate, that a waxen army is not likely to stand fire well.

To the lady, I answer thus beforehand, that if, in the late times of war, our present army has been of no more use than a waxen one, a waxen one will now, in time of peace, be as useful as they; and as to any other reasons, that she or her whole sex may have, for preferring a live standing army to this, they are considerations of a private nature, and must not weigh against so general and public a good.

To the pleasant 'squire I reply, that this army will stand its own fire very well; which is all that seems requisite.

But give me leave to say too, that an army thus constituted will be very far from being without its terror, and will doubtless strike all the fear that is consistent with the liberties of a free people; wax, it is well known, being the most natural and ex-

* The Free Briton, by Francis Walsingham esq; (published under the direction of sir Robert Walpole), was written by William Arnall, who was bred an attorney, but commenced party-writer when under twenty. See the notes on the Dunciad, Book II; where Arnall is said to have received, for Free Britons and other writings, in four years, the sum of 10997 *l.* 6 *s.* 8 *d.* out of the treasury.

preſſive imitation of life, as it unites in itſelf the different advantages of painting and ſculpture.

Our Britiſh monarchs in the Tower are never beheld but with the profoundeſt reſpect and reverence; and that bold and manly repreſentation of Henry the eighth never fails to raiſe the ſtrongeſt images of one kind or another in its beholders of both ſexes. Such is the force of divine right, though but in wax, upon the minds of all good and loyal ſubjects.

Nobody ever ſaw the court of France, lately exhibited here in wax-work, without a due regard; inſomuch that an habitual good courtier was obſerved reſpectfully bowing to their moſt Chriſtian majeſties, and was at laſt only convinced of his error by the ſilence of the court. An army of the ſame materials will certainly have ſtill a ſtronger effect, and be more than ſufficient to keep the peace, without the power of breaking it.

My readers will obſerve, that I only propoſe a reduction of the private men, for, upon many accounts, I would by no means touch the commiſſions of the officers. In the firſt place, they moſt of them deſerve very well of the public; and in the next place, as they are all in parliament, I might, by propoſing to deprive them of their commiſſions, be ſuſpected of political views, which I proteſt I have not. I would therefore deſire, that the preſent ſet of officers may keep the keys, to wind up their ſeveral regiments, troops, or companies; and that a maſter-key to thé whole army be lodged in the hands of the general in chief for the time being, or, in default of ſuch, in the hands of the prime miniſter.

From

From my ſecond *poſtulatum*, that the preſent army is expenſive, and gives uneaſineſs to many of his majeſty's good ſubjects, the further advantages of my ſcheme will appear.

The chief expence here will be only the prime coſt; and I even queſtion whether that will exceed the price of live men, of the height, proportions, and tremendous aſpects, that I propoſe theſe ſhould be of. But the annual ſaving will be ſo conſiderable, that I will appeal to every ſenſible and impartial man in the kingdom, if he does not ſincerely think that this nation would have been now much more flouriſhing and powerful, if, for theſe twenty years laſt paſt, we had had no other army.

Another conſiderable advantage conſiſts in the great care and convenience with which theſe men will be quartered in the countries; where, far from being an oppreſſion or diſturbance to the public houſes, they will be a genteel ornament and decoration to them, and, inſtead of being inflicted as a puniſhment upon the diſaffected, will probably be granted as a favour to ſuch inn-keepers as are ſuppoſed to be the moſt in the intereſt of the adminiſtration, and that too poſſibly with an excluſive privilege of ſhewing them. So that I queſtion, whether a certain great city may not be eloquently threatened with having no troops at all.

As I am never for carrying any project too far, I would, for certain reaſons, not extend this, at preſent, to Gibraltar, but would leave the garriſon there alive as long as it can keep ſo.

Let

Let nobody put the Jacobite upon me, and ſay, that I am paving the way for the pretender, by diſbanding this army. That argument is worn threadbare; beſides, let thoſe take the Jacobite to themſelves, who would exchange the affections of the people for the fallacious ſecurity of an unpopular ſtanding army.

But, as I know I am ſuſpected by ſome people to be no friend to the preſent miniſtry, I would moſt carefully avoid inſerting any thing in this project that might look peeviſh, or like a deſign to deprive them of any of the neceſſary means of carrying on the government. I have therefore already declared, that I did not propoſe to affect the commiſſions of any of the officers, though a very great ſaving would ariſe to the public thereby. And I would further provide, that, in the diſbanding the preſent army, an exact account ſhould be taken of every ſoldier's right of voting in elections, and where; and that the like number of votes, and for the ſame places, ſhall be reſerved to every regiment, troop, or company, of this new army; theſe votes to be given collectively, by the officers of the ſaid regiment, troop, or company, in as free and uninfluenced a manner as hath at any time been practiſed within theſe laſt twenty years.

Moreover, I would provide, that *Mann* and *Day** ſhall, as at preſent, have the entire cloathing of this new army; ſo ſcrupulous am I of diſtreſſing the adminiſtration.

* Two very conſiderable woollen-drapers, in the Strand; the firſt of them was grandfather to ſir Horatio Mann.

People

People are generally fond of their own projects, and, it may be, I look upon this with the partiality of a parent; but I protest I cannot find any one objection to it. It will save an immense expence to the nation, remove the fears that at present disturb the minds of many, and answer every one of the purposes to which our present army has been applied. The numbers will sound great and formidable abroad, the individuals will be gentle and peaceable at home; and there will be an increase to the public of above fifty thousand hands for labour and manufactures, which at present are either idle, or but scurvily employed.

I cannot, I own, help flattering myself, that this scheme will prevail, and the more so from the very great protection and success wax-work has lately met with; which, I imagine, was only as an essay or *tentamen* to some greater design of this nature. But, whatever be the event of it, this alternative I will venture to assert, that, by the 25th of March next, either the army or another body of men must be of wax.

II.

FOG'S *JOURNAL.*

SATURDAY, Jan. 24, 1736. N° 377.

HUMAN nature, though every where the same, is so seemingly diversified by the various habits and customs of different countries, and so blended with

with the early impressions we receive from our education, that they are often confounded together, and mistaken for one another. This makes us look with astonishment upon all customs that are extremely different from our own, and hardly allow those nations to be of the same nature with ourselves, if they are unlike in their manners; whereas all human actions may be traced up to those two great motives, the pursuit of pleasure, and the avoidance of pain: and, upon a strict examination, we shall often find, that those customs, which at first view seem the most different from our own, have in reality a great analogy with them.

What more particularly suggested this thought to me, was an account which a gentleman, who was lately returned from China, gave, in a company where I happened to be present, of a pleasure held in high esteem, and extremely practised by that luxurious nation. He told us, that the tickling of the ears was one of the most exquisite sensations known in China; and that the delight, administered to the whole frame through this organ, could, by an able and skilful tickler, be raised to whatever degree of extasy the patient should desire.

The company, struck with this novelty, expressed their surprize, as is usual on such occasions, first by a silly silence, and then by many silly questions. The account too, coming from so far as China, raised both their wonder and their curiosity, much more than if it had come from any European country, and opened a larger field for pertinent questions. Among others, the gentleman was asked, whether the Chinese

ears

ears and fingers had the leaſt reſemblance to ours; to which having anſwered in the affirmative, he went on thus:

"I perceive, I have excited your curioſity ſo much by mentioning a cuſtom ſo unknown to you here, that I believe it will not be diſagreeable, if I give you a particular account of it.

"This pleaſure, ſtrange as it may ſeem to you, is in China reckoned almoſt equal to any that the ſenſes afford. There is not an ear in the whole country untickled; the ticklers have, in their turn, others who tickle them, inſomuch, that there is a circulation of tickling throughout that vaſt empire. Or if, by chance, there be ſome few unhappy enough not to find ticklers, or ſome ticklers clumſy enough not to find buſineſs, they comfort themſelves at leaſt with ſelf-titillation.

"This profeſſion is one of the moſt lucrative and conſiderable ones in China, the moſt eminent performers being either handſomely requited in money, or ſtill better rewarded by the credit and influence it gives them with the party tickled; inſomuch, that a man's fortune is made as ſoon as he gets to be tickler to any conſiderable mandarin.

"The emperor, as in juſtice he ought, enjoys this pleaſure in its higheſt perfection; and all the conſiderable people contend for the honor and advantage of this employment, the perſon who ſucceeds the beſt in it being always the firſt favourite, and chief diſpenſer of his imperial power. The principal mandarins are allowed to try their hands upon his majeſty's ſacred ears, and according to their dexterity

and

and agility, commonly rise to the posts of first ministers. His wives too are admitted to try their skill; and she among them, who holds him by the ear, is reckoned to have the surest and most lasting hold. His present imperial majesty's ears, as I am informed, are by no means of a delicate texture, and consequently not quick of sensation; so that it has proved extremely difficult to nick the tone of them: the lightest and finest hands have utterly failed; and many have miscarried, who, from either fear or respect, did not treat the royal ears so roughly as was necessary. He began his reign under the hands of a bungling operator, whom for his clumsiness he soon dismissed: he was afterwards attempted by a more skilful tickler; but he sometimes failed too, and, not being able to hit the humour of his majesty's ears, his own have often suffered for it.

" In this public distress, and while majesty laboured under the privation of auricular joys, the empress, who, by long acquaintance, and frequent little trials, judged pretty well of the texture of the royal ear, resolved to undertake it, and succeeded perfectly, by means of a much stronger friction than others durst either attempt, or could imagine would please.

" In the mean time, the skilful mandarin, far from being discouraged by the ill success he had sometimes met with in his attempts upon the emperor's ears, resolved to make himself amends upon his imperial consort's: he tried, and he prevailed; he tickled her majesty's ear to such perfection, that, as the emperor would trust his ear to none but the empress, she would trust hers to none but this light-fingered mandarin,

who,

who, by these means, attained to unbounded and uncontrouled power, and governed ear by ear.

"But, as all the mandarins have their ear-ticklers too, with the same degree of influence over them, and as this mandarin was particularly remarkable for his extreme sensibility in those parts, it is hard to say from what original titillation the imperial power now flows."

The conclusion of the gentleman's story was attended with the usual interjections of wonder and surprize from the company. Some called it strange, some odd, and some very comical: and those who thought it the most improbable, I found by their questions were the most desirous to believe it. I observed too, that, while the story lasted, they were most of them trying the experiment upon their own ears, but without any visible effect that I could perceive.

Soon afterwards, the company broke up; and I went home, where I could not help reflecting, with some degree of wonder, at the wonder of the rest, because I could see nothing extraordinary in the power which the ear exercised in China, when I considered the extensive influence of that important organ in Europe. Here, as in China, it is the source of both pleasure and power; the manner of applying to it is only different. Here the titillation is vocal, there it is manual, but the effects are the same; and, by the bye, European ears are not always unacquainted neither with manual application.

To make out the analogy I hinted at between the Chinese and ourselves in this particular, I will offer to my readers ſome inſtances of the ſenſibility and prevalency of the ears of Great Britain.

The Britiſh ears ſeem to be as greedy and ſenſible of titillation as the Chineſe can poſſibly be; nor is the profeſſion of an ear-tickler here any way inferior, or leſs lucrative. There are of three ſorts, the private tickler, the public tickler, and the ſelf-tickler.

Flattery is, of all methods, the ſureſt to produce that vibration of the air, which affects the auditory nerves with the moſt exquiſite titillation; and, according to the thinner or thicker texture of thoſe organs, the flattery muſt be more or leſs ſtrong. This is the immediate province of the private tickler, and his great ſkill conſiſts in tuning his flattery to the ear of his patient; it were endleſs to give inſtances of the influence and advantages of thoſe artiſts who excel in this way.

The buſineſs of a public tickler is, to modulate his voice, diſpoſe his matter, and enforce his arguments in ſuch a manner as to excite a pleaſing ſenſation in the ears of a number or aſſembly of people: this is the moſt difficult branch of the profeſſion, and that in which the feweſt excel; but to the few who do it, is the moſt lucrative, and the moſt conſiderable. The bar has at preſent but few proficients of this ſort, the pulpit none, the ladder alone ſeems not to decline.

I muſt not here omit one public tickler of great eminency, and whoſe titillative faculty muſt be allowed to be ſingly confined to the ear; I mean the great ſignior Farinelli, to whom ſuch crowds reſort, for the extaſy he adminiſters to them through that organ, and who ſo liberally requite his labours, that,

if

if he will but do them the favour to ſtay two or three years longer, and have two or three benefits more, they will have nothing left but their ears to give him.

The ſelf-tickler is as unhappy as contemptible; for, having none of the talents neceſſary for tickling of others, and conſequently not worth being tickled by others neither, he is reduced to tickle himſelf: his own ears alone receive any titillation from his own efforts. I know an eminent performer of this kind, who, by being nearly related to a ſkilful public tickler, would fain ſet up for the buſineſs himſelf, but has met with ſuch repeated diſcouragements, that he is reduced to the mortifying reſource of ſelf-titillation, in which he commits the moſt horrid exceſſes.

Beſides the proofs abovementioned, of the influence of the ear in this country, many of our moſt common phraſes and expreſſions, from whence the genius of a people may always be collected, demonſtrate, that the ear is reckoned the principal and moſt predominant part of our whole mechaniſm. As for inſtance:

To have the ear of one's prince is underſtood by every body to mean having a good ſhare of his authority, if not the whole, which plainly hints how that influence is acquired.

To have the ear of the firſt miniſter is the next, if not an equal, advantage. I am therefore not ſurprized, that ſo conſiderable a poſſeſſion ſhould be ſo frequently attempted, and ſo eagerly ſollicited, as we may always obſerve it is. But I muſt caution the perſon, who would make his fortune in this way, to confine his attempt ſtrictly to the ear in the ſingular number; a deſign upon the ears, in the plural, of a

 firſt

first minister being for the most part rather difficult and dangerous, however just.

To give ear to a person implies, giving credit, being convinced, and being guided by that person; all this by the success of his endeavours upon that prevailing organ.

To lend an ear is something less, but still intimates a willingness and tendency in the lender to be prevailed upon by a little more tickling of that part. Thus the lending of an ear is a sure presage of success to a skilful tickler. For example, a person, who lends an ear to a minister, seldom fails of putting them both in his power soon afterwards; and, when a fine woman lends an ear to a lover, she shews a disposition at least to further and future titillation.

To be deaf, and to stop one's ears, are common and known expressions, to signify a total refusal and rejection of a person or proposition; in which case I have often observed the manual application to succeed by a strong vellication or vigorous percussion of the outward membranes of the ear.

There cannot be a stronger instance of the great value that has always been set upon these parts, than the constant manner of expressing the utmost and most ardent desire people can have for any thing, by saying they would "give their ears" for it; a price so great, that it is seldom either paid or required. Witness the numbers of people actually wearing their ears still, who in justice have long since forfeited them.

Over head and ears would be a manifest *pleonasmus*, the head being higher than the ears, were not the ears

reckoned

reckoned ſo much more valuable than all the reſt of the head, as to make it a true climax.

It were unneceſſary to mention, as farther proofs of the importance and dignity of thoſe organs, that pulling, boxing, or cutting off the ears, are the higheſt inſults that choleric men of honor can either give or receive; which ſhews that the ear is the ſeat of honor as well as of pleaſure.

The anatomiſts have diſcovered, that there is an intimate correſpondence between the palm of the hand and the ear, and that a previous application to the hand communicates itſelf inſtantly, by the force and velocity of attraction, to the ear, and agreeably prepares that part to receive and admit of titillation. I muſt ſay too, that I have known this practiſed with ſucceſs upon very conſiderable perſons of both ſexes.

Having thus demonſtrated, by many inſtances, that the ear is the moſt material part in the whole mechaniſm of our ſtructure, and that it is both the ſeat and ſource of honor, power, pleaſure, and pain, I cannot conclude without an earneſt exhortation to all my country-folks, of whatſoever rank or ſex, to take the utmoſt care of their ears. Guard your ears, O ye princes, for your power is lodged in your ears. Guard your ears, ye nobles, for your honor lies in your ears. Guard your ears, ye fair, if you would guard your virtue. And guard your ears, all my fellow-ſubjects, if you would guard your liberties and properties.

III.

FOG'S *JOURNAL.*

SATURDAY, April 10, 1736. N° 388.

HAVING in a former paper ſet forth the valuable privileges and prerogatives of the EAR, I ſhould be very much wanting to another material part of our compoſition, if I did not do juſtice to the EYES, and ſhew the influence they either have, or ought to have, in Great Britain.

While the eyes of my countrymen were in a great meaſure the part that directed, the whole people ſaw for themſelves; ſeeing was called believing, and was a ſenſe ſo much truſted to, that the eyes of the body and thoſe of the mind were, in ſpeaking, indifferently made uſe of for one another. But I am ſorry to ſay that the caſe is now greatly altered; and I obſerve with concern an epidemical blindneſs, or, at leaſt, a general weakneſs and diſtruſt of the eyes, ſcattered over this whole kingdom, from which we may juſtly apprehend the worſt conſequences.

This obſervation muſt have, no doubt, occurred to all who frequent public places, whom, inſtead of ſeeing ſo many eyes employed, as uſual, either in looking at one another, or in viewing attentively the object that brings them there, we find modeſtly delegating their faculty to glaſſes of all ſorts and ſizes, to ſee for them. I remarked this more particularly at an opera I was at, the beginning of this winter, where Polypheme was almoſt the only perſon in the houſe that

that had two eyes; the reſt had but one apiece, and that a glaſs one.

As I cannot account for this general decay of our optics from any natural cauſe, not having obſerved any alteration in our climate or manner of living, conſiderable enough to have brought ſo ſuddenly upon us this univerſal ſhort-ſightedneſs; I cannot but entertain ſome ſuſpicions, that their pretended helps to the ſight are rather deceptions of it, and the inventions of wicked and deſigning perſons, to repreſent objects in that light, ſhape, ſize, and number, in which it is their inclination or intereſt to have them beheld. I ſhall communicate to the public the grounds of my ſuſpicion.

The honeſt plain ſpectacles and reading-glaſſes were formerly the refuge only of aged and decayed eyes; they accompanied grey hairs, and in ſome meaſure ſhared their reſpect: they magnified the object a little, but ſtill they repreſented it in its true light and figure. Whereas now the variety of refinements upon this firſt uſeful invention have perſuaded the youngeſt, the ſtrongeſt, and the fineſt eyes in the world out of their faculty, and convinced them, that, for the true diſcerning of objects, they muſt have recourſe to ſome of theſe *media*; nay, into ſuch diſrepute is the natural ſight now fallen, that we may obſerve, while one eye is employed in the glaſs, the other is carefully covered with the hand, or painfully ſhut, not without ſhocking diſtortions of the countenance.

It is very well known, that there are not above three or four eminent operators for theſe portable or pocket-eyes, and that they engroſs that whole buſineſs. Now, as theſe perſons are neither of them people of quality, *who are always above ſuch infamous and dirty motives*, it is not unreaſonable to ſuppoſe that they may be liable to a pecuniary influence; nor conſequently is it improbable that an adminiſtration ſhould think it worth its while, even at a large expence, to ſecure thoſe few that are to ſee for the bulk of the whole nation. This ſurely deſerves our attention.

It is moſt certain, that great numbers of people already ſee objects in a very different light from what they were ever ſeen in before by the naked and undeluded eye; which can only be aſcribed to the miſrepreſentations of ſome of theſe artificial *media*, of which I ſhall enumerate the different kinds that have come to my knowledge.

The looking-glaſs, which for many ages was the miniſter and counſellor of the fair ſex, has now greatly extended its juriſdiction; every body knows that that glaſs is backed with quickſilver, to hinder it from being diaphanous; ſo that it ſtops the beholder, and preſents him again to himſelf. Here his views center all in himſelf, and dear ſelf alone is the object of his contemplations. This kind of glaſs, I am aſſured, is now the moſt common of any, eſpecially among people of diſtinction, inſomuch that nine in ten of the glaſſes that we daily ſee levelled at the public are in reality not diaphanous, but agreeably return the looker to himſelf, while his attention ſeems to be employed upon others.

The

The reflecting telescope has of late gained ground considerably, not only among the ladies, who chiefly view one another through that medium, but has even found it's way into the cabinets of princes; in both which cases it suggests reflections to those, who before were not apt to make many.

The microscope, or magnifying glass, is an engine of dangerous consequence, though much in vogue: it swells the minutest object to a most monstrous size, heightens the deformity, and even deforms the beauties of nature. When the finest hair appears like a tree, and the finest pore like an abyss, what disagreeable representations may it exhibit, and what fatal mistakes may it mutually occasion between the two sexes! Nature has formed all objects for that point of view in which they appear to the naked eye; their perfection lessens in proportion as they leave out that point, and many a Venus would cease to appear one, even to her lover, were she, by the help of a microscope, to be viewed in the ambient cloud of her insensible perspiration. I bar Mrs. Osborne's returning my microscope upon me, since I leave her in quiet possession of the spectacles, and even of the reading-glasses, if she can make use of them.

There is another kind of glass now in great use, which is the oblique glass, whose tube, leveled in a strait line at one object, receives another in at the side, so that the beholder seems to be looking at one person, while another intirely engrosses his attention. This is a notorious engine of treachery and deceit; and yet, they say, it is for the most part made use of by miniſters to their friends, and ladies to their huſbands.

The ſmoked glaſs, that darkens even the luſtre of the ſun, muſt of courſe throw the blackeſt dye upon all other objects. This, though the moſt infernal invention of all, is far from being unpractiſed; and I knew a gentlewoman, who, in order to keep her huſband at home, and in her own power, had his whole houſe glazed with it, ſo that the poor gentleman ſhut up his door, and neither went abroad, nor let any body in, for fear of converſing, as he thought, with ſo many devils.

The dangers that may one day threaten our conſtitution in general, as well as particular perſons, from the variety of theſe miſchievous inventions, are ſo obvious, that they hardly need be pointed out: however, as my countrymen cannot be too much warned againſt it, I ſhall hint at thoſe that terrify me the moſt.

Suppoſe we ſhould ever have a ſhort-ſighted prince upon the throne, though otherwiſe juſt, brave, and wiſe; who can anſwer for his glaſs-grinder, and conſequently, who can tell through what medium, and in what light, he may view the moſt important objects? or who can anſwer for the perſons that are to take care of his glaſſes, and preſent them to him upon occaſion? may not they change them, and ſlip a wrong one upon him, as their intereſt may require, and thus magnify, leſſen, multiply, deform, or blacken, as they think proper; nay, and by means of the oblique glaſs abovementioned, ſhew him even one object for another? Where would the eye of

the

the maſter be then? where would be that eye divinely deputed to watch over? but ſhrunk and contracted within the narrow circle of a deceitful tube.

On the other hand, ſhould future parliaments, by arts of a deſigning miniſter, with the help of a corrupted glaſs-grinder, have deluſive and perverſive glaſſes ſlipped upon them, what might they ſee? or what might they not ſee? nobody can tell. I am ſure every body ought to fear they might poſſibly behold a numerous ſtanding army in time of peace, as an inoffenſive and pleaſing object, nay, as a ſecurity to our liberties and properties. They might ſee our riches increaſe by new debts, and our trade by high duties; and they might look upon the corrupt ſurrender of their own power to the crown, as the beſt protection of the rights of the people. Should this ever happen to be the caſe, we may be ſure it muſt be by the interpoſition of ſome ſtrange medium, ſince theſe objects were never viewed in this light by the naked and unaſſiſted eyes of our anceſtors.

In this general conſideration, there is a particular one that affects me more than all the reſt, as the conſequence of it would be the worſt. There is a body of men, who, by the wiſdom and for the happineſs of our conſtitution, make a conſiderable part of our parliament; all, or, at leaſt, moſt of theſe venerable perſons, are, by great age, long ſtudy, or a low mortified way of living, reduced to have recourſe to glaſſes. Now ſhould their *media* be abuſed, and political tranſlative ones be ſlipped upon them, what ſcandal would their innocent, but miſguided conduct bring upon religion, and what joy would it give, at

this

this time particularly, to the diſſenters? Such as, I am ſure, no true member of our church can think of without horror! I am the more apprehenſive of this, from the late revival of an act that flouriſhed with idolatry, and that had expired with it, I mean the ſtaining of glaſs. That medium, which throws ſtrange and various colours upon all objects, was formerly ſacred to our churches, and conſequently may, for aught I know, in the intended revival of our true church diſcipline, be thought a candidate worthy of our favour and reception, and ſo a ſtained medium be eſtabliſhed as the true, orthodox, and canonical one.

I have found it much eaſier to point out the miſchiefs I apprehend, than the means of obviating or remedying them, though I have turned it every way in my thoughts.

To have a certain number of perſons appointed to examine and licenſe all the glaſſes that ſhould be uſed in this kingdom, would be lodging ſo great a truſt in thoſe perſons, that the temptations to betray it would be exceedingly great too; and it is to be feared that people of quality would not take the trouble of it, ſo that, *Quis cuſtodiat ipſos cuſtodes?* (By whom will theſe keepers be kept?)

I once thought of propoſing, that a committee of both houſes of parliament ſhould be veſted with that power: but I immediately laid that aſide, for reaſons which I am not obliged to communicate to the public.

At laſt, deſpairing to find out any legal method that ſhould prove effectual, I reſolved to content myſelf

ſelf with an earneſt exhortation to all my country-folks, of whatſoever rank or ſex, to ſee with their own eyes, or not ſee at all, blindneſs being preferable to error.

See then with your own eyes, ye princes, though weak or dim: they will ſtill give you a fairer and truer repreſentation of objects, than you will ever have by the interpoſition of any medium whatſoever. Your ſubjects are placed in their proper point of view for your natural ſight; viewing them in that point, you will ſee that your happineſs conſiſts in theirs, your greatneſs in their riches, and your power in their affections.

See likewiſe with your own eyes, ye people, and reject all proffered *media:* view even your princes with your natural ſight; the true rays of majeſty are friendly to the weakeſt eye, or, if they dazzle and ſcorch, it is owing to the interpoſition of burning-glaſſes. Deſtroy thoſe pernicious *media*, and you will be pleaſed with the ſight of one another.

In ſhort, let the natural retrieve their credit, and reſume their power; we ſhall then ſee things as they really are, which muſt end in the confuſion of thoſe whoſe hopes and intereſts are founded upon miſrepreſentations and deceit.

IV.

COMMON SENSE*.

SATURDAY, February 5, 1737. Nº 1.

Rarus enim ferme sensus communis—JUV.
Nothing so rare as common sense.

A PREFACE is, by long custom, become so necessary a part of a book, that, should an author now omit that previous ceremony, he would be accused of presumption, and be supposed to imagine that his performance was above wanting any recommendation. By a preface, an author presents himself to the public, and begs their friendship and protection; if he does it gracefully and genteelly, he is well received, like many a fine gentleman upon the strength of his first address. Besides, were it not for the modest encomiums, which authors generally bestow upon themselves in their prefaces, their works would often die unpraised, and sometimes unread.

A weekly writer, I know, is not of a rank to pretend to a preface; but an humble introduction is ex-

* This paper, in which several persons of eminence were concerned, was partly political, and on the side of opposition, but mostly moral, and calculated for the improvement of manners and taste. Lord Lyttelton was one of the writers; and the papers which fell from his pen have been inserted in the collection of his works.

Those which are here given sufficiently shew, by the original turn and admirable management of irony discernible in them, the masterly hand from which they came. Our authority, however, for producing them as lord Chesterfield's, is that of one of his particular friends, to whom his lordship gave the list, which we have followed.

pected

pected from him. He muſt make his bow to the public at his firſt appearance, let them a little into his deſign, and give them a ſample of what they are to expect from him afterwards.

In this caſe, it may be equally unhappy for him to give himſelf out, like Æſop's fellow-ſlaves, for one that can do every thing, or, like Æſop, for one that can do nothing; for, if he ſpeaks too aſſumingly, the world will revolt againſt him, and, if too modeſtly, be apt to take him at his word.

Theſe conſiderations determined me to make this firſt paper ſerve as an introduction to my future labours, though I am ſenſible that a weekly author is in a very different ſituation from an author in the lump.—If a wholeſale dealer can, by an inſinuating preface, prevail with people to buy the whole piece, his buſineſs is done, and it is too late for the deluded purchaſer to repent, be the goods never ſo flimſy; but a weekly retailer is conſtantly bound to his good behaviour. He, like ſome others, holds both his honors and profits only *durante bene placito*; and whatever may be the ſucceſs of his firſt endeavours, as ſoon as he flags in his painful hebdomadal courſe, he is rigorouſly ſtruck off at once from his two-penny eſtabliſhment.

Another difficulty, that occurred to me, was the preſent great number of my weekly brethren, with whom all people, except the ſtationers and the Stamp-office, think themſelves already over-ſtocked; but this difficulty upon farther conſideration leſſened.

As for the London Journal, it cannot poſſibly interfere with me, as appears from the very title of my

paper;

paper; moreover, I was informed, that paper of the ſame ſize and goodneſs as the London Journal, being to be had much cheaper unprinted and unſtamped, and yet as uſeful to all intents and purpoſes, was now univerſally preferred.

Fog's Journal, by a natural progreſſion from Miſt to Fog, is now condenſed into a cloud, and only uſed by way of wet brown paper, in caſe of falls and contuſions.

The Craftſman was the only rival that gave me any concern; that being the only one, I thought there was world enough for us both, and perſuaded myſelf that, wiſer than Cæſar and Pompey, we ſhould content ourſelves with dividing it between us; beſides that, I never obſerved Mr. D'Anvers to be an enemy to common ſenſe.

Being a man of great learning, I have, in chuſing the name of my paper, had before my eyes that excellent precept of Horace to authors, to begin modeſtly, and not to promiſe more than they are able to perform, and keep up to the laſt.—I have therefore only entitled it Common Senſe, which is all I pretend to myſelf, and no more than what, I dare ſay, the humbleſt of my readers pretends to likewiſe.

But, as a farther encouragement and invitation to the public to try me, I declare, that though I only promiſe them common ſenſe, yet if I have any wit they ſhall have it into the bargain. Wherefore I deſire my cuſtomers to look upon this weekly expence as a two-penny ticket in a lottery: it may poſſibly come up wit, and if a blank, at worſt, common ſenſe.

But,

But, as modesty is the best recommendation to great minds, on the other side it is apt to prejudice little ones, who mistake it for ignorance, or guilt; therefore, that I may not suffer by it with the latter, I must repeat a known observation, that common sense is no such common thing. I could give many instances of this truth, if I would, but decline it at present, and chuse to refer my readers to their several friends and acquaintance.

Should I here be asked then what I mean by common sense, if it is so uncommon a thing, I confess I should be at a loss to know how to define it. I take common sense, like common honesty, rather to be called common, because it should be so, than because it is so. It is rather that rule, by which men judge of other people's actions, than direct their own; the plain result of right reason admitted by all, and practised by few.

An ingenious dramatic author has considered common sense as so extraordinary a thing, that he has lately, with great wit and humor, not only personified it, but dignified it too with the title of a queen. Though I am not sure that had I been to personify common sense, I should have borrowed my figure from that sex, yet as he has added the regal dignity, which by the law of the land removes all defects, I wave any objection.—The fair sex in general, queens excepted, are infinitely above plain downright common sense; sprightly fancy and shining irregularities are their favourites, in which despairing to satisfy, though desirous to please them, I have, in order to be of some use to them, stipulated with my stationer, that my paper ſhall be of the propereſt ſort for pinning up of their hair. As the new French faſhion is very favourable to me in this particular, I flatter myſelf, they will not diſdain to have ſome common ſenſe about their heads at ſo eaſy a rate.

Should I ever, as poſſibly I often may, be extremely dull, I will not, as ſome of my predeceſſors have done, pretend that it was by deſign, for I proteſt that I do not intend it; but in that caſe, I claim my ſhare in the preſent general indulgence to dulneſs, of being thought the wiſer for it, and hope to meet with ſympathetic nods of approbation from the moſt ſolid of my readers. Moreover, I ſhall go on the longer and the ſafer for it, dulneſs being the ballaſt of the mind, that fits it for a long voyage, keeps it ſteddy, and ſecures it from the guſts of fancy and imagination.

I cannot help thinking how very advantageous it may be to a great many people to purchaſe my paper, were it only for the ſake of the title.—Have you read common ſenſe? Have you got common ſenſe? are queſtions which one ſhould be very ſorry not to be able to anſwer in the affirmative; and yet, in order to be able to do it with truth, a precaution of this kind may poſſibly not be unneceſſary, at leaſt it can do no hurt.

As to the deſign of my paper, it is to take in all ſubjects whatſoever, and try them by the ſtandard of common ſenſe. I ſhall erect a kind of tribunal, for the *crimina læſi ſenſûs communis*, or the pleas of common ſenſe. But the method of proceeding muſt be different from that of other courts, or it would be

 contrary

contrary to the meaning and inſtitution of this. The cauſe of common ſenſe ſhall be pleaded in common ſenſe. Let not the guilty hope to eſcape, or the innocent fear being puzzled, delayed, ruined, or condemned.

It would be endleſs for me to enumerate the various branches of the juriſdiction of this court, ſince every thing, more or leſs, falls under its cognizance. The poſſeſſion or the want of common ſenſe appears proportionably in the loweſt, as well as in the higheſt, tranſactions; and a king, and a cobler, without it, will equally bungle in their reſpective callings. The *quicquid agunt homines* (actions of men) is my province; and *homines* comprehends, not only all men, but all women too, that is, as far as they are to be comprehended. The conduct of the fair ſex will therefore come under my conſideration; but with this indulgence, which is due to them, that, in trying their actions by the ſtraight rule of common ſenſe, I ſhall make proper allowances for thoſe pretty obliquities and deviations from it, which great vivacity, lively paſſions, and conſcious beauty, frequently occaſion, and in ſome meaſure juſtify.

The fine gentlemen cannot hope to eſcape trial, were it only as acceſſaries to their fair principals. I am aware, that they will cavil at the juriſdiction of the court, and will alledge, if they know how, that they are brought *coram non judice* (before an incompetent judge). I acknowledge too, that they have a preſumptive kind of exemption from inquiries and proſecutions of this nature; but as this connivance, if too long indulged, might grow into a right, I muſt insist upon their appearing sometimes in court, where they shall meet with all the lenity that is due to their birth and education.

But let all authors, from right honorable, or right reverend, down to the humblest inhabitant in Grub-street, respect and tremble at the jurisdiction of the court. With them I disclaim all lenity, as they are generally the most daring and boldest offenders. I shall try them by my rule, as the tyrant Procrustes tried his subjects by his bed, and will, without mercy, stretch out those that fall short of it, and cut off from those who go beyond it.

I am sensible that common sense has lately met with very great discouragement in the noble science of politics; our chief professors having thought themselves much above those obvious rules that had been followed by our ancestors, and that lay open to vulgar understandings; they have weighed the interests of Europe in nicer scales, and settled them in so delicate a balance, that the least blast affects it. For my part, I shall endeavour to bring them back to the old solid English standard of common sense; but if by that means any gentlemen, who distinguish themselves in that sublime sphere, should be at a loss for business, and appear totally unqualified for it, I hope they will not lay their misfortunes to my charge, since it is none of my fault, if their interests and those of common sense happen to be incompatible.

If, in domestic affairs too, I should find that common sense has been neglected, I shall take the liberty to assert its rights, and represent the justice, as well as the expediency, of reſtoring it to its former credit and dignity. Our conſtitution is founded upon common ſenſe itſelf, and every deviation from one is a violation of the other. The ſeveral degrees and kinds of power, wiſely allotted to the ſeveral conſtituent parts of our legiſlature, can only be altered by thoſe who have no more common ſenſe than common honeſty. Such offenders ſhall be proceeded againſt as guilty of high-treaſon, and ſuffer the ſevereſt puniſhment.

I foreſee all the difficulties I am to ſtruggle with in the courſe of this undertaking; and ſee the improbability, if not the impoſſibility, that common ſenſe ſhould ſingly, by its own weight and merit, make its way into the world, and retrieve its loſt empire. But as many valuable things in themſelves have owed their reception and eſtabliſhment, not to their own intrinſic worth, but to ſome lucky hit, or favourable concurrence of circumſtances; ſo ſome ſuch accident in my favour is what I more rely upon than the merit of my paper, ſhould it have any. Faſhion, which prevails nobody knows how, can introduce what reaſon would in vain recommend; and as, by the circulation of faſhions, the old ones revive after a certain interval, the faſhion of common ſenſe ſeems to have been laid aſide long enough to have a fair chance now for revival.

If therefore any fine woman, in good humour on a Saturday morning, would be pleaſed to drop a word in my favour, and ſay, "It is a good comical paper;" or any man of quality, at the head of taſte, be ſo kind as to ſay, "It is not a bad thing;" I ſhould become the faſhion, and be univerſally bought up at leaſt: and as for being read or not, it is other people's buſineſs, not mine.

As I am ſcrupulous even to delicacy in all my engagements, I muſt premiſe that, in intitling my paper Common Senſe, I only mean the firſt half-ſheet, or it may be a column of the next; the reſt of the paper, which will contain the events foreign and domeſtic, I am very far from promiſing ſhall have any relation at all to common ſenſe. But, as the chief profits of a weekly writer ariſe from thence, the world, which at leaſt reaſons very juſtly upon that ſubject, would, I am ſure, think that I wanted common ſenſe myſelf, if I neglected them.

Upon the whole, my intention is to rebuke vice, correct errors, reform abuſes, and ſhame folly and prejudice, without regard to any thing but common ſenſe; which, as it implies common decency too, I ſhall confine myſelf to things, and not attack perſons; it being my deſire to improve or amuſe every body, without ſhocking any body.

I do not think it neceſſary, at leaſt yet, to give the public any information as to my perſon; let my paper ſtand upon its own legs. My preſent reſolution is to keep my name concealed, unleſs my ſucceſs ſhould ſome day or other tempt my vanity to diſcover it. All I will ſay at preſent is, that I never appeared in print before; and if I ſhould not meet with ſome encouragement now, I ſhall withdraw myſelf to my former retirements, and there indulge thoſe oddneſſes that compoſe my character; the de-

ſcription

ſcription of which, if I go on, may ſome time or other entertain my readers.

V.

COMMON SENSE.

SATURDAY, February 19, 1737. N° 3.

BERNIER informs us of a very extraordinary cuſtom, which prevails to this day in the empire of the Mogol. His imperial majeſty is annually weighed upon his birth-day; and if it appears that, ſince his former weighing, he has made any conſiderable acquiſition of fleſh, it is matter of public rejoicings throughout his whole dominions. Upon that great day too, his ſubjects are obliged to make him preſents, which ſeldom amount to leſs than thirty millions.

This ſeems to be a cuſtom which, like many cuſtoms in other countries, is merely obſerved for antiquity or form-ſake; but the original purpoſe, for which it was at firſt wiſely eſtabliſhed, is either neglected or quite forgotten: or it is impoſſible to imagine, that his Mogol majeſty's good and loyal ſubjects ſhould find ſuch matter of joy in the literal increaſe of their ſovereign's materiality, which muſt of courſe render him leſs qualified for the functions and duties of his government; ſo that it is more reaſonably to be preſumed, that, as all the oriental nations chuſe to convey their precepts of religion, morality, and government, through hieroglyphics, types, and

 emblems,

emblems, this cuſtom was originally allegorical, and ſignified the political increaſe of his majeſty's weight as to credit, power, and dominion; which might juſtly adminiſter great joy to his faithful ſubjects.

Or, to carry my conjecture a little farther, is it impoſſible that his now abſolute empire might formerly have been a limited one; the equal balance of which it might be neceſſary often to examine, in order to preſerve it in its juſt equilibrium? In which caſe, it is highly probable, that his majeſty was weighed againſt ſome counterpoiſe; or, to ſpeak plainer, the prerogative of the prince might be examined with relation to the rights and privileges of the ſubject. What confirms me the more in this opinion, is the choice of the day for the operation. It was his ſacred majeſty's birth-day, a day in which he was ſuppoſed to be in good humour; and the preſents were of a nature to put him in good humour, in caſe they had not found him ſo: which circumſtances ſeem to be meant as preparatory ſweeteners to a ceremony, that would not otherwiſe have been very agreeable to him.

It will be no objection to my conjecture to alledge the preſent abſolute form of that government; ſince a very little knowledge of hiſtory will ſhew us, that the moſt abſolute governments now in the world have been originally free ones, and only bought, bullied, or beaten, out of their liberties.

This may very probably have been the caſe in Indoſtan, where the nobles and repreſentatives of the people might think it both civil and prudent not to weigh quite fair againſt his majeſty; but to lighten their own ſcale, that he might preponderate a little.

This

This little by degrees increaſed the bulk of their ſucceſſors, by continually adding more and more to it.

The ſuperiority of weight probably pleaſed his majeſty, and gave him a reliſh for more; which theſe great annual preſents, ſwelling up his civil liſt, enabled him the better to gratify, by having wherewithal to corrupt the weighers on the part of the nobles and the people, till by degrees the whole weight was thrown into the royal ſcale, without any counterpoiſe. By ſuch gradations this cuſtom, originally eſtabliſhed for the ſecurity of the conſtitution, may have dwindled into a mere pompous ceremony, and an expenſive rareeſhow annually exhibited to a cozened people, in exchange for their liberties.

Would I follow the example of the moſt eminent critics, I could ſupport theſe my criticiſms and conjectures by innumerable authorities both antient and modern; and prove, beyond contradiction, from the natural hiſtory of fat, that it is impoſſible a ſovereign can deſire that great increaſe of his corporal bulk, or a good ſubject rejoice in it. But I ſhall content myſelf with a few.

Fat and ſtupidity are looked upon as ſuch inſeparable companions, that they are uſed as ſynonymous terms; and all the properties of corporal materiality, when applied to the mind, intimate ſlowneſs, heavineſs, dulneſs, and ſuch like qualities.

The *pinguis Minerva* of the antients ſhews us their opinion, that, if even the goddeſs of arts and wiſdom herſelf were to grow fat, ſhe would grow ſtupid too; which, if ſauce for a god or goddeſs, may ſurely, with all due regard, be ſauce for a king or queen.

Horace's *pingue ingenium*, or fat head, means by the ſame figure a puzzled, dull, impenetrable one.

The very air the Bœotians breathed was, from their ſtupidity, called a fat one; and at this day, a neighbouring nation, not leſs eminent than the Bœotians for the ſedateneſs and tranquillity of their genius, are likewiſe diſtinguiſhed by the weight and circumference of their bodies.

After theſe inſtances, it would not only be uncandid, but indecent, to ſuppoſe that any ſovereign would deſire to clog and encumber, by a load of fleſh, thoſe faculties upon whoſe clearneſs and quickneſs the welfare of his ſubjects, and his own glory, ſo much depend; beſides that even bodily agility is highly neceſſary for a prince. A light, clever, active monarch can with more frequency and celerity viſit his remoteſt dominions, where his preſence may often be required. His military operations too may receive great luſtre and advantage from the agility of his perſon; not to mention what a fatal hindrance a prominent abdomen would prove to his royal exercitations in the ſeraglio.

Having thus proved that this cuſtom muſt originally have been only emblematical, and never meant literally as an annual regiſter, or rather bill of fare, of the real pounds of fleſh his Indian majeſty may get or loſe in the courſe of a year, let us examine a little whether this cuſtom may not deſerve, in future times, adoption here, and be advantageouſly introduced into our conſtitution.

Methinks even our conſtitution itſelf points out to us this very method of preſerving it; the three constituent parts of the supreme legislative power form a kind of a political *trilanx*, to each scale of which a due sort and proportion of weight is wisely allotted, that they may all hang even, and yet, with all submission to a right reverend prelate, independent of each other. What then more natural than an annual examination and inspection of this *trilanx?*

That this method of weighing states and empires is very antient, appears from Homer, who tells us, that Jupiter himself weighed the fates of Greece and Troy: by what kind of scale he weighed them, I do not find, either in Eustathius, or any other commentator; but it is only evident by the side that prevailed, that it could not be Troy weight.

Such, I acknowledge, is the happiness of our present times, such the wisdom and integrity of all those who now compose the legislative power, and such the nice equality of the scales, that any caution of this nature would be altogether unnecessary; but common sense looks farther, and wisely provides against future, remote, and possible dangers.

As therefore I apprehend no danger this century, I only propose this measure to commence in the year of our Lord 1800, when, as it is naturally to be presumed that all the persons, of which the legislative power shall be composed, will be such as are now unborn, nobody can tell what may happen, nor how necessary it may be to weigh them frequently, and with the greatest exactness. This too is the more practicable here, because we have the balance of Europe now ready in our hands for the purpose: we have held it with vast credit and success, and infinite

advantage

advantage of late, and no doubt ſhall continue long in poſſeſſion of it; ſo that the legiſlature may certainly borrow it of the miniſtry a couple of days in the year for this domeſtic purpoſe.

In the performing of this operation, it ſeems abſolutely neceſſary that all interchangeable preſents, betwixt the parties to be weighed, be ſtrictly prohibited, as they might give an undue ſhare of weight to the ſcale in which they may be thrown, and have the ſame fatal conſequences here, that, in my opinion, they have already had in Indoſtan; and ſhould it ever happen that, through politeneſs, or any other motive, grains and drachms ſhould be annually thrown into the regal ſcale, it muſt in the end ſo far preponderate, that it will be difficult, if not impoſſible, to retrieve it: nay, another caſe might happen, that would be very ridiculous, which is, if the regal ſcale and the popular ſcale, at the two extremities of the beam, ſhould both be loaded with the ſpoils of the middle one, that middle one would ſtill keep dangling, though quite empty.

What has been ſaid hitherto relates only to metaphorical weight, and is meant to recommend to the ſerious care and attention of poſterity the preſervation of our happy conſtitution, and to adviſe them to be watchful of any the leaſt innovation in any part of it. But I am not ſure, whether the real literal weighing of many individuals may not greatly contribute to this good end; and I am the more confirmed in this opinion by an experiment of that kind, which, I am informed, has been for ſome years laſt paſt tried with great ſucceſs. I am aſſured that in a great hall, at

the

the country ſeat of a very conſiderable perſon in Chriſtendom, there is a very magnificent pair of man ſcales, where the maſter of the houſe and his numerous gueſts are annually weighed, and are as annually found to increaſe immenſely. This hint, I think, may admit of great improvements; ſomething of this kind, whether ſcales or ſteel-yards, can be moſt advantageouſly made uſe of the firſt and laſt day of every ſeſſion of parliament; though, in my humble opinion, the ſcale muſt be found the more decent of the two, becauſe it muſt appear ludicrous, and conſequently turn the whole ceremony into a kind of farce, to ſee the people of the firſt rank, both in church and ſtate, dangling and ſprawling at the end of a ſteel-yard.

But it is certain, that to come ſome way or other at the intrinſic weight of the individuals who compoſe our legiſlature, and to diſtinguiſh exactly betwixt that intrinſic weight and the extraneous weight they may be apt to acquire, would greatly tend to preſerve a due equilibrium between the collective bodies that form our conſtitution.

I muſt own, many difficulties occur to me in this undertaking; but, as I am unwearied in my endeavours for the good of my country, I will turn this matter in my thought, till I have reduced it to ſome method that may appear to me to be practicable, when I ſhall not fail communicating it to the world for the good of poſterity. In the mean time, I ſhall think myſelf obliged to any ingenious perſon who ſhall ſend me his thoughts upon this ſubject, and help me to ascertain the due weight of every individual, as well as a true method of coming at it.

VI.

COMMON SENSE.

SATURDAY, February 26, 1737. N° 4.

THE Romans used to say, *ex pede Herculem*, or, you may know Hercules by his foot, intimating, that one may commonly judge of the whole by a part. I confess, I am myself very apt to judge in this manner, and may, without pretending to an uncommon share of sagacity, say, that I have very seldom found myself mistaken in it. It is impossible not to form to one's self some opinion of people the first time one sees them, from their air and dress; and a suit of cloaths has often informed me, with the utmost certainty, that the wearer had not common sense. The Greeks (to display my learning) said ἱμάτιον ἀνήρ, or, the dress shews the man; and it is certain, that of all trifling things, there is none by which people so much discover their natural turn of mind, as by their dress. In greater matters they proceed more cautiously, nature is disguised, and weaknesses are concealed by art or imitation; but in dress they give a loose to their fancy, and, by declaring it an immaterial thing, though at the same time they do not think it so, promise themselves at least impunity in their greatest oddnesses and wildest excesses. I shall therefore, in this paper, consider the

the ſubject of dreſs by certain plain rules of common ſenſe, which I ſhall ſtrictly charge and require all perſons to obſerve.

As dreſs is more immediately the province, not to ſay the pleaſure, not to ſay the care, not to ſay the whole ſtudy, of the fair ſex, I make my firſt application to them; and I humbly beg their indulgence, if the rules I ſhall lay down ſhould prove a little contrary to thoſe they have hitherto practiſed. There is a proper dreſs for every rank, age, and figure, which thoſe who deviate from are guilty of petty-treaſon againſt common ſenſe; to prevent which crime for the future, I have ſome thoughts of diſpoſing, in proper parts of the town, a certain number of babies in the ſtatutable dreſs for each rank, age, and figure, which, like the 25th of Edward III, ſhall reduce that matter to a preciſion.

Dreſs, to be ſenſible, muſt be properly adapted to the perſon; as, in writing, the ſtyle muſt be ſuited to the ſubject, which image may not unaptly be carried on through the ſeveral branches of it. I am far from objecting to the magnificence of apparel, in thoſe whoſe rank and fortune juſtify and allow it; on the contrary, it is a uſeful piece of luxury, by which the poor and the induſtrious are enabled to live, at the expence of the rich and the idle. I would no more have a woman of quality dreſſed in doggrel, than a farmer's wife in heroics. But I hereby notify to the profuſe wives of induſtrious tradeſmen and honeſt yeomen, that all they get by dreſſing above themſelves is the envy and hatred of their inferiors and their

their equals, with the contempt and ridicule of their ſuperiors.

To thoſe of the firſt rank in birth and beauty, I recommend a noble ſimplicity of dreſs; the ſubject ſupports itſelf, and wants none of the borrowed helps of external ornaments. Beautiful nature may be disfigured, but cannot be improved, by art; and as I look upon a very handſome woman to be the fineſt ſubject in nature, her dreſs ought to be epic, modeſt, noble, and entirely free from the modern tinſel. I therefore prohibit all *concètti*, and luxuriancies of fancy, which only depreciate ſo noble a ſubject; and I muſt do the handſomeſt women I know the juſtice to ſay, that they keep the cleareſt from theſe extravagances. Delia's good ſenſe appears even in her dreſs, which ſhe neither ſtudies nor neglects; but, by a decent and modeſt conformity to the faſhion, equally ſhuns the triumphant pageantry of an overbearing beauty, or the inſolent negligence of a conſcious one.

As for thoſe of an inferior rank of beauty, ſuch as are only pretty women, and whoſe charms reſult rather from a certain air and *je ne ſais quoi* in their whole compoſition, than from any dignity of figure, or ſymmetry of features, I allow them greater licences in their own ornaments, becauſe their ſubject, not being of the ſublimeſt kind, may receive ſome advantages from the elegancy of ſtyle, and the variety of images. I, therefore, permit them to dreſs up to all the flights and fancies of the ſonnet, the madrigal, and ſuch-like minor compoſitions. Flavia may ſerve for a model of this kind; her ornaments are her

amuſement,

amusement, not her care; though she shines in all the gay and glittering images of dress, the prettiness of the subject warrants all the wantonness of the fancy. And if she owes them a lustre, which, it may be, she would not have without them, she returns them graces they could find no where else.

There is a third sort, who, with a perfect neutrality of face, are neither handsome nor ugly, and who have nothing to recommend them, but a certain smart and genteel turn of little figure, quick and lively. These I cannot indulge in a higher style than the epigram, which should be neat, clever, and unadorned, the whole to lie in the sting; and where that lies, is unnecessary to mention.

Having thus gone through the important article of dress, with relation to the three classes of my country-women, who alone can be permitted to dress at all, *viz.* the handsome, the pretty, and the genteel, I must add, that this privilege is limited by common sense to a certain number of years, beyond which no woman can be any one of the three. I therefore require, that, when turned of thirty, they abate of the vigor of their dress; and that, when turned of forty, they utterly lay aside all thoughts of it. And, as an inducement to them so to do, I do most solemnly assure them, that they may make themselves ridiculous, but never desirable by it. When they are once arrived at the latitude of forty, the propitious gales are over; let them gain the first port, and lay aside their rigging.

I come now to a melancholy subject, and upon which the freedom of my advice, I fear, will not be kindly

kindly taken; but, as the cause of common sense is most highly concerned in it, I shall proceed without regard to the consequences: I mean the ugly, and, I am sorry to say it, so numerous a part of my country-women. I must, for their own sakes, treat them with some rigor, to save them not only from the public ridicule, but indignation. Their dress must not rise above plain humble prose; and any attempts beyond it amount at best to the mock-heroic, and excite laughter. An ugly woman should by all means avoid any ornament that may draw eyes upon her which she will entertain so ill. But if she endeavours, by dint of dress, to cram her deformity down mankind, the insolence of the undertaking is resented; and when a Gorgon curls her snakes to charm the town, she would have no reason to complain if she lost head and all by the hand of some avenging Perseus. Ugly women, who may more properly be called a third sex, than a part of the fair one, should publickly renounce all thoughts of their persons, and turn their minds another way; they should endeavour to be honest good-humoured gentlemen; they may amuse themselves with field sports, and a chearful glass, and, if they could get into parliament, I should, for my own part, have no objection to it. Should I be asked how a woman shall know she is ugly, and take her measures accordingly; I answer, that, in order to judge right, she must not believe her eyes, but her ears, and, if they have not heard very warm addresses and applications, she may depend upon it, it was the deformity, and not the

the ſeverity, of her countenance, that prevented them.

There is another ſort of ladies, whoſe daily inſults upon common ſenſe call for the ſtrongeſt correction, and who may moſt properly be ſtyled old offenders. Theſe are the ſexagenary fair-ones, and upwards, who, whether they were handſome or not in the laſt century, ought at leaſt in this to reduce themſelves to a decency and gravity of dreſs ſuited to their years. Theſe offenders are exceedingly numerous: witneſs all the public places, where they exhibit whatever art and dreſs can do, to make them compleatly ridiculous. I have often obſerved ſeptuagenary great-grandmothers adorned, as they thought, with all the colours of the rainbow, while in reality they looked more like the decayed worms in the midſt of their own ſilks. Nay, I have ſeen them proudly diſplay withered necks, ſhriveled and decayed like their marriage-ſettlements, and which no hand, but the cold hand of time, had viſited theſe forty years. The utmoſt indulgence I can allow here, is extreme cleanlineſs, that they may not offend more ſenſes than the ſight; but for the dreſs, it muſt be confined to the elegy and the *triſtibus*.

What has been ſaid with relation to the fair ſex, holds true with relation to the other, only with ſtill greater reſtrictions, as ſuch irregularities are leſs pardonable in men than in ladies. A reaſonable compliance with the faſhion is no diſparagement to the beſt underſtanding, and an affected ſingularity would; but an exceſs, beyond what age, rank, and character will juſtify, is one of the worſt ſigns the body can hang out, and will never tempt people to call in. I ſee with indulgence the youth of our nation finely bound, and gilt on the back, and wiſh they were lettered into the bargain. I forgive them the unnatural ſcantineſs of their wigs, and the immoderate dimenſions of their bags, in conſideration that the faſhion has prevailed, and that the oppoſition of a few to it would be the greater affectation of the two. Though, by the way, I very much doubt whether they are all of them gainers by ſhewing their ears; for it is ſaid that Midas, after a certain accident, was the judicious inventer of long wigs. But then theſe luxuriancies of fancy muſt ſubſide, when age and rank call upon judgement to check its excreſcencies and irregularities.

I cannot conclude this paper without an animadverſion upon one prevailing folly, of which both ſexes are equally guilty, and which is attended with real ill conſequences to the nation; I mean that rage of foreign fopperies, by which ſo conſiderable a ſum of ready money is annually exported out of the kingdom, for things which ought not to be ſuffered to be imported even *gratis*. In order therefore to prevent, as far as I am able, this abſurd and miſchievous practice, I hereby ſignify, that I will ſhew a greater indulgence than ordinary to thoſe who only expoſe themſelves in the manufactures of their own country; and that they ſhall enjoy a connivance, in the nature of a drawback, to thoſe exceſſes, which otherwiſe I ſhall not tolerate.

I muſt add, that if it be ſo genteel to copy the French, even in their weakneſſes, I ſhould humbly hope it might be thought ſtill more ſo, to imitate them where they really deſerve imitation, which is, in preferring every thing of their own to every thing of other people's. A Frenchman, who happened to be in England at the time of the laſt total eclipſe of the ſun, aſſured the people, whom he ſaw looking at it with attention, that it was not to be compared to a French eclipſe: would ſome of our fine women emulate that ſpirit, and aſſert, as they might do with much more truth, that the foreign manufactures are not to be compared to the Engliſh; ſuch a declaration would be worth two or three hundred thouſand pounds a year to the kingdom, and operate more effectually than all the laws made for that purpoſe. The Roman ladies got the Oppian law, which reſtrained their dreſs, repealed, in ſpite of the unwearied oppoſition of the elder Cato. I exhort the Britiſh ladies to exert their power to better purpoſes, and to revive, by their credit, the trade and manufactures of their own country, in ſpite of the ſupine negligence of thoſe whoſe more immediate care it ought to be to cultivate and promote them.

VII.

COMMON SENSE.

SATURDAY, April 30, 1737. N° 14.

THOSE who attack the fundamental laws of virtue and morality, urge the uncertainty of them, and alledge their variations in different countries, and even in different ages in the ſame countries. Morality, ſay they, is local, and conſequently an imaginary thing, ſince what is rejected in one climate as a vice, is practiſed in another as a virtue; and, according to them, the voice of nature ſpeaks as many different languages as there are nations in the world.

The dangers and ill conſequences of this doctrine are obvious, but ſurely the falſity of it is not leſs ſo; and the moſt charitable opinion one can entertain of thoſe who propagate it, is, that they miſtake faſhion and cuſtom for nature and reaſon. The invariable laws of juſtice and morality are the firſt and univerſal emanations of human reaſon, while unprejudiced and uncorrupted; and we may as well ſay, that ſickneſs is the natural ſtate of the body, as that injuſtice and immorality are the natural ſituation of the mind. We contract moſt of the diſtempers of the one, by the irregularity of our appetites, and of the other, by yielding to the impetuoſity of our paſſions; but, in both caſes, reaſon, when conſulted, ſpeaks a different language.

I admit, that the prevailing cuſtoms and faſhions of moſt countries are not founded upon reaſon, and, on the contrary, are too frequently repugnant to it: but then the reaſonable people of thoſe countries condemn and abhor, though, it may be, they too wittingly comply with, or, at leaſt, have not courage enough openly to oppoſe, them.

The people of rank and diſtinction, in every country, are properly called the people of faſhion; becauſe, in truth, they ſettle the faſhion. Inſtead of ſubjecting themſelves to the laws, they take meaſure

of

of their own appetites and passions, and then make laws to fit them; which laws, though neither founded in justice, nor enacted by a legal authority, too often prevail over, and insult, both justice and authority. This is fashion.

In this light, I have often considered the word *honor* in its fashionable acceptation in this country, and must confess, that, were that the universal meaning of it throughout this kingdom, it would very much confirm the doctrine I endeavour to confute; and would be so contrary to that honor which reason, justice, and common sense, point out, that I should not wonder, if it inclined people to call in question the very existence of honor itself.

The character of a man of honor, as received in the *beau monde*, is something so very singular, that it deserves a particular examination; and, though easier observed than described, I shall endeavour to give my readers a description of it, illustrated with some original pieces, which have luckily fallen into my hands.

A man of honor is one, who peremptorily affirms himself to be so, and who will cut any body's throat that questions it, though upon the best grounds. He is infinitely above the restraints which the laws of God or man lay upon vulgar minds, and knows no other tyes but those of honor; of which word he is to be the sole expounder. He must strictly adhere to a party denomination, though he may be utterly regardless of its principles. His expence should exceed his income considerably, not for the necessaries, but for the superfluities of life, that the debts he contracts may do him honor. There should be a haughtiness and insolence in his deportment, which is supposed to result from conscious honor. If he be choleric, and wrong-headed into the bargain, with a good deal of animal courage, he acquires the glorious character of a man of nice and jealous honor: and, if all these qualifications are duly seasoned with the genteelest vices, the man of honor is compleat; any thing his wife, children, servants, or tradesmen, may think to the contrary, notwithstanding.

Belville is allowed to be a man of the most consummate honor, that this or any age ever produced. The men are proud of his acquaintance, and the women of his protection; his party glories in being countenanced by him, and his honor is frequently quoted as a sanction for their conduct. But some original letters, which I shall give my readers, will let them more intimately into the particulars of so shining a character, than mere description would do.

He had run out a considerable fortune by a life of pleasure, particularly by gaming, and, being delicately scrupulous in points of honor, he wrote the following letter to his attorney after an ill run at play:

"SIR,

"I HAD a damned tumble last night at hazard, "and must raise a thousand within a week; get "it me upon any terms, for I would rather suffer the "greatest incumbrance upon my fortune, than the least "blemish upon my honor. As for those clamorous "rascals the tradesmen, insist upon my privilege, and "keep

"keep them off as long as poſſible; we may chance "to ruin ſome of them, before they can bring us "to trial.

"Yours, &c.

"BELVILLE.

"To Mr. Tho. Gooſetree, attorney,
"in Furnival's Inn."

But, leſt the endeavours of Mr. Gooſetree ſhould prove ineffectual, Belville, from the ſame principle of honor, reſolved, at all events, to ſecure that ſum collaterally, and therefore wrote the following letter to the firſt miniſter:

"SIR,

"I WAS applied to yeſterday in your name by "*** to vote for the point which is to come "into our houſe to-morrow; but, as it was extremely "contrary to my opinion and principles, I gave him "no explicit anſwer, but took ſome time to con-"ſider of it. I have therefore the honor now to "acquaint you, that I am determined to give my "concurrence to this affair; but muſt deſire, at the "ſame time, that you will immediately ſend *** "to me, with the fifteen hundred pounds he offered "me yeſterday, and for which I have a preſſing oc-"caſion this morning. I am perſuaded you know "me too well to ſcruple this payment beforehand, and "that you will not be the firſt perſon that ever "queſtioned the honor of,

"SIR,

"Your moſt faithful humble ſervant,

"BELVILLE."

I find another letter, of the same date, to a lady, who appears to be the wife of his most intimate friend:

"MY DEAR,

"I HAVE just now received yours, and am very "sorry for the uneasiness your husband's behaviour has given you of late; though I cannot be "of your opinion, that he suspects our connection. "We have been bred up together from children, and "have lived in the strictest friendship ever since; so "that I dare say he would as soon suspect me of a design to murder, as wrong him this way. And you "know it is to that confidence and security of his, "that I owe the happiness that I enjoy. However, "in all events, be convinced that you are in the "hands of a man of honor, who will not suffer you "to be ill-used; and, should my friend proceed to "any disagreeable extremities with you, depend upon "it, I will cut the cuckold's throat for him.

"Yours most tenderly."

The fourth and last letter is to a friend, who had, probably, as high notions of honor as himself, by the nature of the affair in which he requires his assistance:

"DEAR CHARLES,

"PRYTHEE come to me immediately, to serve "me in an affair of honor. You must know, I "told a damned lye last night in a mixed company; "and a formal odd dog, in a manner, insinuated that "I did so: upon which, I whispered him to be in "Hyde-Park this morning, and to bring a friend

"with

"with him, if he had ſuch a thing in the world. "The booby was hardly worth my reſentment; but "you know my delicacy, where honor is concerned.

"Yours,

"BELVILLE."

It appears, from theſe authentic pieces, that Mr. Belville, filled with the nobleſt ſentiments of honor, paid all debts but his juſt ones; kept his word ſcrupulouſly in the flagitious ſale of his conſcience to a miniſter; was ready to protect, at the expence of his friend's life, his friend's wife, whom, by the opportunities that friendſhip had given him, he had corrupted; and puniſhed truth with death, when it intimated, however juſtly, the want of it in himſelf.

This perſon of refined honor, conſcious of his own merit and virtue, is a moſt unmerciful cenſor of the leſſer vices and failings of others; and laviſhly beſtows the epithets of ſcoundrel and raſcal upon all thoſe who, in a ſubordinate rank of life, ſeem to aſpire to any genteel degree of immorality. An awkward country gentleman, who ſells his ſilent vote cheap, is with him a ſad dog. The induſtrious tradeſmen are a pack of cheating raſcals, who ſhould be better regulated, and not ſuffered to impoſe upon people of condition; and ſervants are a parcel of idle ſcoundrels, that ought to be uſed ill, and not paid their wages, in order to check their inſolence.

It is not to be imagined how pernicious the example of ſuch a creature is to ſociety; he is admired, and conſequently imitated: he not only immediately corrupts his own circle of acquaintance, but the contagion

tagion ſpreads itſelf to infinity, as circles in water produce one another, though gradually leſs marked out, in proportion as they are remoter from the cauſe of the firſt.

To ſuch practice and ſuch examples in higher life, may juſtly be imputed the general corruption and immorality which prevail through this kingdom. But, when ſuch is the force of faſhion, and when the examples of people of the firſt rank in a country are ſo prevalent as to dignify vice and immorality, in ſpite of all laws divine and human, how popular might they make virtue, if they would exert their power in its cauſe! and how muſt they, in their cooler moments, reproach themſelves, when they come to reflect, that, by their fatal examples, they have beggared, corrupted, and it may be, enſlaved, a whole nation!

VIII.

COMMON SENSE.

SATURDAY, May 14, 1737. N° 16.

I HAVE lately read with great pleaſure father Du Halde's account of China, where I have found ſeveral rules of morality and good government, which the politeſt nations in Europe might adopt with honor, and practiſe with advantage. Many of them are conveyed, according to the oriental cuſtom, in allegories and fables, ſo that they ſtrike one more ſenſibly, and imprint themſelves deeper in the memory,

mory, by their connexion with ſome familiar image. Among others, I obſerved this remarkable one, which I ſhall now give my readers.

Hoen Kong aſked his miniſter Koan Tchong, "What was the moſt to be feared in a government?" Koan Tchong anſwered, "In my mind, ſir, nothing "is more to be dreaded than what they call *the rat* "*in the ſtatue.*" Hoen Kong not underſtanding the allegory, Koan Tchong explained it to him. "You "know, ſir, ſaid he, that it is a common practice to "erect ſtatues to the genius of the place: theſe "ſtatues are of wood, hollow within, and painted "without. If a rat gets into one of them, one does "not know how to get him out: one does not care "to make uſe of fire, for fear of burning the wood; "one cannot dip it in water, for fear of waſhing off "the colours; ſo that the regard one has for the "ſtatue ſaves the rat that is got into it. Such, ſir, "are in every government thoſe, *who, without virtue* "*or merit, have gained the favour of their prince:* "*they ruin every thing*; *one ſees it, one laments it, but* "*does not know how to remedy it.*"

I approve of the moral of the ſtory, and am very much of Koan Tchong's mind, that nothing is to be dreaded more in a government than this rat in the ſtatue; but how he came to be of that mind himſelf, I cannot eaſily comprehend, for our author ſays he was a miniſter, and conſequently of the rat kind. But as he does not indeed ſay, that he was the firſt, or ſole miniſter, I am inclined to think that he was only one of thoſe who have the name and ſalary of miniſters, without any of the power, and who are often glad to

give

give a ſlap by the bye to the firſt miniſter, though they have not courage enough openly to attack him.

After this ſhort remark, I return to the allegory itſelf, which I cannot ſay is ſo apt as I expected, from a people ſo much verſed in that manner of inſtruction. The parallel drawn between the emperor and a wooden ſtatue is ſo diſreſpectful and uncourtly, that I could have wiſhed our author had informed us, how his Chineſe majeſty had reliſhed the ſimilitude, that is, in caſe he took all the force of it; for, in reality, it was making no difference between an anointed head and a wooden one. A rat may very well eat his way into a ſtatue unſeen, unfelt, and unſmelt: but can a miniſter, eſpecially ſuch a one as is here deſcribed, without virtue or merit, nibble himſelf into a prince's favour, and the prince not ſmell a rat? It is impoſſible; and the bare ſuppoſition of it was highly injurious to his royal wiſdom and penetration. I will admit, in favour of Koan Tchong, that the eaſtern monarchs have not that degree of ſagacity, which ſo eminently diſtinguiſhes and adorns the European ones; and I will allow, that they are more likely to be ſurprized and impoſed upon by the artifices of a deſigning miniſter; their indolent and retired way of life, ſoaking in the arms of their imperial conſorts, or wantoning in the embraces of their concubines, not giving them the ſame opportunity of ſeeing, or being informed. But ſtill, when this general rule is univerſally ſeen and lamented, as Koan Tchong expreſſes it, the unanimous voice, the juſt complaints, the groans, and the deſolation, of a ruined and oppreſſed people, muſt reach, muſt affect, and must rouze his majesty, if he be but ever so little above a statue. If not, if such an impossibility could be supposed, I must then confess, that the allegory of the painted wood is so far just, as that the king's head would properly be *but the sign of the government*.

The conclusion Koan Tchong draws from this allegory is no less false and absurd; for, says he, when the rat is got into the statue, one does not know how to get him out. One does not dare to make use of fire, for fear of burning the wood; one cannot dip it in water, for fear of washing off the colours: so that the regard one has for the statue saves the rat that is got into it. This tender regard for the statue would, with all submission to Koan Tchong, in my opinion, much better have become an Hibernian courtier, than a Chinese one; for it is saying, in very good Irish, that the statue, from regard one has for it, shall be entirely devoured, for fear of being a little damaged or defaced. Whereas I should rather think, that the best way of shewing that regard for the statue would be, by saving as much as ever one could of it from the further depredations of the rat; even though it were to cost a limb or two, as is frequently practised upon human bodies. But, to do Koan Tchong justice, I do not impute his reasoning to want of parts; I rather think it was a piece of ministerial logic, which has been used in other countries besides China. Here the minister breaks out, and the minister too, who seems to have no opinion of the distinguishing faculty of his prince, when he tries such a piece of sophistry upon him, which, I dare

I dare ſay, he would not have ventured in any other company. For he ſo cloſely connects the rat and the ſtatue, and conſequently the king and the miniſter, that, in effect, he makes them but one fleſh, and one would think they grew together like the two Hungarian girls*; by this way of reaſoning, whoever attacked this all-devouring rat, *alias* miniſter, was an enemy to the ſtatue, *alias* king; and, *vice verſa*, thoſe that were friends to rat and miniſter were friends to ſtatue and king.

This indiſſoluble union would, I own, be moſt excellent doctrine for a miniſter to inculcate, could he find either king or nation weak enough to believe it; but I can never imagine that any thing ſo abſurd could be received by the Chineſe, who are a wiſe and ſenſible people: at leaſt, it could not extend itſelf beyond the walls of the palace.

Let us now conſider the allegory literally. Theſe ſacred, painted, tawdry images, are erected to the genii of the place: they are the productions of ſuperſtition, and, probably, the creatures of the bonzes, who dub them ſacred, and exhibit them as repreſentations, wooden ones, alas! of the divinity. Sacrilegious rats eat their way into them, and endanger their wooden exiſtence. What is to be done? Why truly they are to devour with impunity, for fear the ſtatue ſhould receive ſome ſmall damage in the reſcue; as if there were not a thouſand ways of coming at the rat, with little or no danger to the ſtatue. For inſtance, ſhaking it ſoundly might probably make the dwelling of

* Two Hungarian girls, that were ſhewn ſome years ago as a fine ſight, and were faſtened together by the rump.

the

the rat ſo uneaſy, that he might be willing to quit it, for fear of ſomething worſe afterwards.

There is another obvious expedient that occurs, which is that of ſending a cat up after him: but to this, I own, I have ſome objection myſelf, becauſe, though the cat would kill the rat, he would poſſibly remain in his place, and be as unwilling to quit it. But is it poſſible that the uſeful art of rat-catching ſhould be unknown to ſo ingenious a people as the Chineſe? If it is, I would adviſe our Eaſt-India company to ſend them a rat-catcher or two next voyage, for whom they might expect as conſiderable returns, and advantages, as Whittington is reported to have made by his cat. Though, I am very ſorry to ſay it, the noble art and myſtery of rat-catching has greatly declined even here of late; and I ſhould be at a loſs to find an honeſt and ſkilful artiſt to recommend to them.

But can one ſuppoſe, that the religion and piety of the bonzes would ſuffer them to remain indifferent ſpectators of ſuch ſacrilegious outrages; and that they, who can diſlodge a devil, cannot get out a rat; unleſs one has little charity enough to believe, that the bonzes, by a ſort of commutation, are not unwilling to let the rats take ſanctuary in their ſtatues, to be rid of them themſelves, and ſo, by an intereſted and impious connivance, give up their gods to ſave their bacon?

To come now to the allegorical ſenſe, which Koan Tchong had ſuch a mind to eſtabliſh. A miniſter without virtue or merit gains the favour of his prince: he ruins every thing; one ſees it, one laments it, but one

one does not know how to remedy it. To me the remedy ſeems very eaſy and obvious; take the miniſter away from him, and prevent the ruin, that threatened both him and his country. I do not doubt, indeed, but the miniſter would, during the operation, cry out, like Koan Tchong; you attack the king, you deface the king, you wound the king through my ſides, and would plead the king, as women do their bellies, to reſpite execution: but, ſurely, upon examination, a degree of ſagacity, much inferior to that of matrons, would be ſufficient to bring him in not quick with king, but a diſtinct and ſeparate body, eaſily removed, without the leaſt danger to the ſovereign.

Having fully diſcuſſed this allegory, I ſhall conclude with adopting one part of it, which is, that nothing is ſo much to be dreaded in a government, as a miniſter without virtue or merit, who gains the favour of his prince; but with entirely rejecting the latter part, that one ſees and laments it, but, out of regard to the prince, one does not know how to remedy it; ſince that very regard for the prince ſhould excite one to endeavour it, and common ſenſe points out the means of doing it, if there be bur common honeſty enough to put them in practice.

IX *.

COMMON SENSE.

SATURDAY, June 4, 1737. N° 19.

To the Author of COMMON SENSE.

— *Vocem Comœdia tollit.* HOR.

Comedy lifts her voice.

SIR,

AS the cause of common ſenſe and the ſtage are jointly concerned, ſome obſervations on the bill depending at preſent for the regulation of the latter cannot be thought improper for your paper; eſpecially ſince I believe it will appear by them to be ineffectual to the end propoſed, and injurious to the poet, the player, and the public.

The end, propoſed by this bill, is the regulation of theatrical entertainments, which, from their exceſs, fill both town and country with idleneſs and debauchery; and, from being under no reſtraint, exhibit to the public encomiums on vice, and laugh away the ſober principles of modeſty and virtue.

A deſign of this kind is certainly worthy the care of the legiſlature; ſince every one, who thinks in the juſt mean between libertiniſm and ſeverity, muſt be con-

* The act for licenſing the theatres was attacked with great ſtrength of reaſoning by our nobleman in his famous ſpeech on that ſubject, and with great humour and delicacy in this eſſay. But, notwithſtanding his efforts, the bill was carried through both houſes with an amazing rapidity, and received the royal aſſent the 21ſt of June, 1737.

vinced that a well-governed ſtage is an ornament to the ſociety, an encouragement to wit and learning, and a ſchool of virtue and good manners; while a licentious one is the parent of looſe deſires, a nurſery of vice, effeminacy, and irreligion.

But let us examine the preſent bill by the end propoſed—

Will it tend to a regulation by decreaſing the number?

I think it is plain, that it will have the contrary effect; ſince, while a diſcretionary power of licenſing them remains in any one perſon whatſoever, a way is left open for APPLICATION, which, it cannot be thought, will be always unſucceſsful. And I ſee no reaſon why it is not as well worth the charge of a miniſtry to ſend companies of ſtrollers round to the corporations, to entertain them *gratis* with political plays before an election, as it has been to circulate political news-papers upon the like occaſion. For it may very well be preſumed, that Caleb * hanged in effigy, and dropping limb from limb like Harlequin, will conduce as much to render him unpopular in a country audience, as the wit and ſatire of a Gazetteer †. And no one can doubt, but that com-

* The Craftſman.

† The Daily Gazetteer was a title given very properly to certain papers, each of which laſted but a day. Into this, as a common ſink, was received all the traſh which had been before diſperſed in ſeveral journals, and circulated at the public expence of the nation. The authors were the ſame obſcure men: though ſometimes relieved by occaſional eſſays from ſtateſmen, courtiers, biſhops, deans, and doctors. The meaner ſort were rewarded with money; others with places or benefices, from an hundred to a thouſand pounds a year. See the Dunciad, Book II.

mon

mon ſenſe will be expoſed upon ſuch ſtages, and ridiculed, for the diverſion of a mayor and aldermen, with great ſucceſs. Nor can this conjecture of mine be thought improbable, from any difficulty to ſupply ſuch a number of inferior play-houſes with actors and poetry; ſince, in the preſent ſtate of trade, the exciſe officers may, at their leiſure hours, ſupply the firſt, and the ſeveral ingenious authors of the Gazetteer * club for the other. The miraculous ſir A. B. muſt have an excellent head for a political pantomime; and Mrs. Oſborne herſelf can condeſcend to be waggiſh for the ſervice of the government.

This ſcheme, in time, muſt affect the freedom of election, ſince a purſe-proud court-candidate might eaſily draw into his intereſt the governing part of moſt corporations, I mean the women, by this terrible menace, "D—mn me, madam, if you do not "make Mr. mayor return me, you ſhall have no "more plays, by G—d."

As it is plain therefore that this ſcheme muſt increaſe the number, will it produce any good effect by any reſtraint that will probably be laid on the pieces performed?

The anſwer that will be given to this queſtion is, that they muſt all undergo my lord chamberlain's inſpection. Is then every lord chamberlain a wit and a critic, juſt as every Merry Andrew is a phyſician, by his office? or is it reaſonable to ſuppoſe that one man can peruſe all the dramatic poetry that is produced in this ſcribbling kingdom of Great Britain;

* Of theſe, Oſborne and Arnall, mentioned above, p. 2, and p. 7, appear to have been the moſt reſpectable perſonages.

or even in that ſmall retreat of the Muſes, where moſt of theſe pieces are generated, and from whence, for the future, we muſt expect a ſupply? As this is in its nature impoſſible, my lord will probably delegate this authority to ſome of his domeſtics; the chaplain, for tragedy; the cook, or the porter, may execute the office of comedy-inſpector. And when that is the caſe, beſides the abuſe of juſtice, which is always ſeen in inferior juriſdictions, nobody can ſuppoſe theſe delegates can have equal taſte in the politer ſtudies, or be as good judges of wit and morality, as my lord himſelf: nor will they be inclined to men of merit in the profeſſion of poetry, who are ſo little verſed in the proper methods of making court to their ſuperiors.

Beſides, if the ſcheme above-mentioned is put into execution, wit and ſatire will be poſtponed for party reflection and abuſe. The comic glaſs, inſtead of expoſing vice and folly, will be made a corrupt uſe of, to magnify the features of ſome honeſt country ſquire in the oppoſition into a papiſt or a ſaracen, to the affright of himſelf and his neighbours; while the curioſity of the vulgar, and the opportunities of indulging it at theſe entertainments, will ſtill continue, and have the ſame tendency to produce idleneſs and luxury as they have at preſent; though it may be preſumed that the taſte for theſe entertainments will, by this method, gradually decay.

I think I have, by theſe few obſervations above, demonſtrated that this bill cannot have its deſired effect. I ſhall now endeavour to prove that it will

be

be injurious to the poet, the player, and the public in general.

It is very well known how difficult it is at preſent for merit, without intereſt, to bring any play upon the ſtage: and will the pride and ſelf-conceit of the manager be abated by this regulation? or, can a poet's temper be brought to ſubmit to ſtrike out whatever offends ſo many critics, as will have a judicial authority to blot by virtue of this act? The neceſſitous indeed will, perhaps with reluctance, comply: but what can be expected from that band, who prefer ſolid pudding to empty praiſe? Can it be thought that a man, who has ſenſe and learning enough to write a play fit for the ſtage, and who has ſtood the judgment of a play-houſe monarch and his privy-council of critics, will be induced to cringe to a chaplain, a porter, a cook, or a ſecretary?

If I might preſume to ſpeak my judgment, formed on experience, I ſcarce believe he would ſubmit to my lord himſelf.

Here then is a manifeſt diſcouragement to that ſpecies of learning, which inſtructs youth, and delights in age; which is an ornament to the man of fortune, a comfort and ſupport of neceſſity; which entertains in the cloſet, and diverts abroad; ſhortens the journey of the traveller, and is a chearful companion in ſolitude and exile *.

As this is a diſcouragement to poetry, ſo it lays ſuch a reſtraint on the actor, and ſo ſubjects him to the arbitrary will of an inſolent patentee, that few I believe, will think it worth their while to leave to

* Cicero, Orat. pro Archia Poëta.

law, the counter, or Ireland itself, to get a poor tawdry subsistence on the stage.

If dramatic poesy is, under proper regulations, a benefit, the discouragement of it in general, which, from what has been observed above, will be effected by this act, must be injurious to the public; and if this bill should pass into a law, a Wycherley or Congreve will never rise again on the English stage: for there will be always fools enough to fill the licensed play-houses, that delight in farce, noise, and show; and, while that is the case, no manager will run the hazard of endeavouring to refine the taste of the vulgar, by complying with that of the learned.

Besides the loss of the little wit still remaining among us, I am afraid that the swarm of insignificant mortals, who are now employed in the study of this kind of poetry, will, upon the disadvantage this bill will lay them under, desert this only fertile spot of Parnassus, and join in an insurrection with the distillers *, or turn from robbing the dead to the plunder of the living.

I need not here mention the infringement attempted by this act on the liberty of the press.

* The act, for restraining the sale of spirituous liquors in small quantities, had failed of its effect. The informers, who dared to give intelligence against offenders, were so roughly treated by the populace, and so ill protected by the ministry, that the abuse became intolerable. It was so manifestly the interest of the distillers to defeat the bill, that they were supposed to have had a hand in these insurrections; and the noble author of this essay humorously hints, that writers of plays, being now disappointed, for want of proper licences, in their retail of wit, would suffer themselves to be employed by the composers, retailers, or consumers, of liquors, to join in these riots, and perhaps take to the road.

But if, notwithſtanding theſe few haſty objections, the wiſdom of the legiſlature ſhould think proper to paſs this bill, I would beg leave to ſubmit the two following amendments to their conſideration.

Firſt, that the ſtrolling companies, licenſed, be reſtrained to ſome particular number, and not be permitted to act in any borough or corporation.

Secondly, ſince wit and modeſty, morality and religion, ought chiefly to be regarded in theſe entertainments, that every thing deſtructive of either may be ſure to be expunged: and ſince the fair ſex have lately ſhewn ſo laudable a zeal for wit, that they may have a ſhare in the adminiſtration of it.

I propoſe that the lord chamberlain's power, given by this act, be transferred to a committee of the maids of honor and biſhops, who ſhall act in joint commiſſion in this important affair; ſince the firſt are the beſt judges of wit and modeſty, the latter of morality and religion, in this kingdom.

Yours,

A. Z.

X.

COMMON SENSE.

SATURDAY, July 16, 1737. N° 25.

IT is the complaint of moſt men, who have lived any time in the world, that the preſent age is much degenerated in its morals within the memory of man. I am afraid this complaint is not altogether without foundation. That there has been a gradual decay of public ſpirit for ſome years, cannot be denied; and which owes its original, if I am not very much miſtaken, to our party diviſions.

There is a particular maxim among parties, which alone is ſufficient to corrupt a whole nation; which is, to countenance and protect the moſt infamous fellows who happen to herd amongſt them. There is no man, let his private character be ever ſo ſcandalous, that can be of ſome uſe to ſerve a turn, but immediately grows to be a man of conſequence with his party.

It is ſomething ſhocking to common ſenſe, to ſee the man of honor and the knave, the man of parts and the blockhead, put upon an equal foot; which is often the caſe amongſt parties. In the ſtruggles that happen about elections, when ſome candidate of a fair character has been ſet up on one ſide, how often have you ſeen the moſt abandoned knave of the other party put up to oppoſe him, and both ſupported with equal zeal! Parties will always find ſomething or other, in the worſt of men, to reconcile them to the obnoxious parts of their characters. He, that has ſenſe enough to diſtinguiſh right from wrong, can make a noiſe; nay, the leſs ſenſe, the more obſtinacy, eſpecially in a bad cauſe; and the greater knave, the more obedient to his leaders, eſpecially when they are playing the rogue. Theſe are the beſt tools; and ſuch are the qualities neceſſary for putting in execution the bad meaſures which the corrupt leaders of parties intend to carry on, if they are uppermoſt.

Party

Party zeal changes the name of things; black is white, vice is virtue, a bribe in an office is called a perquiſite, and the moſt ſtudied and concerted fraud, that can enter into the head of the moſt thorough-paced knave, ſhall be voted a little negligence. In fine, party merit takes away all blots and ſtains out of the blackeſt characters; and he that deſerves to be hanged, by all laws human and divine, for his conduct in private life, may, at the ſame time, be an angel with his party.

Mendax, while he held an office in the ſtate, is detected in a little mean fraud; for Mendax was of a complection ſo delicate, and had ſomething in his conſcience ſo ſcrupulouſly nice, that he fancied he wronged his family, if he did not play the rogue whenever any thing was to be got by it; but, however, Mendax, in a public capacity, has been always true to the troop. The chiefs of the party having met, to conſider how to behave with reſpect to Mendax in this critical juncture, all the men of honor amongſt them were for giving him up, and even joining in any puniſhment that might be laid upon him, in order to convince the world, that they would not protect the man that had wronged his country; but a veteran, who was grown old in all the iniquitous practices of party, and who had acquired authority by his experience, was quite of another opinion. "Mendax," ſays he, "has always been an active "member of the cauſe:" and what have we to do with his morals, or his honor? adding, "The man that "is true to the troop muſt always be ſkreened, let "him be guilty of what he will."

Thus,

Thus, by the deteſtable politics of party, Mendax was countenanced and careſſed under the infamy of a moſt ſcandalous fraud; and lived to do his country more miſchief, by the corruption which he afterwards ſpread through it, than a famine, a plague, or a war, could have done.

If we look back into the hiſtory of a few years paſt, we ſhall find that the immenſe eſtates that have been made, by the numerous fraudulent projects with which this virtuous age has abounded, have been by perſons who pretended to be zealous party men, and have gone great lengths in party: nay, ſome have been ſo cunning as to ſhift ſides, and go over to the ſtrongeſt, juſt before they have reſolved to ſtrike ſome bold ſtroke, wiſely ſecuring a good retreat before they enter upon action; ſo that I have often thought, that a ſtrong party is the ſame thing to a cheat, that a ſtrong iſland in the Weſt-Indies is to a pirate, a place of ſafety to lay up all he has ſtolen.

As I have intitled my paper, Common Senſe; the public may depend upon it, that I ſhall not write the ſenſe of a party, becauſe common ſenſe muſt be free from all prejudice, and party ſenſe is obſerved to be rarely ſo. I will farther add, that I take common ſenſe and common honeſty to be ſo near akin, that, whenever I ſee a man turn knave, I ſhall not ſtick to pronounce him a fool. I have the experience of the times in which I have lived, to juſtify me in this opinion. I never knew a man, that ſet out with good principles, and afterwards became a proſtitute to men in power, but ſome creature of a little, narrow, mean underſtanding. A piece of ribbon, or a word

added

added to a name, ſhall reconcile a fool to the moſt deſtructive meaſures that the moſt corrupt miniſter or miniſters can enter upon: but common ſenſe has ſome modeſty; it has a ſenſe of ſhame, and cannot act in direct oppoſition to truth and honor.

But I am farther of opinion, that, if a writer ſhould at this time expect to make his way in the world, and to become popular, by running violently into all the prejudices of a party, he would meet with a reception from the public very different from what he expected. Party prejudice is not the ſame thing it was. The malignity of the diſtemper is worn out; and it muſt be a ſingular pleaſure to a man who loves his country, to find that thoſe two odious diſtinctions of Whig and Tory, with which we formerly reproached one another, are uſed no more. All men unplaced, and unpenſioned, talk and think alike; and we ſee gentlemen, who were bred up in oppoſite principles, and, though in other reſpects men of honor, had imbibed all the prejudices of their reſpective parties, now meet and ſhake hands, and, upon comparing notes, wonder that they had ever differed: and what makes it more extraordinary is, that all this ſhould happen without their being reproached, either by their country, or their particular friends, of changing their principles; which ſhews there is ſomething in an honeſt and an upright conduct, that will carry it through the world, and ſupport it againſt all the ſuggeſtions that calumny can invent.

I will not ſay, that it is proſperity that has wrought this great change. I am afraid this union of minds is not owing to a univerſal content of the nation: the

cauſes

causes of it are too well known to need any explanation; but, be it as it will, it is certain that the cure of any grievances that may fall upon us can come from nothing else but this union. This is not only my opinion; it is certainly the opinion of those whose safety, next to the corruption of the times, depends upon our divisions.

When a nation is divided against itself, how great must be the providence that must save it from sinking! When the people are broken into parties and factions, worrying and reviling one another, what a fine harvest it yields to the common enemy! If I should be asked, who is that common enemy? I shall only answer, that there are banditti in time of peace as well as in time of war; there are free-booters, who are not regularly listed on either side, and who, while both sides are engaged against each other, will certainly plunder the nation.

I will only say, beware of those who are labouring to keep alive the animosities of party: it is true, they have laboured in vain; and Providence has so confounded their devices, that they have united us by the very methods they took to keep us asunder; but they have not yet given up the game for lost. They are continually throwing out bones of contention; they are raking up the dying embers of party, in hopes of kindling a new flame.

There is a set of men, who are governed by no principles, and have no friends or followers but such as are attached to them for mercenary ends. These assume to themselves the name of a party, though they do not carry so much as the appearance of it: it is they

who

who are for fomenting divisions, in hopes that, when the madness of party shall again seize the people, both sides will by turns fall in with them, in order to be revenged and undo each other, which will save a great deal in bribes; a method of doing business, which must have an end, when there is no money left in the nation. But it happens, that they have been so awkward in concealing their foul play, that all the world has seen through it; and it looks as if Providence had infatuated their cunning, with a kind intention of putting us upon our guard, and of rouzing that antient spirit of our people which has preserved this nation when any incroachments have been made upon its liberties.

But though there may be no dangerous designs at present, and the whole body of the people may entertain the same opinion of the good intentions and of the great abilities of our present set of ministers as they really merit, yet it is not amiss to have our eyes about us. Political jealousy is inseparable from the minds of good patriots; it is their duty to be watchful for the public, and suspicious of the designs of men in power. A certain degree of this jealousy is absolutely necessary to be kept up at all times, for the preservation of liberty. This jealousy, I say, is our great security; and it cannot decay till public spirit decays.

The individuals of that great body called *the people*, are so taken up with their several avocations, that they are not always at leisure to examine well the designs of men in power, and to see through those disguises which they endeavour to throw over bad measures;

 therefore

therefore it is the duty of every private man to give the alarm whenever he perceives any thing doing which muſt have a tendency to alter and impair that plan of government under which we and our anceſtors have lived free.—And this we propoſe ſhall be partly the buſineſs of this paper.

The adverſaries, that in all probability will oppoſe us in this deſign, are not much to be feared. That paper, which is looked upon as the work of the greateſt wits, and moſt profound politicians of the faction, for they are not to be called a party, might be excelled by the loweſt productions in Grub-ſtreet; yet here you ſee all the good ſenſe that is amongſt them, and it would be reaſon enough for making the people uneaſy, if they ſhould have a notion that the public affairs were to be managed by ſuch hands as publiſh the moſt idle, the moſt inconſiſtent, and moſt ſlaviſh ſchemes of politics, that the world ever ſaw.

I cannot help thinking, that they have taken up a notion, that the only qualification of a political writer is a hardy and intrepid manner of aſſerting what is not, and of denying what is. As to their profligate manner of endeavouring to turn public ſpirit into ridicule, they have done it with ſo little wit, that they have not been able to gain the very laughers on their ſide. Thanks be to their dullneſs, it riſes againſt their oppoſition: he that laughs with them, muſt laugh without a jeſt; and therefore, as often as I ſaw my predeceſſors employ their wit againſt thoſe who never uſed that weapon againſt them, I own I did not look upon it as very generous in them; methinks, if I were maſter of that weapon called wit, I ſhould be as much

much ashamed of drawing it against an Osborne, or a Walsingham, as I should of drawing a sword against a naked man.

Upon the whole, though I have promised never to be dull with design, yet I would not have the public expect much from me at such times as I shall be drawn into a dispute with that paper, which has a mob of Swiss writers to support it; it is a Briareus with an hundred hands, but not one head: and as there is neither conduct, nor order, nor discipline, nor honor, amongst them, they will be as easily defeated as any other rabble.

XI.

COMMON SENSE.

SATURDAY, August 20, 1737. N° 30.

THOUGH the separation of the parliament generally suspends the vigor of political altercations, I doubt it creates domestic ones, not less sharp and acrimonious; and, possibly, the individuals of both houses may find as warm debates at home, as any they have met with during the course of the session.

Their motion for adjourning into the country is, I believe, seldom seconded by their wives and daughters; and, if at last they carry it, it is more by the exertion of their authority, than by the cogency of their reasoning.

This

This act of power so strenuously withstood at first, and so unwillingly submitted to at last, lays but an indifferent foundation of domestic harmony during their retirement; and I am surprized that the throne, which never fails, at the end of the session, to recommend to both houses certain wholesome and general rules for their behaviour and conduct, when scattered in their respective counties, should hitherto have taken no notice of their ladies, nor have made them the least excuse for the disagreeable consequences which result to them from the recess. Nay, even in the female reigns of queen Elizabeth and queen Anne, I cannot discover that any advice, or application of this nature, has ever been directed to the fair sex; as if their uneasiness and dissatisfaction were matters of no concern to the peace and good order of the kingdom in general.

For my own part, I see this affair in a very different light; and I think I shall do both my country and the ministry good service, if, by any advice and consolation I can offer to my fair countrywomen, in this their dreadful time of trouble and trial, I can alleviate their misfortunes, and mitigate the horrors of their retirement; since it is obvious, that the people in the country, who see things but at a distance, will never believe that matters go right, when they observe a general discontent in every one but the master of the family, whose particular tranquillity they may, possibly, ascribe to particular reasons, and not to the happy state of the public. Besides that, my real concern and regard for the fair sex excites my compassion for them; and I sympathize with them

them in that ſcene of grief and deſpair which the proſpect of their ſix months exile preſents to them.

I own I have been ſo ſenſibly touched, as I have gone along the ſtreets, to ſee, at the one pair of ſtairs windows, ſo many fine eyes bathed in tears, and diſmally fixed upon the fatal waggons loading at their doors, that I reſolved, my endeavours ſhould not be wanting to adminiſter to them whatever amuſement or comfort I could think of, under their preſent calamity.

The antient philoſophers have left us moſt excellent rules for our conduct, under the various afflictions to which we are liable. They bid us not be grieved at misfortunes, nor pleaſed with proſperity; and undeniably prove, that thoſe imaginary ills of old age, ſickneſs, the loſs of friends, fortune, &c. would really not be ills, if we were but wiſe enough not to be affected by them. But I have no where found, in their writings, any conſolation offered to the fair ſex, to ſupport and ſtrengthen them under the rigors of a country life. Whether this barbarous cuſtom of confining the ladies half the year in the country was not practiſed among the antients, whether the caſe was not looked upon as above comfort or below attention, or whether the Goths and Vandals may not have deprived the learned world of thoſe valuable treatiſes, I cannot tell: but this is certain, that I know no caſe of greater compaſſion, and few of greater conſequence, than that of a fine woman, hurried, not only by her huſband, but *with* her huſband, from all the joys of London, to all the horrors of the manſion-ſeat in the country; where, not to mention many other circumſtances of this tyranny, in one particular, I fear it too often reſembles the Mezentian cruelty of tying a living body to a dead one.

I firſt addreſs myſelf to thoſe ladies, whoſe diſtinguiſhed beauty, delicacy, and accompliſhments, juſtly place them at the head of the pleaſures and faſhion of the town. Their will is the law, and their example the model, of the polite world: poſſeſſed, one half of the year, of more than imperial ſway; the other half, they groan under the uſurped power of their huſbands. Nay, even the ſuperior beauty of many ladies, like the ſuperior merit of many illuſtrious Athenians, has often both cauſed and prolonged their exile. Can kings depoſed and impriſoned experience a more cruel reverſe of fortune than this? Their caſe is certainly above comfort; and I own I am at a loſs what to recommend to them. *Succedanea* there are none; I ſhall only endeavour to ſuggeſt lenitives.

I am not abſurd enough, even to hint the uſual rural recreations, of fetching a walk, a horſe-race, an aſſize-ball, or a ſillabub under the red cow; which muſt all of them be exceedingly ſhocking to their delicacy. Beſides, I know, that, at their firſt arrival in the country, they entirely give up all hopes, not only of pleaſure, but of comfort, and, from a juſt contempt of whatever they are to ſee or hear, plunge themſelves at once into an auguſt melancholy, and a ſullen deſpair, like captive princeſſes in a tragedy.

I wiſh I could procure them a ſix-months ſleep or annihilation; but, as that is not in my power, the beſt advice I can give them, is to carry down a proviſion of the tendereſt books, which will at once improve their

their ſtyle, nouriſh all the delicacy of their ſentiments, and keep imagination awake.

The moſt voluminous romances are the moſt ſerviceable, and wear the beſt in the country, ſince four or five of them will very near hold out the ſeaſon. Beſides that, the pleaſing deſcriptions of the flowery vales, where the tender heroines ſo often bewailed the abſence of their much-loved heroes, may, by the help of a little imagination and an elegant ſympathy, render the ſolitary proſpect of the neighbouring fields a little more ſupportable.

This ſerious ſtudy may ſometimes be diverſified by ſhort and practical novels, of which the French language furniſhes great abundance. Here the cataſtrophe comes ſooner, and nature has its ſhare, as well as ſentiments; ſo that a lady may exactly fit the humour ſhe happens to be in.

If a gentle languor only inſpires tender ſentiments, ſhe may find, in the cleareſt light, whatever can be ſaid upon *le cœur & l'eſprit* (the heart and the mind), to indulge thoſe thoughts; or, if intruding nature breaks-in with warmer images, ſhe will likewiſe find in thoſe excellent manuals ſuitable and correſponding paſſages. The pleaſing tumult of the ſenſes, the ſoft annihilation, and the expiring ſighs of the diſſolving happy pair, may agreeably recall the memory of certain tranſactions in the foregoing winter, or anticipate the expected joys of the enſuing one.

Some time too may be employed in epiſtolatory correſpondence with diſtreſſed, ſympathizing, friends in the ſame ſituation, pathetically deſcribing all the diſagreeable circumſtances of the country: with this juſt exception only, "that one could bear with it "well enough for two or three months in the ſum- "mer, with the company one liked, and without "the company one diſliked."

As for the more ſecret and tender letters, which are to go under two or three directions, and as many covers, the uppermoſt to be directed by truſty Betty, and by her given into the poſtman's own hand, they of courſe furniſh out the moſt pleaſing moments of the confinement; and I dare ſay, I need neither recommend them, nor the attentive and frequent peruſal of the anſwers returned to them.

But, as theſe occupations will neceſſarily meet with ſome interruption, and as there will be intervals in the day, when thoughts will claim their ſhare, as at dinner with my lord or his neighbours, or on Sundays at church; I adviſe that they ſhould be turned as much as poſſible from the many diſagreeable, to the few agreeable proſpects, which the country affords.

Let them reflect, that theſe abſences, however painful for the time, revive and animate paſſions, which, without ſome little ceſſation, might decay and grow languid. Let them conſider, how propitious the chapter of accidents is to them in the country, and what charming events they may reaſonably flatter themſelves with, from the effuſion of ſtrong beer and port, and the friendly interpoſition of hedges, ditches, and five-barred gates: not to mention another poſſible contingency, of their huſbands meeting with Actæon's fate from their own hounds, which, whether probable or not, they know beſt.

With

With theſe proſpects, and theſe diſſipations, I ſhould hope they may paſs, or rather kill, the tedious time of their baniſhment, without very great anxiety; but, if that cannot be, there is but one expedient more which occurs to me, and which I have often known practiſed with ſucceſs; that is, the colic, and pains of the ſtomach, to ſuch a degree, as abſolutely to require the aſſiſtance of the Bath. The colic, in the ſtomach I mean, is a clean genteel diſtemper, and by no means below women of the firſt condition, and they ſhould always keep it by them, to be uſed as occaſion requires; for as its diagnoſtics are neither viſible nor certain, it is pleadable againſt huſband, neighbours, and relations, without any poſſibility of being traverſed.

As for thoſe ladies who move but in a ſecond ſphere in town, their caſe is far from being ſo compaſſionate, their fall from London to the country being by no means ſo conſiderable; nay, in ſome particulars, I am not ſure if they are not gainers by it. For they are indiſputably in the country, what they never are in town, the firſt. They give currency to faſhions and expreſſions; they are ſtared at, admired, and conſulted; and the female diſtrict forms itſelf upon their model. They are likewiſe of a more accommodating temper, and can let themſelves down to country recreations; they do not diſdain the neighbouring aſſembly, nor the captain of dragoons who commands at it. They can ſwallow a glaſs of red wine and a macaroon in the evening, when hoſpitably tendered them by the ſquire's lady, or the parſon's wife; and, upon a pinch, can make up a country dance at night, with the help of the butler, the houfe-keeper, and a couple of chairs.

It is true, thefe are but condefcenfions too, which they would be horribly afhamed of, fhould they be detected in the fact by any of their London acquaintance; but ftill, with thefe helps, the fummer goes off tolerably well, till bad roads, bad weather, and long evenings, change the fcene. Then comes the dire domeftic ftruggle: the lady expofes with fatire and contempt the ruftic pleafures that detain them in the country; the hufband retorts the pleafures of a different nature, which, he conceives, invite her ladyfhip up to town: warmth enfues, the lady grows eloquent, the hufband coarfe, and from that time, till the day is fixed for going to London, peace is banifhed the family.

The Bath would be of fovereign efficacy in this cafe too, and, like the waters of Lethé, would wafh away the remembrance of thefe difagreeable incidents; but, if that cannot be compaffed, the laft refort I can recommend to thefe ladies is, by the alternate and proper ufe of clamor and fullennefs, invectives and tears, to reduce their hufbands to feek for quiet in town.

How ufeful thefe my endeavours for the fervice of my fair countrywomen may prove, I cannot pretend to fay; but I hope, at leaft, they will be acceptable to them; and that, in return for my good intentions, they will admit my paper, with their tea tables, to diffipate fome of the tedious moments of their retirement.

XII.

COMMON SENSE.

SATURDAY, Sept. 3, 1737. N° 32.

MONSIEUR de la Rochefoucault very juſtly obſerves, that people are never ridiculous from their real, but from their affected, characters; they cannot help being what they are, but they can help attempting to appear what they are not. A hump-back is by no means ridiculous, unleſs it be under a fine coat; nor a weak underſtanding, unleſs it aſſumes the luſtre and ornaments of a bright one. Good-nature conceals and pities the inevitable defects of body or mind, but is not obliged to treat acquired ones with the leaſt indulgence. Thoſe, who would paſs upon the world talents which they have not, are as guilty in the common courſe of ſociety, as thoſe who, in the way of trade, would put off falſe money, knowing it to be ſuch; and it is as much the buſineſs of ridicule to expoſe the former, as of the law to puniſh the latter.

I do not here mean to conſider the affectation of moral virtues, which comes more properly under the definition of hypocriſy, and juſtly excites our indignation and abhorrence, as a criminal deceit; but I ſhall confine myſelf now to the affectation of thoſe leſſer talents and accompliſhments, without any of which a man may be a very worthy valuable man, and only becomes a very ridiculous one by pretending to them. Thoſe people are the proper, and, it may be, the only proper objects of ridicule; for they are above fools, who are below it, and below wise men, who are above it. They are the coxcombs lord Rochester describes as self-created, and of whom he says, that God never made one worth a groat. Besides, as they are rebels and traitors to common sense, whose natural-born subjects they are, I am justified in treating them with the utmost rigor.

I cannot be of the general opinion, that these coxcombs have first imposed upon themselves, and really think themselves what they would have others think them. On the contrary, I am persuaded that every man knows himself best, and is his own severest censor; nay, I am convinced that many a man has lived and died with faults and weaknesses, which nobody but himself ever discovered. It is true, they keep their own secrets inviolate, which makes people believe they have not found it out. Why do we discern the failings of our friends sooner and better than we do other people's, but because we interest ourselves more in them? By the same rule, we feel our own still sooner. And possibly, in this case alone, we are kinder to our friends than to ourselves; since I very much question if a man would love his friend so well if he were faultless, and he would certainly like himself the better for being so. If this supposition be true, as I think it is, my coxcombs are both the more guilty, and the more ridiculous, as they live in a constant course of practical lying, and in the absurd and sanguine hopes of passing undetected.

Fatuus, the most consummate coxcomb of this or any other age or country, has parts enough to have excelled

excelled in almoſt any one thing he would have applied himſelf to. But he muſt excel in all. He muſt be at once a wit, a lover, a ſcholar, and a ſtateſman; yet, conſcious of the impracticability of the undertaking, he parcels out his accompliſhments, and compounds to have the ſeveral branches of his merit admired in ſeparate diſtricts.

Hence, he talks politics to his women, wit to miniſters of ſtate, diſplays his learning to beaux, and brags of his ſucceſs in gallantry to his country neighbours. His caution is a proof of his guilt, and ſhews that he does not deceive himſelf, but only hopes to impoſe upon others. Fatuus's parts have undone him, and brought him to a bankruptcy of common ſenſe and judgement; as many have been ruined by great eſtates, which led them into expences they were not able to ſupport.

There are few ſo univerſal coxcombs as Fatuus, to whom I therefore gave the poſt of honor; but infinite are the numbers of minor coxcombs, who are coxcombs *quoad hoc*, and who have ſingled out certain accompliſhments, which they are reſolved to poſſeſs in ſpite of reluctant nature. Their moſt general attempts are at wit and women, as the two moſt ſhining and glittering talents in the *beau monde*.

Thus Protervus, who has a good ſerious underſtanding, contrives to paſs almoſt for a fool, becauſe he will be a wit. He muſt ſhine; he admires and purſues the luſtre of wit, which, like an *ignis fatuus*, leads him out of his way into all ſorts of abſurdities. He is awkwardly pert; he puns, twiſts words, inverts ſentences, and retails in one company the ſcraps he has

has picked up in another; but ſtill, conſcious of his own inſufficiency, he cautiouſly ſeeks to ſhine where he hopes he may dazzle, and prudently declines the encounter of the ſtrongeſt eyes. How often have I ſeen his unnatural alacrity ſuddenly confounded, and ſhrinking into ſilence, at the appearance of ſomebody of avowed and unqueſtioned wit!

Ponderoſus has a ſlow, laborious underſtanding, a good memory, and, with application, might ſucceed in buſineſs; but truly he muſt be a fine man, and ſucceed with women. He expoſes his clumſy figure by adorning it, makes declaration of love with all the form and ſolemnity of a proclamation, and ridiculouſly conſumes in revels the time he might uſefully employ at the deſk. He cannot be ignorant of his ill ſucceſs; he feels it, but endeavours to impoſe upon the world, by hinting, in one ſet of company, his ſucceſſes in another; and by whiſpering, in public places, with an air of familiarity, ſuch indifferent trifles, as would not juſtify the woman in refuſing to hear them. But how have I ſeen him ſkulk at the approach of the real favourite, and betray his conſciouſneſs of his affected character! Be it known to Ponderoſus, and all thoſe of his turn, that this vanity, beſides the abſurdity of it, leads them into a moſt immoral attempt; and that this practical defamation of a woman more juſtly deſerves an action at law, than a coarſe word raſhly uttered.

Garrulus hopes to paſs for an orator, without either words or matter; it is plain he knows his own poverty, by his laborious robbery of authors. He paſſes the nights in book-breaking, and puts off in the day-

time

time the ſtolen goods as his own; but ſo awkwardly and unſkilfully, that they are always brought back to their true owners.

Bavius, ballaſted with all the lead of a German, will riſe into poetry, without either ear or invention: he recites, what he calls his verſes, to his female relations, and his city acquaintance, but never mentions them to Pope.

Perplexus inſiſts upon being a man of buſineſs, and, though formed, at beſt, for a letter-carrier, will be a letter-writer; but, conſcious that he can neither be neceſſary nor uſeful, endeavours to be tolerated by an implicit conformity to men and times.

In ſhort, there are as many ſpecies of coxcombs, as there are deſirable qualifications and accompliſhments in life; and it would be endleſs to give inſtances of every particular vanity and affectation, by which men either make themſelves ridiculous, or, at leaſt, depreciate the other qualities they really poſſeſs. Every one's obſervation will furniſh him with examples enough of this kind. But I will now endeavour to point out the means of avoiding theſe errors; though, indeed, they are ſo obvious in themſelves, that one ſhould think it unneceſſary, if one did not daily experience the contrary.

It is very certain, that no man is fit for every thing; but it is almoſt as certain too, that there is ſcarce any one man, who is not fit for ſomething, which ſomething nature plainly points out to him, by giving him a tendency and propenſity to it. I look upon common ſenſe to be to the mind, what conſcience is to the heart, the faithful and conſtant monitor

monitor of what is right or wrong. And I am convinced that no man commits either a crime or a folly, but againſt the manifeſt and ſenſible repreſentations of the one or the other. Every man finds in himſelf, either from nature or education, for they are hard to diſtinguiſh, a peculiar bent and diſpoſition to ſome particular character; and his ſtruggling againſt it is the fruitleſs and endleſs labor of Siſyphus. Let him follow and cultivate that vocation, he will ſucceed in it, and be conſiderable in one way at leaſt; whereas, if he departs from it, he will at beſt be inconſiderable, probably ridiculous. Mankind, in general, have not the indulgence and good-nature to ſave a whole city for the ſake of five righteous; but are more inclined to condemn many righteous, for the ſake of a few guilty. And a man may eaſily ſink many virtues by the weight of one folly, but will hardly be able to protect many follies by the force of one virtue. The players, who get their parts by heart, and are to ſimulate but for three hours, have a regard, in chooſing thoſe parts, to the natural bent of their genius. Penkethman never acted Cato; nor Booth, Scrub; their invincible unfitneſs for thoſe characters would inevitably have broke out in the ſhort time of their repreſentation. How then ſhall a man hope to act with ſucceſs all his life long a borrowed and ill-ſuited character? In my mind, Pinkey got more credit by acting Scrub well, than he would have got by acting Cato ill; and I would much rather be an excellent ſhoemaker, than a ridiculous and inept miniſter of ſtate. I greatly admire our induſtrious neighbours, the Germans, for many things; but for nothing more than their ſteady adherence to the voice of nature: they indefatigably purſue the way ſhe has chalked out to them, and never deviate into any irregularities of character. Thus many of the firſt rank, if happily turned to mechanics, have employed their whole lives in the incatenation of fleas, or the curious ſculpture of cherry-ſtones; while others, whoſe thirſt of knowledge leads them to inveſtigate the ſecrets of nature, ſpend years in their elaboratory, in purſuit of the philoſopher's ſtone: but none, that I have heard of, ever deviated into an attempt at wit. Nay, even due care is taken in the education of their princes, that they may be fit for ſomething, for they are always inſtructed in ſome other trade beſides that of government; ſo that, if their genius does not lead them to be able princes, it is ten to one but they are excellent turners.

I will conclude my remonſtrance to the coxcombs of Great Britain with this admonition and engagement, that "they diſband their affectations, and "common ſenſe ſhall be their friend." Otherwiſe I ſhall proceed to further extremities, and ſingle out, from time to time, the moſt daring offenders.

I muſt obſerve, that the word *coxcomb* is of the common gender, both maſculine and feminine; and that the male coxcombs are equalled in number by the female ones, who ſhall be the ſubject of my next paper.

XIII.

COMMON SENSE.

SATURDAY, Sept. 10, 1737. N° 33.

HAVING, in my former paper, cenfured, with freedom, the affectations and follies of my own fex, I flatter myfelf, that I fhall meet with the indulgence of the ladies, while I confider, with the fame impartiality, thofe weakneffes and vanities to which their fex is as liable as ours, and, if I dare fay fo, rather more, as their fphere of action is more bounded and circumfcribed. Man's province is univerfal, and comprehends every thing, from the culture of the earth, to the government of it; men only become coxcombs, by affuming particular characters, for which they are particularly unfit, though others may fhine in thofe very characters. But the cafe of the fair fex is quite different; for there are many characters which are not of the feminine gender, and, confequently, there may be two kinds of women coxcombs; thofe who affect what does not fall within their department; and thofe who go out of their own natural characters, though they keep within the female province.

I fhould be very forry to offend, where I only mean to advife and reform; I therefore hope the fair fex will pardon me, when I give ours this preference. Let them reflect, that each fex has its diftinguifhing characteriftic: and if they can with juftice, as certainly they may, brand a man with the name of a

cott-

cott-quean, if he invades a certain female detail, which is unqueſtionably their prerogative, may not we, with equal juſtice, retort upon them, when, laying aſide their natural characters, they aſſume thoſe which are appropriated to us? The delicacy of their texture, and the ſtrength of ours, the beauty of their form, and the coarſeneſs of ours, ſufficiently indicate the reſpective vocations. Was Hercules ridiculous and contemptible with his diſtaff? Omphale would not have been leſs ſo at a review or a council-board. Women are not formed for great cares themſelves, but to ſooth and ſoften ours: their tenderneſs is the proper reward for the toils we undergo for their preſervation; and the eaſe and chearfulneſs of their converſation, our deſirable retreat from the labors of ſtudy and buſineſs. They are confined within the narrow limits of domeſtic offices; and, when they ſtray beyond them, they move excentrically, and conſequently without grace.

Agrippina, born with an underſtanding and diſpoſitions, which could, at beſt, have qualified her for the ſordid help-mate of a pawnbroker or uſurer, pretends to all the accompliſhments that ever adorned man or woman, without the poſſeſſion, or even the true knowledge, of any one of them. She would appear learned, and has juſt enough of all things, without comprehending any one, to make her talk abſurdly upon every thing. She looks upon the art of pleaſing as her maſter-piece, but miſtakes the means ſo much, that her flattery is too groſs for ſelf-love to ſwallow, and her lies too palpable to deceive for a moment; ſo that ſhe ſhocks thoſe ſhe would gain.

Mean

Mean tricks, ſhallow cunning, and breach of faith, conſtitute her miſtaken ſyſtem of politics. She endeavours to appear generous at the expence of trifles, while an indiſcreet and unguarded rapaciouſneſs diſcovers her natural and inſatiable avidity. Thus miſtaking the perfections ſhe would ſeem to poſſeſs, and the means of acquiring even them, ſhe becomes the moſt ridiculous, inſtead of the moſt complete, of her ſex.

Eudoſia, the moſt frivolous woman in the world, condemns her own ſex for being too trifling. She deſpiſes the agreeable levity and chearfulneſs of a mixed company; ſhe will be ſerious, that ſhe will; and emphatically intimates, that ſhe thinks reaſon and good ſenſe very valuable things. She never mixes in the general converſation, but ſingles out ſome one man, whom ſhe thinks worthy of her good ſenſe, and in a half voice, or *ſotto voce*, diſcuſſes her ſolid trifles in his ear, dwells particularly upon the moſt trifling circumſtances of the main trifle, which ſhe enforces with the proper inclinations of head and body, and with the moſt expreſſive geſticulations of the fan, modeſtly confeſſing every now and then, by way of parentheſis, that poſſibly it may be thought preſumption in a woman to talk at all upon thoſe matters. In the mean time, her unhappy hearer ſtifles a thouſand gapes, aſſents univerſally to whatever ſhe ſays, in hopes of ſhortening the converſation, and carefully watches the firſt favourable opportunity, which any motion in the company gives him, of making his eſcape from this excellent ſolid underſtanding. Thus deſerted, but not diſcouraged, ſhe takes the whole

company

company in their turns, and has, for every one, a whiſper of equal importance. If Eudoſia would content herſelf with her natural talents, play at cards, make tea and viſits, talk to her dog often, and to her company but ſometimes, ſhe would not be ridiculous, but bear a very tolerable part in the polite world.

Sydaria had beauty enough to have excuſed, while young, her want of common ſenſe. But ſhe ſcorned the fortuitous and precarious triumphs of beauty. She would only conquer by the charms of her mind. An union of hearts, a delicacy of ſentiments, a mental adoration, or a ſort of tender quietiſm, were what ſhe long ſought for, and never found. Thus nature ſtruggled with ſentiment till ſhe was five and forty, but then got the better of it to ſuch a degree, that ſhe made very advantageous propoſals to an Iriſh enſign of one and twenty: equally ridiculous in her age and in her youth.

Canidia, withered by age, and ſhattered by infirmities, totters under the load of her miſplaced ornaments, and her dreſs varies according to the freſheſt advices from Paris, inſtead of conforming itſelf, as it ought, to the directions of her undertaker. Her mind, as weak as her body, is abſurdly adorned: ſhe talks politics and metaphyſics, mangles the terms of each, and, if there be ſenſe in either, moſt infallibly puzzles it; adding intricacy to politics, and darkneſs to myſteries, equally ridiculous in this world and the next.

I ſhall not now enter into an examination of the leſſer affectations (moſt of them are pardonable, and many of them are pretty, if their owners are ſo); but confine my present animadversions to the affectations of ill-suited characters, for I would by no means deprive my fair countrywomen of their genteel little terrors, antipathies, and affections. The alternate panicks of thieves, spiders, ghosts, and thunder, are allowable to youth and beauty, provided they do not survive them. But what I mean is, to prevail with them to act their own natural parts, and not other peoples; and to convince them, that even their own imperfections will become them better than the borrowed perfections of others.

Should some lady of spirit, unjustly offended at these restrictions, ask what province I leave to their sex? I answer, that I leave them whatever has not been peculiarly assigned by nature to ours. I leave them a mighty empire, Love. There they reign absolute, and by unquestioned right, while beauty supports their throne. They have all the talents requisite for that soft empire, and the ablest of our sex cannot contend with them in the profound knowledge and conduct of those *arcana*. But then, those who are deposed by years or accidents, or those, who by nature were never qualified to reign, should content themselves with the private care and œconomy of their families, and the diligent discharge of domestic duties.

I take the fabulous birth of Minerva, the goddess of arms, wisdom, arts, and sciences, to have been an allegory of the antients, calculated to shew, that women of natural and usual births must not aim at those accomplishments. She sprang armed out of Jupiter's head, without the co-operation of his consort Juno;

and as ſuch only had thoſe great provinces aſſigned her.

I confeſs, one has read of ladies, ſuch as Semiramis, Thaleſtris, and others, who have made very conſiderable figures in the moſt heroic and manly parts of life; but, conſidering the great antiquity of thoſe hiſtories, and how much they are mixed up with fables, one is at liberty to queſtion either the facts, or the ſex. Beſides that, the moſt ingenious and erudite Conrad Wolfang Laborioſus Nugatorius, of Hall in Saxony, has proved to a demonſtration, in the 14th volume, page 2981, of his learned treatiſe *De Hermaphroditis*, that all the reputed female heroes of antiquity were of this Epicene ſpecies, though, out of regard to the fair and modeſt part of my readers, I dare not quote the ſeveral facts and reaſonings with which he ſupports this aſſertion; and as for the heroines of modern date, we have more than ſuſpicions of their being at leaſt of the epicene gender. The greateſt monarch that ever filled the Britiſh throne, till very lately, was queen Elizabeth, of whoſe ſex we have abundant reaſon to doubt, hiſtory furniſhing us with many inſtances of the manhood of that princeſs, without leaving us one ſingle ſymptom or indication of the woman; and thus much is certain, that ſhe thought it improper for her to marry a man. The great Chriſtina, queen of Sweden, was allowed by every body to be above her ſex; and the maſculine was ſo predominant in her compoſition, that ſhe even conformed, at laſt, to its dreſs, and ended her days in Italy. I therefore require that thoſe women, who inſiſt upon going beyond the bounds allotted to their ſex, ſhould previouſly declare themſelves in form hermaphrodites, and be regiſtered as ſuch in their ſeveral pariſhes; till when, I ſhall not ſuffer them to confound politics, perplex metaphyſics, and darken myſteries.

How amiable may a woman be, what a comfort and delight to her acquaintance, her friends, her relations, her lover, or her huſband, in keeping ſtrictly within her character! She adorns all female virtues with native female ſoftneſs. Women, while untainted by affectation, have a natural chearfulneſs of mind, tenderneſs and benignity of heart, which juſtly endears them to us, either to animate our joys, or ſooth our ſorrows; but how are they changed, and how ſhocking do they become, when the rage of ambition, or the pride of learning, agitates and ſwells thoſe breaſts, where only love, friendſhip, and tender care, ſhould dwell!

Let Flavia be their model, who, though ſhe could ſupport any character, aſſumes none, never miſled by fancy or vanity, but guided ſingly by reaſon: whatever ſhe ſays or does is the manifeſt reſult of a happy nature, and a good underſtanding, though ſhe knows whatever women ought, and, it may be, more than they are required to know. She conceals the ſuperiority ſhe has with as much care, as others take to diſplay the ſuperiority they have not; ſhe conforms herſelf to the turn of the company ſhe is in, but in a way of rather avoiding to be diſtanced, than deſiring to take the lead. Are they merry, ſhe is chearful; are they grave, ſhe is ſerious; are they abſurd, ſhe is ſilent. Though ſhe thinks and ſpeaks as a man

would

would do, ſhe effeminates, if I may uſe the expreſſion, whatever ſhe ſays, and gives all the graces of her own ſex to the ſtrength of ours; ſhe is well-bred without the troubleſome ceremonies and frivolous forms of thoſe who only affect to be ſo. As her good-breeding proceeds jointly from good-nature and good ſenſe, the former inclines her to oblige, and the latter ſhews her the eaſieſt and beſt way of doing it. Woman's beauty, like men's wit, is generally fatal to the owners, unleſs directed by a judgement, which ſeldom accompanies a great degree of either: her beauty ſeems but the proper and decent lodging for ſuch a mind; ſhe knows the true value of it, and far from thinking that it authorizes impertinence and coquetry, it redoubles her care to avoid thoſe errors that are its uſual attendants. Thus ſhe not only unites in herſelf all the advantages of body and mind, but even reconciles contradictions in others; for ſhe is loved and eſteemed, though envied, by all.

XIV.

COMMON SENSE.

SATURDAY, October 8, 1737. N° 37.

SOMEBODY told the late regent of France *, that a very ſilly pariſh prieſt had abuſed him moſt groſly in the pulpit; to which the regent, who was much above reſenting the inſults of fools, anſwered

* The duke of Orleans, who was regent during the minority of Lewis XV.

very coolly, "Why does the blockhead meddle with "me? I am not of his pariſh."

In this manner I reply to all the anger and indignation, which the grave Mr. Oſborne, and the facetious ſir A. B. C. have been pleaſed to expreſs againſt me. Cannot they let me alone? I am ſure they have nothing to do with common ſenſe. Nay, I even return them good for evil, and do for them what I believe nobody in the kingdom does but myſelf; for I take-in their papers at my own expence. It is true, I find my account in it, for the Gazetteer makes me laugh, and the London Journal makes me ſleep. I take the former in the morning, and the latter at night. Sir A. B. C. and his aſſociates have ſuch an abſurd pertneſs, and ſo inimitable an alacrity in ſinking, that it is impoſſible not to laugh at firſt, though, I confeſs, they are below it, and that it is a little ill-natured into the bargain. But one can no more help it, than one can help laughing at an awkward fellow, who, going to ſit down, miſſes his chair, and falls ridiculouſly upon his breech; though, to be ſure, there is no joke in it, and very probably the poor man has hurt himſelf too. Mr. Oſborne has quite a different effect upon me; his ſolid uniform dulneſs is the ſureſt ſoporific I have met with; and every Saturday night, as ſoon as I am in bed, my man conſtantly aſks me, "Does your honor take your London Journal to-"night?" I never refuſe his offer, and, to do him juſtice, he reads with a ſlow monotony, ſo excellently adapted to the performance, that one would think he was the author of it himſelf.

Thus,

Thus, after taking theſe two authors regularly, night and morning, they are carefully laid by in a little cloſet, where I ultimately take them, as they happen to lie next my hand.

I have lately heard, with concern, that I ſhall ſoon be deprived of theſe benefits, and that my two favourite authors will withdraw their weekly and daily labors from the public, in order to exhibit themſelves in other ſhapes. Mr. Oſborne, I am told, has engaged himſelf to ſupply the ſtage with tragedies, and ſir A. B. C. with comedies; that it may not be ſaid, that the late act of parliament has prevented the production of excellent dramatic performances, as ſome of the malecontents pretended it would. Though this will diſturb the preſent regular courſe of my preſent laughter, which I muſt afterwards take by the lump, and in twelve-penny doſes, yet I muſt acknowledge them to be the propereſt authors to anſwer the true meaning and intendment of the bill: for I will defy the moſt inveterate and ingenious malice, even that of the Craftſman, to apply any thing out of their writings. With what impatience do I long to ſee the tragic ſcenes of our laureat diſgraced and eclipſed by Oſborne's ſolid drama! Yes, Oſborne ſhall ſnatch the poppies from Cibber's brow, and plant them on his own. I cannot help ſuggeſting, as a friend, to this hopeful young tragic poet, that there is in the Rehearſal both a ſleeping ſcene, and a yawning one, incomparably well written, which I would adviſe him to have before his eyes, while he can keep them open.

I condole with the ingenious author of "Love in "a hollow tree *," who muſt, indiſputably, reſign the comic ſcenes to ſir A. B. C.

As I am perſuaded theſe two young writers will have the ſtage entirely to themſelves, I moſt humbly repreſent it to the lord chamberlain, as a piece of juſtice, to have their labors equally divided between the managers of the two only theatres now ſubſiſting. The comedy, I believe, muſt belong to Mr. Rich; for, I preſume, ſir A. B. C. after the diſtinguiſhed zeal he has manifeſted for the proteſtant religion, in oppoſition to the attempts of Mr. Ward, would by no means aid and abet a perſon of Mr. Fleetwood's principles of religion.

Having ſaid thus much to my two friends, to whom I give my word I will never ſay any thing more, I cannot conclude, without addreſſing myſelf a little to their patron and pay-maſter. He has certainly parts, a pretty turn to waggery, a little coarſe indeed, but yet not without ſalt; and one muſt allow him to be what Tully allowed Nævius, "*ſcurra non parum facetus*," (a buffoon not deſtitute of ſome humor). I therefore cannot imagine why he will ſuffer, much

* This comedy was written by the late lord Grimſton when a boy, and printed in 1705. When he grew up, he was juſtly aſhamed of it, and endeavoured to ſuppreſs it: and this he would have effected, but that the dutcheſs of Marlborough, to ſerve an election purpoſe, cauſed a new impreſſion to be printed, with an elephant in the title-page dancing on a rope. All this edition the author purchaſed; but her grace, being determined to accompliſh her deſign, ſent a copy to be re-printed in Holland, and diſtributed the whole impreſſion among the electors of St. Albans. See the Original Works, in verſe and proſe, of Dr. William King of the Commons, 1776, vol. III. p. 66. *note.*

leſs

leſs pay, ſuch blockheads to write for him. I know he will ſay, they are the beſt he can get. I admit it, I dare ſay they are: but then why will he have any? He had much better have none. Sylla bought-off a dunce who would be writing for him, and Auguſtus paid a bad poet, in bad verſes, as the ſureſt way to prevent any more. If theſe fellows are to be paid for their zeal, let the honorable perſon oblige them to throw him their ſilence into the bargain. Formerly, a right reverend or two uſed to draw their pens in his defence, but of late we have ſeen nothing from that quarter neither; whether thoſe reverend perſons have too much wit, or too much biſhoprick, to go on, I cannot tell: but this piece of advice I will give him, whenever he can get another author of that kind to write for him, not to *tranſlate* him too ſoon.

This certainly never happened in any reign, or under any adminiſtration, before; for, excepting a late imitation of Horace, by Mr. Pope, who but ſeldom meddles with public matters, I challenge the miniſterial advocates to produce one line of ſenſe, or Engliſh, written on the ſame ſide of the queſtion for theſe laſt ſeven years. Has there been an eſſay in verſe or proſe, has there been even a diſtich, or an advertiſement, fit to be read on the ſide of the adminiſtration? But on the other ſide, what numbers of diſſertations, eſſays, treatiſes, compoſitions of all kinds in verſe and proſe, have been written, with all that ſtrength of reaſoning, quickneſs of wit, and elegance of expreſſion, which no former period of time can equal? Has not every body got by heart ſatires, lampoons, ballads, and ſarcaſms, againſt the adminiſtration?

ſtration? and can any body recollect, or repeat, one line for it? What can be the cauſe of this? It cannot be, that thoſe who are able to ſerve the honourable perſon deſpair of being rewarded by him, ſince the known inſtances of his liberality to the worſt of writers are ſure pledges of his profuſion to the beſt. Is it then the rigid virtue, the inflexible honor, of the brighteſt geniuſes of this age, that hinders them from engaging in that cauſe, for which they would be ſo amply recompenſed? If ſo, I congratulate the preſent times, for that was not uſually the characteriſtic of wit, and they were formerly accuſed of flattery at leaſt, if not of proſtitution, to miniſterial favour and rewards.

In all former reigns, the wits were of the ſide of the miniſters; the Oſbornes and the A. B. C's againſt them. And how would the Godolphins, the Somers's, the Halifax's, and the Dorſets, have bluſhed, to have been the Mæcenas of ſuch wretched ſcribblers? But they were not reduced to ſuch an ignominious neceſſity. They found the beſt writers as proud to engage in their cauſe, as able to ſupport it. Even the infamous and pernicious meaſures of King Charles the ſecond's reign, as they are now called, were palliated, varniſhed, or juſtified, by the ableſt pens. By what uncommon fatality then is this adminiſtration deſtitute of all literary ſupport?

One would be apt to ſuppoſe, if one did not know the contrary, that there was ſomething in the meaſures ſo low, ſo corrupt, and ſo diſgraceful, that common decency would not ſuffer wit, or good ſenſe, to appear on that ſide, but made them, in

this

this case, withstand those temptations, to which heretofore they have too often yielded. Nay, the misfortune extends still farther: for I am told, that among those very few, who engaged in the measures, and are able to countenance them in two certain places, the best withhold their eloquence, and only swell the numbers by a silent and sullen concurrence. So that, as Pliny observed in his time, *Vota nunc numerantur, non ponderantur* (votes now are counted, not weighed).

As this case is really compassionate in itself, and particularly hard upon us anti-ministerial writers, as we are called, who cannot possibly answer what we do not understand; I will offer what expedients occur to me, for our mutual relief.

I should think Mr. Wreathcock and Mr. Justice, who are both happily returned from transportation, might be of singular use in this distress. The experienced knowledge of the former in the useful parts of the law, and the known skill of the latter in books of all sorts, must qualify them excellently well for political writers; and if they clubbed their talents, they would amply repair the loss of the deceased Francis Walsingham, esq; or, at least, they would infinitely exceed any now extant. But, if this cannot be brought about, and the avocations of these two gentlemen will not allow them the leisure to turn authors, the last shift I can think of, and which seems to me the most likely to be put in practice, is for the administration to employ their authors of acts of parliament, who answered certain humorous theatrical pieces very effectually last year, with a "Be it en-

"acted *," and who, with a "Be it further enacted," will probably reply next year, with the ſame ſpirit and vigor, to all other performances of what kind ſoever.

XV.

COMMON SENSE.

SATURDAY, Jan. 15, 1738. N° 51.

MY ingenious predeceſſor the Spectator, whom I wiſh to imitate, but without pretending to equal, bid his fair countrywomen, "beware the Ides "of May," looking upon that ſeaſon to be as fatal to their virtue, as the Ides of March had formerly proved to Cæſar's life. I am ſure I heartily concur with him, in his regard and concern for that beautiful part of our ſpecies: but I cannot help differing with him greatly, as to the time and cauſes of their danger, and thinking that he has left the moſt critical part of the year unguarded and defenceleſs. Beware, therefore, ye fair, ſay I, the Ides of January; and muſter-up all the collected force of habit, education, and virtue, to withſtand the operations of the winter campaign, or you may happen to fall with leſs decency than Cæſar.

The Spectator founds his apprehenſions of the month of May upon three ſuppoſitions, all which,

* In alluſion to a thought of Mr. Gay, who addreſſed a poem to his ingenious and worthy friend Mr. Lowndes, "author of that ce-"lebrated treatiſe in folio, called *The Land Tax Bill.*"

with

with ſubmiſſion, I think groundleſs. The firſt is, " that the ſpirits, after having been, as it were, frozen " and congealed by the winter, are then turned looſe, " and ſet a rambling."

Surely the ſpirits may more juſtly be ſaid to be turned looſe, and ſet a rambling, in January, after a tedious ſix months confinement in the country, than they can be in May, after a four months evaporation in London. For my own part, I conſider January as the general gaol-delivery of the fair ſex. It is then that they come to town, fluſhed with the health, and irritated with the confinement, of the country. It is then that, with an appetite whetted for pleaſure by long abſtinence, they taſte more exquiſitely their regained liberty, and feel all the benefits of their *habeas corpus*. And if ever conſtitution or reſentment can be ſuppoſed to have any ſhare in a fine woman's tranſactions, it is then that their effects are moſt to be dreaded.

The Spectator's next ſuppoſition is, " that the gay " proſpect of the fields and the meadows, with the " courtſhip of the birds on every tree, naturally un- " bend the mind, and ſoften it to pleaſure." What effect this rural ſcene may have upon a milkmaid, I cannot ſay; but I can never imagine that women of faſhion and delicacy can be affected by ſuch objects. The fields and the meadows are their averſion, and the periodical anniverſary loves of the birds their contempt. It is the gay London ſcene, where ſucceſſive pleaſures raiſe the ſpirits and warm the imagination, which prepares the faireſt breaſts to receive the tendereſt impreſſions.

The

The laſt conjecture is, "that a woman is prompted "by a kind of inſtinct to throw herſelf upon a bed "of flowers, and not to let thoſe beautiful couches, "which nature has provided, lye uſeleſs." This again evidently relates to the ruddy milkmaid; for, not to mention the danger of catching cold upon one of theſe beds, to any body above a milkmaid, ſurely the privacy, conveniency, and ſecurity, of a good damaſk-bed, or couch, are much ſtronger temptations to a woman of faſhion, to recline a little, than all the dazies and cowſlips in a meadow.

Having thus briefly anſwered the arguments of my predeceſſor, or at leaſt ſhewn, that his care and concern were only calculated for the inferior part of the ſex; I ſhall, now, humbly lay before thoſe of ſuperior rank the many "difficulties and dangers," to which the winter expoſes them.

I believe I may take it for granted, that every fine woman, who comes to town in January, comes heartily tired both of the country and of her huſband. The happy pair have yawned at one another at leaſt ever ſince Michaelmas, and the two indiviſible halves, of man and wife, have been exceedingly burthenſome to each other. The lady, who has had full leiſure moſt minutely to conſider her other moiety, has either poſitively or comparatively found out, that he is by no means a pretty man, and meditates indemnification to herſelf, either by her return to the pretty man, or by enliſting one for the current ſervice of the year. In theſe diſpoſitions ſhe opens the winter, but at the ſame time, with firm and ſtedfaſt purpoſe of not tranſgreſſing the bounds,

or

or even violating the appearances, of virtue. But alas! how frail are all our beſt reſolves! The lover appears firſt in the innocent form of value and eſteem, his converſation is liſtened to with attention, and approved of: it grows frequent and particular; how can one help that? Where is the harm of being diſtinguiſhed by the friendſhip of a man of ſenſe and faſhion? can it be wondered at, that one converſes more with him, than with a thouſand fools, that would be always plaguing one? Beſides, he ſays nothing one has reaſon to take ill, or that would juſtify one in not being civil to him.

With theſe early and juſt diſtinctions in his favour, the pretty man proceeds, and gains the more ground, as his approaches are the leſs perceived or apprehended. He is admitted to the toilette, as an agreeable friend and companion, where he improves the morning moments, which I take to be the *mollia tempora*, ſo propitious to *tête-à-têtes*: here the converſation inſenſibly grows more ſerious, particular applications are made of general topics, ſentiments of love and conſtancy are diſcuſſed; the pretty man confeſſes and laments his unfortunate diſpoſition to both, and wiſhes to heaven that he knew neither; the lady, not without ſome emotion, and an awkward ſmartneſs, tells him that ſhe believes they will neither of them ever do him any great hurt. This unjuſt reproach extorts from him, what otherwiſe he could never have had the courage to have ſaid, *viz.* that, "that depends entirely upon her." Here it is out, the ice is broke. What is to be done? The lady now plainly perceives his meaning, which ſhe never

before

before sufpected. She flattered herself that he had a friendship and value for her, but she now finds the contrary. She is sorry he has put it out of her power to have any longer that esteem for him which she confesses she once had; but they must never meet any more, if that is to be the language. The lover, for now I may call him so, deprecates her wrath, bids her blame her own beauty, and his fate, but pity him, and pressing her hand, which, it may be, in her anger, she forgets to pull away, faithfully promises, never to hold that language more, if he can help it. Upon this solemn engagement, he is forgiven, re-admitted, and all danger is looked upon to be over. Short and fallacious security! for, this point once gained, the besieger, if I may borrow some military metaphors, is most advantageously posted, is in a situation to parley with the garrison, and stands fair for the *horn work*. Here he can argue the case fully, shew the negligence, the injustice, or the oppression, of the present governor, offer terms of honor, safety, and better usage, and, by persuasions, either bring about a willing surrender, or at least so far abate the vigor of the resistance, as with a little force to make himself master of the place.

Having thus represented the danger, I will now point out the best preservatives, I can think of, against it; for in this case prevention alone can be used, remedy comes too late.

I therefore recommend to my countrywomen, to be particularly upon their guard against the very man whose conquest they most wish for, and to be assured that the reasons which determine their choice are so

many

many inſtances of their danger. Let them begin to reflect as ſoon as ever they begin to find a particular pleaſure in his converſation, and let them tremble when they firſt make him a graver curteſy than they do to other people. But if, when he approaches them, they pull up their gloves, adjuſt their tucker, and count the ſticks of their fan, let them deſpair, for they are further gone than they imagine. And though they may, for a time, deceive themſelves with the notion that it is his underſtanding only that engages their attention, they will find at laſt that man, like the ſerpent, when he has once got his head in, the reſt will ſoon follow. Friendſhip and eſteem are the bearded arrows of love, that enter with eaſe, but, when torn out, leave the wound greater.

A conſtant diſſipation, and hurry of various trifles, is of great uſe in this caſe, and does not give leiſure to the mind to receive laſting impreſſions; but beware of ſelect *coteries*, where, without an engagement, a lady paſſes but for "an odd body."

A courſe of viſiting-days is alſo an excellent preſervative againſt an attachment. The rigorous ſentences of thoſe tremendous tribunals, fulminated by the old and ugly upon the young and fair, and where, as in the inquiſition, the ſlighteſt ſuſpicions amount to proofs, muſt neceſſarily ſtrike great terror, and inſpire wholeſome reſolutions.

I abſolutely prohibit balls; the agitation of country-dances putting the blood into an unuſual ferment, too favourable to the partner. Beſides, they often encourage, and cauſe, the firſt ſqueeze by the hand; which, according as it is taken, is either laid to the violence of the paſſion, or excuſed by the impetuoſity of the dance. Morever, there is a certain figure called *ſetting*, that often occaſions a familiar colliſion, which I have often known ominous, and in its conſequences productive of *other figures*.

Maſquerades ſhould be uſed with great care and moderation; for, though I do not look upon them as either convenient or neceſſary for the ratification of mutual love and alliance, I hold them to be exceedingly commodious for the previous negotiations; and there are certain ſecret articles in thoſe treaties, which are better aſked, heard, and adjuſted, between the contracting parties, under a maſque than barefaced.

I have no objection to operas; the innocence of the compoſition admitting of no application, and conveying no idea whatſoever: what little inconveniencies might be apprehended from the ſoftneſs and tenderneſs of the muſic are amply counterbalanced, *Sopranos* being the objects of the attention, and raptures of the ladies. And I have even known this harmleſs muſical attachment ſtand many a fine woman in great ſtead.

But I require them to be very cautious in the choice and uſe of the other theatrical entertainments, and avoid the repreſentation of thoſe dramatic pieces, both tragic and comic, which ſeem only calculated to ſoften the heart, and inflame the imagination. What warm and pleaſing deſcriptions of love are our beſt tragedies filled with! It is commonly what the whole turns upon, and is repreſented as the only comfort, pleaſure, or joy, of life. It is deſcribed, as

"The

"The cordial drop, heaven in our cup has thrown,
"To make the nauſeous draught of life go down."

And can one wonder then, that a lady, who does not find this incomparable drop at home, ſhould ſeek for it elſewhere?

We are told, in another place, that,

"Life without love is load, and time ſtands ſtill:
"What we refuſe to love to death we give,
"And, then, then only when we love we live."

This at once explains the whole thing to them, and accounts for their being tired of their country *tête-à-têtes* with their huſbands, and for their ſaying ſo often, "Well! this is not living!" It ſeems it was all for want of love; an omiſſion which they reſolve not to be much longer guilty of.

Mr. Dryden expreſſes himſelf with ſtill more energy upon this ſubject in Aurengzebe, and paints it in the warmeſt and moſt glowing colors; with him, it is the pleaſure,

"Where nature ſums up all her joys in one;"

and which,

"So fills the ſenſes, that the ſoul ſeems fled,
"And thought itſelf does for the time lie dead."

Muſt not ſuch lively deſcriptions as theſe, independently of certain hints of nature, tempt curioſity to make a trial of the truth? And is it poſſible not to pity, rather than blame, the experiments which a lady is thus ſtrongly prompted to make?

But this is not all: for, leſt theſe tender ſentiments and luſcious deſcriptions ſhould only ſoften the heart, our beſt comedies come in to their aid, with their practical part, and pin the baſket. Here the ways and means are chalked out, the pleaſing progreſs of love delineated, and even the concluſion of it almoſt exhibited. It is unlucky for the audience, that Berynthia, in the Relapſe, had an inner room, where ſhe and her lover retire. But, however, that the audience may not be much longer in the dark than ſhe had been, ſhe takes care to inform them, that ſhe never was better pleaſed in all her life.

Belinda, in taking her leave of Mr. Dorimant, after having paſſed part of the night with him, ſeems moſt penitentially to ſay, "Well, were this to do "again;" but, upon Mr. Dorimant's anſwering, "We ſhould do it, ſhould not we?" ſhe tenderly replies, "I believe we ſhould." Can one refuſe to give credit to the ſo recent teſtimonies and experience of two ladies of ſuch agreeable characters? And the belief of a pleaſure naturally invites to the purſuit of it.

It would be endleſs to ſpecify the particular plays which I muſt totally prohibit; but I believe the beſt and ſhorteſt general rule, that I can give my countrywomen, is abſolutely to abſtain from all thoſe which they like beſt.

There are certain books too, of a moſt ſtimulating and inflammatory nature, a few doſes of which may throw the reader into ſuch a fever, that all the cooling and ſoporific volumes of our modern divines may not be able to abate, and which can only be cured by ſtrong ſudorifics. The catalogue of theſe books would be endleſs: but my fair readers will pretty well gueſs at them, when I tell them, that I mean thoſe which are generally kept under lock and key, and

which

which, when any body comes in, are immediately clapt under the cushion.

I have but one caution more to add; but that is, it may be, the most material one of all; to beware of morning-visits. Breakfast-time is a critical period; the spirits are fresh and active; and, if the watchful lover comes in soon after the drowsy husband is gone out, it presents to the lady a contrast too favourable to the former. The interposing tea-table is but a weak barrier against impatient love. Opportunity invites, resentment provokes, nature at least approves; and, in such a violent situation,

" She, who alone her lover can withstand,
" Is more than woman, or he less than man."

XVI.

COMMON SENSE.

SATURDAY, Feb. 11, 1738. N° 54.

" Ne vitam transeant, veluti pecora; quæ natura prona, atque
" ventri obedientia finxit." SALLUST.

Lest they should pass their time like the beasts, which are by nature disposed to grovel upon this earth, and be slaves to their bellies.

TASTE is now the fashionable word of the fashionable world. Every thing must be done with taste: that is settled; but where and what that taste is, is not quite so certain; for, after all the pains I have taken to find out what was meant by the word, and whether those who use it oftenest had any clear idea annexed to it, I have only been able negatively to discover, that they do not mean their own natural taste, but, on the contrary, that they have sacrificed it to an imaginary one, of which they can give no account. They build houses in taste, which they cannot live in with conveniency *; they suffer with impatience the music they pretend to hear with rapture; and they even eat nothing they like, for the sake of eating in taste.

> Not for himself, he sees, or hears, or eats;
> Artists must chuse his pictures, music, meats. POPE.

It is certain the commandments, now so much neglected, if not abrogated, might be observed with much less self-denial than these imaginary laws of taste, to which so exact and scrupulous an obedience is paid.

I take taste, when not used for the sensation of the palate, which is its proper signification, to be a metaphor, to express that judgement each man forms to himself of those things which are not contained in any certain rules, and which admit of no demonstration: thus circles and equilateral triangles allow of no taste, they must be as they are; but the colors they are drawn in, or the materials they are made of, depend upon fancy or taste.—In building, there are certain necessary rules founded upon nature, as, that the

* This was the case of a general, who, having applied to an English nobleman, celebrated for his taste in architecture, to direct the building of a house for himself, had one constructed indeed with great elegance and regularity on the outside, but altogether destitute of every convenience for a family to live in. Lord Chesterfield, upon seeing it, told the general, "If I had your house, I would hire the "opposite one to live in, and enjoy the prospect."

the ſtronger muſt ſupport the weaker, &c. but the ornamental and convenient parts are the objects of taſte. Hence ariſes the propriety of the metaphor, becauſe taſte in every thing is undetermined and perſonal, as in the palate and all our other ſenſes; nay even our minds are as differently affected as our palates by the ſame things, when thoſe things are not of a nature to be aſcertained and demonſtrated.

However, this right of taſting for one's ſelf, which ſeems to be the natural privilege of mankind, is now totally ſurrendered even in the proper ſenſe of the word; and, if a man would be well received in good company, he muſt eat, though with reluctance, according to the laws of ſome eminent glutton at Paris, promulgated here by the laſt-imported French cook, wiſhing all the while within himſelf, that he durſt avow his natural taſte for good native beef and pudding.

The abſurdity, as well as the real ill conſequences, of this prevailing affectation, has, I confeſs, excited my wrath; and I reſolved that the nobility and gentry of this kingdom ſhould not go on to ruin their fortunes and conſtitutions, without hearing at leaſt the repreſentations and admonitions of common ſenſe.

Eating, itſelf, ſeems to me, to be rather a ſubject of humiliation than of pride, ſince the imperfection of our nature appears in the daily neceſſity we lie under of recruiting it in that manner. So that one would think the only care of a rational being ſhould be, to repair his decaying fabric as cheap as poſſible. But the preſent faſhion is directly contrary: and eating, now, is the greateſt pride, buſineſs, and expence, of life, and that too, not to ſupport, but to deſtroy nature.

The frugal meal was antiently the time of unbending the mind by chearful and improving converſation, and the table-talk of ingenious men has been thought worth tranſmitting to poſterity. The meal is now at once the moſt frivolous and moſt ſerious part of life. The mind is bent to the utmoſt, and all the attention exerted, for what? the critical examination of compound diſhes: and if any two or three people happen to ſtart ſome uſeful or agreeable ſubject of converſation, they are ſoon interrupted, and overpowered by the extatic interjections of, excellent! exquiſite! delicious! Pray taſte this; you never eat a better thing in your life. Is that good? Is it tender? Is it ſeaſoned enough? Would it have been better ſo? Of ſuch wretched ſtuff as this does the preſent table-talk wholly conſiſt, in open defiance of all converſation and common ſenſe. I could heartily wiſh that a collection of it were to be publiſhed, for the honor and glory of the performers; but, for want of that, I ſhall give my readers a ſhort ſpecimen of the moſt ingenious table-talk, I have lately heard carried on with moſt wit and ſpirit.

My lord, having taſted and duly conſidered the Bechamele, ſhook his head, and then offered as his opinion to the company, that the garlick was not enough concealed, but earneſtly deſired to know their ſentiments, and begged they would taſte it with attention.

The company, after proper deliberation, replied, that they were of his lordſhip's opinion, and that the garlick did indeed diſtinguiſh itſelf too much: but the *maître d'hôtel* interpoſing repreſented, that they were now ſtronger than ever in garlick at Paris; upon which the company, one and all, ſaid, that altered the caſe.

My lord, having ſagaciouſly ſmelt at the breech of a rabbit, wiped his noſe, gave a ſhrug of ſome diſſatisfaction, and then informed the company, that it was not abſolutely a bad one, but that he heartily wiſhed it had been kept a day longer. Ay, ſaid ſir Thomas, with an emphaſis, a rabbit muſt be kept. And with the guts in too, added the colonel, or the devil could not eat it. Here the *maître d'hôtel* again interpoſed, and ſaid that they eat their rabbits much ſooner now than they uſed to do at Paris. Are you ſure of that? ſaid my lord, with ſome vivacity. Yes, replied the *maître d'hôtel*, the cook had a letter about it laſt night. I am not ſorry for that, rejoined my lord; for, to tell you the truth, I naturally love to eat my meat before it ſtinks. The reſt of the company, and even the colonel himſelf, confeſſed the ſame.

This ingenious and edifying kind of converſation continued, without the leaſt interruption from common ſenſe, through four courſes, which laſted four hours, till the company could neither ſwallow nor utter any thing more.

A very great perſon among the antients was very properly aſked, if he was not aſhamed to play ſo well upon the fiddle? And one may ſurely with as much

reaſon

reason ask these illustrious moderns, if they are not, ashamed of being such good cooks.

It is really not to be imagined with what profound knowledge and erudition our men of quality now treat these culinary subjects; and I cannot but hope that such excellent critics will at last turn authors themselves; nay, I daily expect to see a digest of the whole art of cookery by some person of honor.

I cannot help hinting, by the way, to these accurate kitchen critics, that it does not become them to be facetious and satyrical upon those dissertations which ladies sometimes hold upon their dress, the subject being by no means so low nor so trifling.

Though such a degree of affected gluttony, accompanied with such frivolous discourses, is pardonable in those who are little superior to the animals they devour, and who are only *fruges consumere nati*, I am surprized and hurt when I see men of parts fall into it, since it not only suspends the exercise of their parts for the present, but impairs them, together with their health, for the future: and, if fools could contrive, I should think they had contrived this method of bringing men of sense down to them; for it is certain, that when a company is thus gorged, glutted, and loaded, there is not the least difference between the most stupid and the wittiest man in it.

What life in all that ample body, say
What heavenly particle inspires the clay?
The soul subsides, and wickedly inclines
To seem but mortal even in sound divines. POPE.

Though an excess in wine is highly blameable, it is surely much more pardonable, as the progressive

steps

ſteps to it are chearful, animating, and ſeducing: the melancholy are for a while relieved, the grave are enlivened, and the witty and the gay ſeem almoſt inſpired; whereas in eating, after nature is once ſatisfied, which ſhe ſoon is, every additional morſel carries dulneſs and ſtupidity along with it.

Moreover, theſe glorious toils are crowned with the juſt rewards of all chronical diſtempers; the gout, the ſtone, the ſcurvy, and the palſy, are the never-failing trophies of their atchievements. Were theſe honors, like ſimple knighthood, only to be enjoyed by thoſe who had merited them, it would be no great matter; but unfortunately, like baronetſhip, they deſcend to and viſit their innocent children. It is already very eaſy to diſtinguiſh at ſight the puny ſon of a compound *entremets*, from the luſty offspring of beef and pudding: and, I am perſuaded, the next generation of the nobility will be a race of pale-faced, ſpindle-ſhanked Lilliputians, the moſt vigorous of whom will not come up to an abortion of John de Gaunt's. Nor does the miſchief even ſtop here; for, as the men of faſhion frequently condeſcend to communicate themſelves to families of inferior rank, but better conſtitutions, they enervate thoſe families too, and preſent them with ſickly helpleſs children, to the great prejudice of the trade and manufactures of this kingdom.

Some people have imagined, and not without ſome degree of probability, that animal food communicates its qualities with its nouriſhment. In this ſuppoſition it was, that Achilles, who was not only born and bred, but fed up too, for a Hero, was nouriſhed with the

the marrow of lions; and we all know what a fine lion he turned out at laſt. Should this rule hold, it muſt be a melancholy reflection to conſider, that the principal ingredients in the food of our principal nobility is eſſence of ſwine.

The Egyptians, who were a wiſe nation, thought ſo much depended upon diet, that they dieted their kings, and preſcribed by law both the quality and quantity of their food. It is much to be lamented, that thoſe bills of fare are not preſerved to this time, ſince they might have been of ſingular uſe in all monarchical governments; but it is reaſonable to be conjectured, from the wiſdom of that people, that they allowed their kings no aliments of a bilious or a choleric nature, and only ſuch as ſweetened their juices, cooled their blood, and enlivened their faculties, if they had any.

The common people of this kingdom are dieted by laws; for, by an act paſſed about two years ago, not leſs advantageous to the crown than to the people, the uſe of a liquor, which deſtroyed both their minds and their bodies, was wiſely prohibited, and, by repeated acts of parliament, their food is reduced to a very modeſt and wholeſome proportion. Surely then the nobility and gentry of the kingdom deſerve ſome attention too, not ſo much indeed for their own ſakes, as for the ſake of the public, which is in ſome meaſure under their care: for if a porter, when full of gin, could not do his buſineſs, I am apt to think a privy counſellor, when loaded with four courſes, will but bungle at his.

Suppoſe,

Suppose, for instance, a number of persons, not over-lively at best, should meet of an evening to concert and deliberate upon public measures of the utmost consequence, grunting under the load and repletion of the strongest meats, panting almost in vain for breath, but quite in vain for thought, and reminded only of their existence by the unsavory returns of an olio; what good could be expected from such a consultation? The best one could hope for would be, that they were only assembled for shew, and not for use; not to propose or advise, but silently to submit to the orders of some one man there, who, feeding like a rational creature, might have the use of his understanding.

I would therefore recommend it to the consideration of the legislature, whether it may not be necessary to pass an act, to restrain the licentiousness of eating, and assign certain diets to certain ranks and stations. I would humbly suggest the strict vegetable as the properest ministerial diet, being exceedingly tender of those faculties in which the public is so highly interested, and very unwilling they should be clogged or incumbered.

But I do most seriously recommend it to those who, from their rank and situation in life, settle the fashions, and whose examples will in these sorts of things always be followed, that they will by their example, which will be more effectual than any law, not only put a stop to, but reform, the ridiculous, expensive, and pernicious luxury of tables; they are the people whom all inferior ranks imitate as far as they are able, and commonly much farther. It is their fatal

example

example that has ſeduced the gentry, and people of ſmaller fortune, into this naſty and ruinous exceſs. Let their example then at laſt reclaim them; let thoſe who are able to bear the expence, and known not to grudge it, give the firſt blow to this extravagant folly; let them avow their own natural taſte, for nature is in every thing plain and ſimple, and gratify it decently at a frugal and wholeſome table, inſtead of purchaſing ſtupidity and diſtempers at the expence of their time and their eſtates. And they may depend upon it, that a faſhion ſo convenient, as to the fortunes and the conſtitutions of their fellow-ſubjects, will chearfully be followed, and univerſally prevail, to the great advantage of the public.

XVII.

COMMON SENSE.

SATURDAY, March 4, 1738. N° 57.

I TOOK my leave ſome time ago of the daily ſilly Gazetteers, and promiſed to take no further notice of them; but then I only promiſed that impunity to their folly and abſurdity. Now, whether they underſtood that amneſty to extend farther than I meant it, or whether, with the laſt three or four ſhillings paid them by Mr. Pounce with a P, they likewiſe received orders to be ſaucy and impertinent, I cannot tell; but, be that as it will, they have of late been ſo impudently perſonal upon one worthy

 gentle-

gentleman *, that I cannot help ſtepping a little out of my way, to give them a kick: nor is this the greateſt provocation they have given me; for, notwithſtanding the regard I have for the character of that young gentleman, with whom they are ſo free, I am more incenſed againſt them for diſturbing the aſhes of the dead, and for preſuming, as they do, to touch Cicero with their impure and unhallowed hands. I therefore begin, by abſolutely forbidding them even to mention, directly or indirectly, the name of Cicero, till they have firſt read and underſtood him in the original; which, as I take it, amounts to a perpetual prohibition.

I have ſo much charity for the poor devils, as to believe they would not write at all, if they could help it, and that they would write better if they could. I never looked upon their daily labors as voluntary, but conſidered them as the production of heads and ſtomachs equally empty, and I really took in their papers out of charity, for, as to any other uſe I make of them, I might be ſupplied cheaper; but I muſt tell them that, if they grow perſonally ſcurrilous, I ſhall withdraw my charity, and common ſenſe ſhall purſue them, though indeed I fear it will never overtake them.

By what I can underſtand of their papers, they ſeem to have a great diſlike to a certain young gentleman, whom they have ſometimes almoſt called by his own name, and of late by a hard Latin name. I

* Mr. afterwards lord Lyttelton, who had been moſt groſsly abuſed, both in doggrel verſe, and in dull proſe, by the authors of the Gazetteer.

confeſs

confess it is very natural they should dislike him, nor am I in the least surprized that he should be the object of their satire, when I consider the useful subjects of their panegyrics; but then I must intimate to them, that they proceed very injudiciously, and do him a service which they little intended. Would they hurt him, they should commend him, for they are very sure that nobody will take their words for any thing; but when such wretched advocates, and profligate panegyrists of corruption, oppression, fraud, and all political immorality, direct their satire at one man, it is marking him out to the public, as a person eminently distinguished by all the opposites of those vices. The execution too of their design is as injudicious, as the design itself. They, somewhere or other, had an imperfect account of one Cicero, who had no mind that one Cæcilius, a young man, should be the prosecutor of one Verres, an old rogue; and that this same Cicero had told this Cæcilius, that he was too vain and enterprizing for so young a man, and wholly unequal to the task he undertook. This they thought was a pure scrap of history for them, and resolved to apply it immediately; when behold the misfortune that always attends ignorance and presumption! all the particular circumstances of that affair made against them, and suggested ugly applications elsewhere. When I saw that they made this young gentleman Cæcilius, I was really afraid for them, and went on with impatience to see whom they would make Verres: but I perceived they had prudently avoided this danger, and wisely, as they thought, dubbed their patron Hortensius, who was a great lover of pictures and ſtatues, was bribed by a ſphynx of curious workmanſhip and of ineſtimable value, to appear as the advocate of the moſt flagitious fellow, and the moſt infamous cauſe, that Rome ever knew. He proſtituted his eloquence to the defence of peculation and corruption, and, by ſkreening the moſt infamous of men, became little leſs ſo himſelf. This circumſtance is an unlucky one; I leave it with them to conſider of.

As to their Cæcilius himſelf, it is well known to every body but them, that he was a ſham proſecutor, ſet on by Verres himſelf, to prevent a real one. He had been a ſharer both of his plunder and of his guilt, and, upon a pretended concerted quarrel between them, offered himſelf as the propereſt perſon to proſecute this affair; but Cicero, who was in earneſt, and determined that juſtice ſhould be done upon ſo notorious an offender, diſcovered and defeated this ſtratagem, obtained the management of the cauſe, puſhed it with vigor and abilities, and got the criminal condemned. Was the character of Cæcilius really applicable to this young gentleman, were there any hopes that he could ever be brought to ſkreen the moſt notorious corruption, I dare ſay, he would meet with the approbation, inſtead of the cenſure, of this virtuous ſociety; and I am apt to think, that it is his unlikeneſs to Cæcilius, and his reſemblance to Tully, which have drawn their indignation upon him.

A late very ingenious author has moſt judiciouſly obſerved, in his incomparable and ſhort eſſay towards a character, &c. that pictures ought to be like the

 perſons

perſons they are drawn for, nay ſo like, as to be known by their acquaintance: but theſe wretched rogues are conſcious they are ſuch bad painters, that, under the ſigns they daub, they always write the name. It is ſometimes a certain young gentleman, who is tall and lean; at other times it is one, who was cofferer about ſeventeen years ago; and indeed if it was not for theſe helps, I, who am their only reader, ſhould be at a great loſs to know whom they mean.

I have often wondered what ſort of fellows this ingenious ſociety was compoſed of; for, that their paper is a moſaic work of folly is evident; and I imagine it conſiſts of a parcel of poor devils, who have either failed in their ſeveral trades, or who had never parts enough to be bound out, aſſiſted ſometimes by what they call *an able hand*, ſuch as a mungrel lawyer, a tattered reverend, or a facetious clerk of an office; who, by ſending them a paper now and then, get them a holiday from their daily drudgery; and here I cannot help condoling with them for the irreparable loſs they have lately ſuſtained, by the untimely and violent death of Mr. Carr *, who, I am told, was reckoned their top hand: ſo far is certain, that the under-ſheriff, to whom that unhappy author gave his papers, was ſo ſtruck with the ſimilitude of ſtyle between them and the Daily Gazetteers, that he was heard to ſay, however juſtly Mr. Carr might have ſuffered, the adminiſtration would ſtill have a great loſs of him.

* He was an attorney, and was concerned in a conſiderable robbery; for which he was tried, caſt, and executed.

As

As to those of his fraternity, who still survive and write, I have no more time to lose upon them, than just to say, that when they answer this, if they are ordered so to do, I absolutely bar their supposing it to be written by the gentleman himself, whom it is designed to vindicate. This they have often practised, and seem to think it very cunning, whereas it cannot possibly pass on any mortal; for there is not, certainly, more than one man in the kingdom, whose condition is so bad, that he could not find a friend to write in defence of him, when attacked, without being paid for it.

Having said thus much to these miserable journeymen, whom the world and I equally despise, I will just drop one word to their paymaster, whoever he may be; which is, that if he either encourages or suffers these scurrilities upon the private concerns and characters of others, who have always scorned to attack him out of his public character, let him strictly examine himself, and his own circumstances, and consider whether ample returns may not be made him by better pens, and with more truth, than ever were or will be employed on his side.

XVIII.

COMMON SENSE.

SATURDAY, Oct. 14, 1738. Nº 89.

SUCH is the uncertainty and unstability of the things of this world, that there is scarce any event which ought to surprise us, or any thing new to be ſaid upon it. The greateſt empires, and beſt-modeled governments, have been ſuddenly overturned by unexpected occurrences of unlucky and unforeſeen accidents. Notwithſtanding which, when one ſees great and ſudden revolutions happen, one cannot help falling into trite obſervations, which a thouſand events of the ſame kind had ſuggeſted to thouſands of people before.

I confeſs this happened to me lately, when I heard that operas were no more, and that too at a time when the vigor and ſucceſs, with which a ſubſcription was carried on, both by the great and the fair, ſeemed to promiſe them in their fulleſt luſtre. "Shall the "kings and the miniſters of the earth, cried I, be "ſurprized when their beſt-concerted ſchemes are de-"feated; ſchemes which it is generally the common "intereſt of mankind to defeat? and muſt we be-"hold, unmoved, the fatal cataſtrophe of that great "deſign, which the common pleaſures of mankind "ſeemed engaged to ſupport?" Many other reflections occurred to me, which, though I thought new at the time, I am ſince perſuaded were made by the Aſſyrians, the Medes, the Perſians, and others, upon the ſubverſion of their ſeveral empires; and therefore I ſhall not trouble my readers with them.

But I came at laſt to conſider, as I always do, how far, and in what manner, this great event might poſſibly affect the public, and whether the ceſſation of operas would prove a national loſs, or a national advantage: for public diverſions are by no means things indifferent; they give a right or a wrong turn to the minds of the people, and the wiſeſt govern-

ments

ments in the world, I mean, to be ſure, our own, thought ſo not above two years ago, and prudently ſubjected all our public entertainments to the wiſdom and care of the lord chamberlain, his licenſer, or his licenſer's deputy-licenſer.

Was I to follow the examples of the greateſt hiſtorians, I ſhould ſearch into, and aſſign, the cauſes of this revolution, and might poſſibly affirm, with more certainty than they commonly do, that the unſkilfulneſs of the compoſers, the immoderate profit of the performers, the partialities of the governors, and the influence of foreign miſtreſſes, naturally produced this event. But I wave, at preſent, theſe reflections, in order to conſider the effects of muſic in general.

Muſic was held in great eſteem among the antients, particularly the Greeks, who looked upon it as the neceſſary part of the education of their youth, and thought the due regulation of it worthy the care of their laws; inſomuch, that Timotheus was condemned by a decree of the Lacedæmonians, for introducing innovations in their muſic, and corrupting the true eſtabliſhed taſte. Which decree Boëtius has preſerved to us in the original. It ſays, that Timotheus of Miletum, being come into their town, had ſhewn great diſregard to the antient muſic, and the antient lyre, that he had multiplied the ſounds of one, and the ſtrings of the other; and that, inſtead of the plain, expreſſive manner of ſinging, he had invented a fantaſtical new one, where he had introduced the chromatic, &c. He was therefore publicly reprimanded by the ephori, and his lyre was ordered to be altered.

 This

This is not to be wondered at, confidering the aftoniſhing effects which the beſt hiſtorians aſſure us muſic had in thoſe days, and of which I ſhall give ſome inſtances.

The Pyrrhic tune, as is well known, had ſuch a martial influence, that, in a very little time, it ſet the audience a fighting, whether they would or not. This tune, by the way, muſt have infinitely exceeded our beſt modern marches, which, by what I have been able to obſerve in Hyde-Park, rather ſets our army a dancing than a fighting. I aſcribe this difference wholly to the unſkilfulneſs of our modern compoſers; for I will never believe that my countrymen have not as much potential courage in them as the Greeks, if properly excited. I therefore wiſh the Pyrrhic tune had been tranſmitted down to us, to have been uſed in proper places, and upon proper occaſions.

The Phrygian muſic inclined as much to love; and Quintilian tells us, that Pythagoras, having obſerved a young man ſo inflamed by this Phrygian modulation, that he was going to offer violence to a lady of condition, immediately ordered the inſtruments to play in a graver meaſure, called the ſpondee, which inſtantly checked the gallant's deſires, and ſaved the lady's chaſtity. A ſtrong inſtance this of the force of muſic, and the ſagacity of the philoſopher! though by the way, if that Phrygian movement had the ſame effect upon the lady, which it had upon the gentleman, the philoſopher's interpoſition might poſſibly be but unwelcome. Our operas have not been known to occaſion any attempts of this violent nature; which I likewiſe impute to the ef-

fects

fects of the compoſition, and not to any degree of inſenſibility or modeſty in our youth, and who, it muſt be owned, give a fair hearing to muſic, and whoſe ſhort bobs ſeem admirably contrived for the better reception of ſounds.

Dion Chryſoſtomus informs us, that the muſician Timotheus, playing one day upon the flute before Alexander the Great, in the movement called Ortios, that prince immediately laid hold of his great ſword, and was with difficulty hindered from doing miſchief, reſtrained, no doubt, by ſome prudent and pacific miniſter. And Mr. Dryden, in his celebrated ode upon St. Cecilia's day, repreſents that hero alternately affected, in the higheſt degree, by tender or martial ſounds, now languiſhing in the arms of his courtezan, Thaïs, and anon furious, ſnatching a flambeau, and ſetting fire to the town of Perſepolis. This we have lately heard, ſet to muſic by the great Mr. Handel, who, for a modern, certainly excels in the Ortios, or warlike meaſure. But we have ſome reaſon to think that the impreſſions, which it was obſerved to make upon the audience, ſoon gave way to the Phrygian or laſcivious movement.

I am apt to believe that in muſic, as in many other arts and ſciences, we fall infinitely ſhort of the antients. For I take it for granted, that we ſhould be open to the ſame impreſſions, if our compoſers had but the ſkill to make them. However, though muſic does not now cauſe thoſe ſurprizing effects which it did formerly, it ſtill retains power enough over men's paſſions to make it worth our care: and I heard ſome perſons, equally ſkilled in muſic and politics, aſſert, that king James was ſung and fiddled out of this kingdom by the proteſtant tune of Lilly-bullero; and that ſomebody elſe would have been fiddled into it again, if a certain treaſonable Jacobite tune had not been timely ſilenced by the unwearied pains and diligence of the adminiſtration.

The bag-pipe, I am credibly informed, has been known to have a wonderful effect upon our countrymen the North Britons, and to influence whole clans; which I am the more inclined to believe, becauſe I have really ſeen it do ſtrange things here.

The Swiſs, who are not a people of the quickeſt ſenſations, have at this time a tune, which, when played upon their fifes, inſpires them with ſuch a love of their country, that they run home as faſt as they can: which tune is therefore, under ſevere penalties, forbid to be played, when their regiments are on ſervice, becauſe they would inſtantly deſert. Could ſuch a tune be compoſed here, it would then be worth the nation's while to pay the piper; and one could eaſily ſuggeſt the proper places for the performance of it: for inſtance, it might be of great uſe, at the opening of certain aſſemblies, where prayers have already proved ineffectual; and the ſerjeant at arms and the gentleman uſher of the black-rod ſhould be inſtructed to play it in perfection. The band of court muſic would of courſe execute it incomparably, where it would doubtleſs have all the effect which could be expected. I would therefore moſt earneſtly recommend it to the learned doctor Green, to turn his thoughts that way. It is not from the leaſt diſtruſt of Mr. Handel's ability, that I addreſs myſelf

preferably

preferably to doctor Green: but Mr. Handel, having the advantage to be by birth a German, might probably, even without intending it, mix ſome modulations in his compoſition, which might give a German tendency to the mind, and therefore greatly leſſen the national benefit I propoſe by it.

How far the polite part of the world is affected by the ceſſation of operas, I am no judge myſelf; but I aſked a young gentleman of wit and pleaſure about town, whether he did not apprehend that he ſhould be a ſufferer by it in his way of buſineſs, for that I preſumed thoſe ſoft and tender ſounds ſoothed and melted the faireſt breaſts, and fitted them to receive impreſſions? He anſwered me very frankly, that, as far as he could judge, the loſs would be but inconſiderable to their profeſſion; that ſome years ago, indeed, the taſte of muſic, being expreſſive and pathetic, had inſpired tender ſentiments, and ſoftened ſtubborn virtue; but the faſhion being of late for both the compoſers and the performers only to ſhew what tricks they could play, had rather taught the ladies to play tricks too, than made the proper impreſſions upon them, and that he oftener found them tired than ſoftened at the end of an opera. But he confeſſed that they might happen to miſs the opera books a little, becauſe, as moſt of his profeſſion could make a ſhift to read the Engliſh verſion at leaſt, they found, in thoſe incomparable dramas, ſentiments proper for all ſituations, which might not otherwiſe have occurred to them, and which, by emphatical ſigns and looks, they could apply to the proper objects; inſomuch that he had often known very

pretty

pretty ſentimental converſations carried on through a whole opera by theſe references to the book.

Having thus ſhewn the power and effects of muſic, both among the antients and the moderns, and the good and ill uſes which may be made of it, I ſhall ſubmit it to perſons wiſer than myſelf, what is to be done in this important criſis. I look upon operas to have been the great national eſtabliſhment of muſic, and I am perſuaded that innumerable ſects will riſe from their ruins, and break into various conventicles of vocal and inſtrumental, which, if not attended to, may prove of ill conſequence. But in this, as in every thing elſe, I put my truſt in the wiſdom of the miniſters, who daily ſhew that nothing is above their ſkill, or below their care. Kingdoms and gin-ſellers tremble at their fleets, and their informers. Terrible abroad, and lovely at home, they put me always in mind of that beautiful deſcription, which Taſſo gives of one of his heroes:

Se'l vedi folminar, fra l'arme, au volto
Marte le ſtimi; Amor ſe ſcopre il volto.

If you were to ſee him, ſays he, glittering in his armour, and in all the thunder of war, you would take him for Mars, the god of it; but when that is over, and he lays by his helmet, you would think him the god of love.

XIX.

COMMON SENSE.

SATURDAY, Nov. 11, 1738. N° 93.

EVERY age has its faſhionable follies, as well as its faſhionable vices: but, as follies are more numerous than vices, they change oftener, and every four or five years produce a new one. I will indulge my fellow-ſubjects in the full enjoyment of ſuch follies, as are inoffenſive in themſelves, and in their conſequences. Men, as well as children, muſt have their play-things: but when *hæ nugæ ſeria ducunt in mala* (theſe trifles lead on to real evils), I ſhall take the liberty to interpoſe, repreſent, and cenſure.

Faſhion, which is always at firſt the offspring of little minds, and the child of levity, gains ſtrength and ſupport by the great number of its relations, till at length it is received and adopted by better underſtandings, who either conform to it to avoid ſingularity, or who are ſurprized into it, from want of attention to an object which they look upon as indifferent in itſelf, and ſo dignify and eſtabliſh the folly.

This is the caſe of a preſent prevailing extravagancy, I mean the abſurd and ridiculous imitation of the French, which is now become the epidemical diſtemper of this kingdom: not confined to thoſe only from whom one expects no better, but it has even infected thoſe whom one ſhould have thought much

much above ſuch weakneſſes; and I behold with indignation the ſturdy conquerors of France ſhrunk and dwindled into the imperfect mimics, or ridiculous *caricaturas*, of all its levity. The *traveſty* is univerſal; poor England produces nothing fit to eat, or drink, or wear. Our cloaths, our furniture, nay our food too, all is to come from France; and I am credibly informed, that a poulterer at Calais now actually ſupplies our polite tables with half their proviſions.

I do not mean to undervalue the French; I know their merit, they are a chearful, induſtrious, ingenious, polite people, and have many things in which I wiſh we did imitate them. But, like true mimics, we only ape their imperfections, and awkwardly copy thoſe parts which all reaſonable Frenchmen themſelves contemn in the originals.

If this folly went no farther than diſguiſing both our meats and ourſelves in the French modes, I ſhould bear it with more patience, and content myſelf with repreſenting only to my country folks, that the one would make them ſick, and the other ridiculous: but when even the materials for the folly are to be brought over from France too, it becomes a much more ſerious conſideration. Our trade and manufactures are at ſtake, and what ſeems at firſt only very ſilly, is in truth a great national evil, and a piece of civil immorality.

There is ſurely ſome obedience due to the laws of the land, which ſtrictly prohibit the importation of theſe fooleries, and, independently of thoſe laws, there is a ſtrong obligation upon every member of a ſociety a ſociety from which he himſelf receives ſo many advantages: theſe are moral duties, if I know what moral duties are, but I preſume they are awkward ones, and not fit to reſtrain the unbounded fancy of fine gentlemen and fine ladies, in their dreſs and manner of living; and it is, certainly, much more reaſonable, that our trade ſhould decay, and our manufactures ſtarve, than that people of taſte and condition ſhould content themſelves with the wretched produce of their own country.

Methinks there is ſomething very mean in being ſuch avowed plagiaries, and I wonder the Britiſh ſpirit will ſubmit to it. Why will our countrymen thus diſtruſt themſelves? Let them exert their own genius and invention, and I make no doubt but they will be able to produce as many original extravagances, as all the marſhals of France can do. How much more glorious would it be for thoſe ladies who eſtabliſh the faſhion here, to conſider at the ſame time their own dignity, and the public good! Let them not ſervilely copy or tranſlate French edicts, but let them enact original laws of their own. I look upon the birth-day cloaths of a fine woman to be the ſtatute of dreſs for that year: and, by the way, the only ſtatute which is complied with. I therefore humbly intreat, that it may be enacted in Engliſh. Seriouſly, if three or four ladies, at the head of the faſhion, would but value themſelves upon being cloathed entirely with the manufactures of their own country, and from the plenitude of their own power pronounce all foreign manufactures ungenteel, awkward, and frippery, the legions,

legions, who dreſs under their banner, would ſoon be as much aſhamed of dreſſing againſt their country, as they are now of being thought even natives of it. This would be moreover the real imitation of the French, who like nothing but their own.

What I have ſaid with relation to my fair countrywomen holds equally true as to my fine countrymen, to whom I cannot help hinting, over and above, that they make very ridiculous Frenchmen, and might be very valuable Engliſhmen. Every nation has its diſtinguiſhing mark and characteriſtic. If we have a ſolidity which the French have not, they moſt certainly have an elaſticity which we have not; and the imitation is equally awkward. Horace juſtly calls imitators *ſervum pecus* (ſlaviſh cattle); and, to do him juſtice, he is himſelf an original. If my countrymen would be thought converſant with Horace, as they moſt of them would be, I am ſure they will find in him no inſtance of foppery, luxury, or profuſion.

We have heard with ſatisfaction that ſome conſiderable perſons in this kingdom, from a juſt and becoming concern for our diſtreſſed tradeſmen and manufacturers, diſcountenance, as far as poſſible, this pernicious folly. And though I make no doubt but, at the end of this long mourning, by which trade has ſuffered ſo immenſely, ſome meaſures will be taken to this effect elſewhere, this would be the moſt likely way of eradicating the evil, and as it is by no means unprecedented to annex certain conditions to the honor and privilege of ſubjects appearing in the preſence of their ſovereign, ſurely none can be juster nor more reasonable than that they should contribute to the good of their country.

But the mischief does not stop here neither; for now we are not content with receiving our fashions and the materials for them from France, but we even export ourselves in order to import them. The matter, it seems, is of too great consequence to trust to hear-say evidence for; but we must go ourselves to view those great originals, be able to say, of our own knowledge, how such a glutton eats, and how such a fool dresses, and return loaded with the prohibited tinsel and frippery of the *palais* *. Half the private families in England take a trip, as they call it, every summer to Paris; and I am assured, that near four hundred thousand pounds have been remitted thither in one year, to supply this extravagancy. Should this rage continue, the act of parliament, proposed in one of Mr. Congreve's comedies, to prohibit the exportation of fools, will in reality become necessary. Travelling is, unquestionably, a very proper part of the education of our youth; and, like our bullion, I would allow them to be exported. But people of a certain age beyond refining, and once stamped here, like our coin, should be confined within the kingdom. The impressions they have received make them current here, but obstruct their currency any where else, and they only return dis-

* The place where the courts of justice and parliament are held at Paris, answering to Westminster-hall. Milliners and toymen are allowed to have shops and stalls; and know how to dispose of their trinkets to young lawyers, foreigners, and other persons, whom curiosity or idleness draws to this place.

guised,

guiſed, defaced, and probably much leſſened in the weight.

The ſober and well-regulated family of a country gentleman is a very valuable part of the community; they keep up good neighbourhood by decent hoſpitality, they promote good manners by their example, and encourage labor and induſtry by their conſumption. But when once they run French, if I may uſe the expreſſion, and are to be poliſhed by this trip to Paris, I will venture to aſſure them, that they may, from that day, date their being ridiculous for ever afterwards. They are laughed at in France, for not being like the French; they are laughed at here, for endeavouring to be like them; and, what is worſe, their mimicking their luxury brings them into their neceſſity, which ends in a moſt compleat imitation indeed, of their mean and ſervile dependance upon the court.

I could point out to theſe itinerant ſpirits a much ſhorter, leſs expenſive, and more effectual method of travelling and frenchifying themſelves; which is, if they would but travel to *Old Soho*, and ſtay two or three months in *le quartier des Grecs* *; lodgings and *legumes* are very cheap there, and the people very civil to ſtrangers. There too they might poſſibly get acquainted with ſome French people, which they never do at Paris, and, it may be, learn a little French, which they never do in France neither: and

* The place where moſt of the deſcendants of the French refugees then lived. Their chapel, in which divine ſervice was, and ſtill continues to be, performed, according to the rites of the church of England, had formerly belonged to a congregation of Greeks, and has given its name to all the *environs* of Soho ſquare.

I appeal

I appeal to any one, who has ſeen thoſe venerable perſonages of both ſexes, of the refugees, if they are not infinitely more genteel, eaſier, and better dreſſed in the French manner, than any of their modern Engliſh mimics.

As for our fair countrywomen in particular, they are ſo valuable, ſo beautiful a part of our own produce, and in which we ſo eminently excel all other nations, that I can by no means allow of their exportation: they are ſurely, if I may ſay ſo, much more valuable commodities than wool or fuller's-earth, the exportation of which is ſo ſtrictly prohibited by our laws, leſt foreigners ſhould have the manufacturing of them; which reaſoning holds ſtronger, upon many accounts, in this caſe, than in the two others.

Let it not be urged, that the loſs ariſing from theſe follies is but a trifling object with relation to our trade in general. This, for aught I know, might have been true ſome years ago: but ſuch is the preſent unhappy ſtate of our trade, that I doubt no object is now a trifling one, or below the attention of every individual. After ſix and twenty years peace, we labor under every one of the taxes which ſubſiſted at the concluſion of the laſt expenſive war, without reckoning ſome new ones laid on ſince; while other nations, gradually eaſed of that burthen, under-work and under-ſell us in every foreign market. The laſt valuable part of our trade, how has it been attacked for theſe many years! and how has it been protected! It would be unreaſonable to expect that the adminiſtration, ingroſſed by much greater cares, ſhould attend to ſo trifling a conſideration as trade;

 nor

nor can one wonder that it has intirely eſcaped the attention of parliaments, when one conſiders, that ſo many affairs of a much higher nature have, of late, ſo advantageouſly employed them. But it therefore becomes more peculiarly the care of every individual; and if, from the reformation only of thoſe follies here mentioned, five or ſix hundred thouſand pounds a year may be ſaved to the nation, which I am convinced is the caſe, how incumbent is it upon every one to ſacrifice a little private folly to ſo much public good! It may at leaſt be a reprieve to our trade and manufactures from that ruin which, at beſt, ſeems to be too near them; and poſſibly too the examples of ſome private people may, at leaſt, ſhame others, whoſe more immediate care it ought to be, into ſome degree of attention to what they have ſo long ſeemed to neglect and deſpiſe.

XX.

COMMON SENSE.

SATURDAY, Jan. 27, 1739. N° 103.

SIR,

I HAVE lately read, with the greateſt ſatisfaction, the account, printed in our public papers, of the ſignal victory obtained by his majeſty's Hanoverian troops over the Danes *, notwithſtanding the great inequality

* A more ſerious account of this tranſaction, which occaſioned a long paper war, and was terminated in 1740, by a treaty with the king

inequality of the numbers, the Danes being at least thirty, and the Hanoverians at most five hundred men; the Danes having moreover the important fortress of Steinhorst to protect, and the counsels of counsellor Wedderkop to direct them.

As the best account of this great action is in the Daily Gazetteer of the 25th of December last, which nobody reads, I will, for the satisfaction of the curious, transcribe it from thence.

"Hanover, December the 12th, O. S. On the "4th instant a detachment of Hanoverians, consisting of five hundred men, with two field-pieces, "marched to take possession of the territory of Steinhorst, which belongs to the privy counsellor Wedderkop, wherein were posted thirty dragoons in "the service of the king of Denmark. The colonel "who commanded the detachment no sooner arrived, "but he sent a lieutenant to the Danish captain in "the castle, to acquaint him, that he was come with "orders to take possession of it, and, if he refused, "to turn him out by force. The Danish captain "having answered the lieutenant, that he was commanded to repel force by force, the two officers "had such high words, that they drew their swords "and fought a duel, in which the Danish captain "was killed on the spot, and the lieutenant mortally "wounded. The Hanoverian colonel having advanced with his troops in the *interim*, to begin the "attack, a very smart skirmish ensued, wherein se-

king of Denmark, is given in the *Farther Vindication of the case of the Hanover Troops*, written by lord Chesterfield and Mr. Waller.

"veral soldiers were killed on both sides. The "Danes then drew up their draw-bridges, and re-"tired into the castle, where they defended them-"selves a while; but the Hanoverians having, by "the means of great hooks, plucked down the "bridges, they entered the castle and took possession "of it, by virtue of an instrument drawn up by a "lawyer, and a scrivener, whom they had sent for "from Hamburg for that purpose."

This action is, in my mind, as great an instance of prudence, generosity, magnanimity, and moderation, as any we read of in antiquity. Considering the strength of the castle and the number of the garrison, it was certainly prudent to send no less than five hundred men to attack it. The colonel shews his generosity, in the first place, by sending a very civil message to the commanding officer, to let him know he was come to take possession of the castle, and to turn him out by force; and then the ardor of his courage, by not staying for an answer, but beginning the attack in the *interim*. After he had possessed himself of the fortress by his hooks, and other warlike instruments, he declines the right of conquest, which he might undoubtedly have insisted upon, but quiets the possession, by virtue of an instrument prepared by a lawyer and scrivener, whom he had sent for from Hamburg for that purpose.

This important fortress, together with the estate about it, I am assured, is worth, as to the *dominium utile*, no less than a thousand pounds a year, and inestimable, as to the *dominium supremum*, as it is a

check

check to the northern powers: but, the title being pretty intricate and doubtful, his majesty bought it a pennyworth of the duke of Holstein, the last time he visited his German dominions, paying, I think, no more than thirty thousand pounds for it.

I have met with some timorous people, who apprehend ill consequences from this affair. The king of Denmark, say they, incensed at this treatment, will certainly throw himself into the arms of France, which has, for some time, been endeavouring to engage him, as well as other northern powers, provisionally in her interests, to facilitate her future schemes of power and greatness. Nay, more, say they, the king of Denmark may probably resent this upon Hanover itself, and march a considerable body of troops there; in which case, Hanover will cry out murther, call upon England for help, and we may be obliged to send more fleets to the Baltic, and be engaged in a war upon account of a disputed possession, too inconsiderable even for a law-suit. But those, who talk in this way, are but shallow politicians, and have not an adequate notion of the strength and importance of our foreign dominions, or of the goodness of those troops. On the contrary, it seems evident to me, that the king of Denmark will think twice before he engages in measures disagreeable to that state, whose strength, courage, and conduct, he has of late so sensibly experienced; but, should he take any rash and inconsiderate step, Hanover alone is more than a match for him, and England neither can nor will be engaged in that quarrel; and especially at a time that our expences and fleets are employed,

 in

in obtaining ample reparation for our merchants, and future ſecurity for our trade, which, it may be, is not quite yet accompliſhed.

Upon this occaſion, give me leave, ſir, to ſuggeſt to you my thoughts upon the luſtre and advantage which England receives from being ſo happily annexed to his majeſty's German dominions, in anſwer to the vulgar prejudices too commonly entertained againſt them.

While England was unconnected with any dominions upon the continent, we had only our fleets to prevent and reſiſt inſults from other powers; whereas, by our happy union with Hanover, we have a body of above twenty thouſand men, moſt excellent troops, to act whenever we think proper, without the leaſt danger or expence to England, by which too particularly we bridle the north.

The dutchy of Bremen is of infinite advantage to England, as it ſupplies us with great quantities of linen, both for home conſumption, and re-exportation, to the great eaſe of our linen manufacturers, who would otherwiſe be obliged to make ten times the quantity they do now.

Hanover may be likewiſe of uſe to us by its example, ſince there cannot be a ſtronger inſtance of the advantages ariſing to a country, from a wiſe and frugal adminiſtration, than the great improvements of that electorate, under the ſucceſſive governments of his late and his preſent majeſty.

The whole revenues of the electorate, at the time of his late majeſty's acceſſion to the throne of theſe realms, did not amount to more than three hundred thouſand

thouſand pounds a year; and yet ſoon afterwards the conſiderable purchaſe of Bremen and Verden were made for above five hundred thouſand pounds ſterling. Not long after this, the number of troops, in the electorate, was raiſed much above what it was before thought able to maintain, and has continued ever ſince upon that high eſtabliſhment.

Since his preſent majeſty's acceſſion to the electorate, ſeveral acquiſitions have alſo been made; and the very laſt time his majeſty viſited thoſe dominions, he bought in, at the price of above a hundred thouſand pounds, the revenues of the poſtage of the electorate, which was an hereditary grant to the counts of Platen: and in Auguſt laſt his majeſty concluded the purchaſe, and paid above thirty thouſand pounds for the fortreſs and eſtates of Steinhorſt. So that upon the whole, notwithſtanding that the expences for the current ſervice of the year equal, at leaſt, the revenue of the electorate, yet, by a prudent and frugal management, a million ſterling at leaſt has been laid out, over and above, in new acquiſitions.

If ſuch frugal means had been purſued, we ſhould have been in a better condition than we now are. I cannot help recommending to the adminiſtration, here, to follow the example of their German brethren, to have ſpirit enough to act, and frugality enough to put the nation in a condition of doing it.

I am ſir,

Your humble ſervant,

ANGLO-GERMANICUS.

XXI.

OLD ENGLAND,

Or the Constitutional Journal;

By Jeffrey Broad-Bottom, of Covent-Garden, Efq; *.

Saturday, Feb. 5, 1743. N° 1.

IT has generally been the cuftom with our hebdomadal and diurnal authors to preface their works with an account of their birth, parentage, and education, the company they keep, and feveral other curious particulars relating to their own perfons: but, as I am of opinion, that it is more proper for a writer to endeavour to recommend his bufinefs than his perfon to the public, I fhall inform my reader of the one, and leave him to indulge the pleafure of conjecture as to the other.

We are told by critics, that definitions ought to be conceived in as plain, concife terms as poffible. The world naturally expect that a public writer fhould, at his

* The refignation of fir Robert Walpole was not attended with that total change of men and meafures which had been expected. The Newcaftle party kept their ground; and, by entering into a private negotiation with Mr. Pulteney and lord Carteret, fucceeded in dividing the oppofition. Very few of them were taken into the miniftry; and lord Chefterfield, who, with feveral more, were excluded, highly complained of having been facrificed by their friends, and loft no opportunity of expreffing their refentment. This paper was undertaken with that view. It made a great deal of noife, and the fuppofed author and printer were taken into cuftody. Lord Chefterfield owned himfelf repeatedly to his chaplain, the prefent bifhop of Waterford, author of the firft number; and I think there can be no doubt but that the third came from the fame hand.

his outſet, acquaint them with his principles, views, and motives of writing; therefore I intend, in compliance with this expectation, to acquaint my reader in very plain terms with thoſe ſeveral particulars. This is fair; if he likes the definition of each, he will be curious to know the ſeveral propoſitions deduced from them, and perhaps be prevailed on to encourage the doctrine ariſing upon the whole: if, on the other hand, he ſhould diſlike them, there is but little harm done; he knows what he is to expect, and will hereafter ſave both himſelf and me the mortification of any farther interviews with one another.

All experience convinces me, that 90 men out of 100, when they talk of forming principles, mean no more than embracing parties; and, when they talk of ſupporting their party, mean ſerving their friends, and the ſervice of their friends implies no more than conſulting ſelf-intereſt. By this gradation, principles are fitted to party, party degenerates into faction, and faction is reduced to ſelf. For this reaſon, I openly declare that I think no honeſt man will implicitly embrace any party, ſo as to attach himſelf to the perſons of thoſe who form it. I am firmly of opinion, that, both in the laſt and preſent age, this nation might have been equally well ſerved either by whigs or tories; and, if ſhe was not, it was not becauſe their principles were contrary to her intereſt, but becauſe their conduct was inconſiſtent with their principles.

To extend this view a little farther, I am entirely perſuaded that, in the words, *our preſent happy eſta-*

bliſhment,

blishment, the happineſs mentioned there is that of the ſubjects; and that, if the eſtabliſhment ſhould make the prince happy and the ſubjects otherwiſe, it would be very juſtly termed our preſent unhappy eſtabliſhment. I apprehend the nation did not think king James unworthy of the crown, merely that he might make way for the prince of Orange; nor can I conceive, that they ever precluded themſelves from dealing by king William in the ſame manner as they had done by king James, if he had done as much to deſerve ſuch a treatment. Neither can I in all my ſearch find, that, when the crown was ſettled in a hereditary line upon the preſent royal family, the people of Great Britain ever ſigned any formal inſtrument of recantation, by which they expreſſed their ſorrow and repentance of what they had done againſt king James, and proteſted that they would never do ſo by any future prince, though reduced to the ſame melancholy neceſſity. I farther think, the people ſettled the crown upon the family of Hanover, neither from any opinion which they entertained of infallibility in all the future princes which that illuſtrious houſe was to produce, nor from their being perſuaded that the crown of this kingdom, in right of blood, belonged to that houſe, but becauſe they thought that the government of thoſe princes bade faireſt to make themſelves happy. They thought, that princes of that houſe, having fewer connections with any intereſt upon the continent deſtructive to that of Great Britain, would be more independent, and leſs incumbered with any foreign concern, and conſequently more at liberty to act for the intereſt of this

this nation. From these considerations, as a subject of Great Britain, and as an honest man, I think myself bound, even in my individual capacity, to oppose all schemes destructive of those effects, which I, in my conscience, believe were the reasons that induced this free people to raise the head of the family of Hanover, from being the youngest elector in Germany, to be one of the most powerful princes in Europe. I think, that there can be no treason equal to that of a minister, who would advise his majesty to sacrifice his great concerns to his little ones; because, as I think his majesty's virtues have firmly riveted him in the hearts of his subjects, he is as sure of the crown of England as of the electorate of Hanover; and therefore every measure in favour of the latter, in prejudice of the former, is the blackest treason both against the king and the people.

Such are my principles with regard to the general system of our constitution and government; as to the particular propositions to be deduced from these principles, they will be the subject of after-disquisition.

I am next to account for the views of my writing. I had always observed, of the late very wicked ministers, that, though they did many infamous scandalous things, and put up with many gross affronts in favour of foreign considerations; yet, I will do them the justice to say it, the odium arising from their measures always fell upon their own persons; and whatever the secret springs of their conduct might have been, yet we never saw the safety and profit of Hanoverian dominions, made in parliament itself,

itſelf, the immediate, open, and avowed cauſe of ſacrificing the neareſt and the deareſt intereſts of this nation. Queſtions indeed were carried for Heſſian troops, for extravagant ſubſidies, for inconſiſtent treaties, and the like; but they never had the impudence, the inſolence, or the wickedneſs, to bring Hanover and Great Britain, as two parties, before the bar of their own corruption, and then to paſs a verdict, by which the latter was rendered a province to the former. It is againſt ſuch, as can be found wicked enough to do this, that this paper is undertaken; it is undertaken againſt thoſe who have found the ſecret of acquiring more infamy in ten months, than their predeceſſors, with all the pains they took, could acquire in twenty years. It is intended to vindicate the honor of the crown of Great Britain, and to aſſert the intereſt of her people againſt all foreign conſiderations; to keep up the ſpirit of virtuous oppoſition to wicked people; to point out the means of completing the great end of the revolution; and, in ſhort, to give the alarm upon any future attacks that may be made, either open or ſecret, of the government upon the conſtitution.

I am now to ſpeak of the motives for an undertaking of this kind: theſe are many, but ſome of them perhaps not quite ſo proper to be committed to the public. We have ſeen the noble fruits of a twenty years oppoſition blaſted by the connivance and treachery of a few, who, by all ties of gratitude and honor, ought to have cheriſhed and preſerved them to the people: but this diſappointment ought to be ſo far from diſcouraging, that it ſhould lend

ſpirit

ſpirit and life to a new oppoſition. The late one labored their point for a much longer term of years, and againſt many greater difficulties, than any oppoſition at preſent can be under any apprehenſions of encountering. They became a majority, from a minority of not above eighty-ſeven or eighty-eight in all; they fought againſt an experienced general and a national purſe; and the queſtions they oppoſed were more plauſible in their nature, and leſs dangerous in their conſequences, than any that have yet fallen within the ſyſtem of their blundering ſucceſſors. At preſent, the friends of their country, who have already declared themſelves, have advantages which their predeceſſors could never compaſs, even after twenty years hard labor.

I know, that the conduct of thoſe, who ſneaked, and abandoned their principles, upon the late change of miniſtry, is ſometimes made uſe of as an argument why all oppoſition muſt be fruitleſs, ſince all mankind, ſay they, employ it only as a means of their preferment, or the inſtrument of their revenge. This argument is in point of fact abſolutely falſe, and in point of reaſoning extremely inconcluſive. To prove it falſe in fact, I need but appeal to an underſtanding reader's own memory; let him recollect the characters of thoſe, who betrayed their party upon the late change, the light in which they ſtood with the public, and the eſtimation they held with their friends. Whoever ſhall take the pains to do this will own, that the part they acted could be no ſurprize upon the diſcerning part of mankind. In all parties and bodies of men, even leſs numerous than thoſe who formed

the

the late oppoſition, there have always been found, and it has been always underſtood there are, men, whoſe virtue is too weak to ſtand the firſt ſhock either of temptation or danger: when ſuch men give way, they leave a party ſtronger, becauſe its rottenneſs is removed.

They, who fell off upon the late turn, are of two ſorts; ſuch as were never ſuſpected of having virtue to reſiſt temptation, and ſuch as were never thought of conſequence enough to deſerve it. The ſurprize, therefore, is not that ſome fell, but that ſo many ſtood. But then how melancholy is the conſideration, when we reflect, that there is a poſſibility, that the great concerns of the nation both at home and abroad may, by ſuch an alteration of affairs, fall into the hands of thoſe who were either the reproach or ſcum of their party? What a proſpect muſt this nation have, if in the moſt deciſive conjuncture, as to the liberties of Europe, the management of foreign concerns ſhould fall into the hands of a perſon of the following character?

A man, who, when in the oppoſition, even his ſincerity could never beget confidence, nor his abilities eſteem; whoſe learning is unrewarded with knowledge, and his experience with wiſdom; diſcovering a haughtineſs of demeanour, without any dignity of character; and poſſeſſing the luſt of avarice, without knowing the right uſe of power and riches. His underſtanding blinded by his paſſions, his paſſions directed by his prejudices, and his prejudices ever hurrying into preſumption; impatient even of an equal, yet ever requiring the correction of a ſuperior.

Right as to general maxims, but wrong in the application; and therefore always ſo intoxicated by the proſpect of ſucceſs, that he never is cool enough to concert the proper meaſures to attain it.

Should a man, I ſay, of ſuch a character as this, ever come to be at the head of foreign affairs, the nation muſt be in greater danger than it was in any time of the late adminiſtration, becauſe her ruin will be more ſwift, diſgraceful, and irretrievable. One might eaſily form a contraſt to this character, and yet not deviate from a living reſemblance. I could point out a perſon, without any other merit but the loweſt ſpecies of proſtitution, enjoying a conſiderable poſt, got by betraying his own party, without having abilities to be of uſe to any other: one, who had that plodding mechanical turn, which, with an opinion of his ſteadineſs, was of ſervice to the oppoſition, but can be of none to a miniſtry: one, whoſe talents were ſo low, that nothing but ſervile application could preſerve him from univerſal contempt, and who, if he had perſevered all his life in the intereſts of his country, might have had a chance of being remembered hereafter as a uſeful man. If there are ſuch characters as thoſe now exiſting, it is at leaſt of ſome conſolation to men of ſenſe and virtue, that, if their inclinations lead them to views deſtructive of the intereſts and conſtitution of Great Britain, yet their abilities and reputation with all mankind are too mean for them to continue ſo long in power as to be able to copy the late miniſter in procuring a ſafe retreat for his crimes.

Having

Having ſaid thus much, I declare that this paper ſhall ceaſe as ſoon as the motives on which it is undertaken have ceaſed; but till then it ſhall be carried on with all the ſpirit which is conſiſtent with decency, law, and the principles of this conſtitution. While the writers in it keep to theſe, they are determined to fear no conſequences; becauſe nothing can ariſe ſo melancholy to their own private intereſt, as an attempt to cruſh the liberty of writing muſt be to thoſe of the public.

JEFFREY BROADBOTTOM.

XXII.

OLD ENGLAND,

Or the CONSTITUTIONAL JOURNAL.

SATURDAY, February 19, 1743. N° 3.

I SCARCE know a more delicate and difficult ſituation, than that of an author at his firſt appearance in public. He preſents himſelf without introductor or credentials. He is his own ambaſſador, ſent by himſelf to ſpeak of himſelf and for himſelf; in which caſe it is almoſt impoſſible for him not to ſay either too little or too much. But the difficulties of a weekly author, or an author by retail, are ſtill greater, as they are perpetual; for even ſhould he get through his firſt audience with ſucceſs, and be graciouſly received, the leaſt ſlip in his ſubſequent conduct undoes the whole, and he is diſgraced. He

is

is bound over, as it were, from week to week, to his good behaviour, and a hundred thouſand judges, not all of them learned or impartial as the twelve, are to determine whether he has forfeited his recognizances or not.

Aware of theſe dangers, I ſhould not have encountered them, had not a full conviction of my own ſuperior merit aſſured me that I was ſafe from them all. Armed with wit, judgment, erudition, and every other eminent qualification, I ruſh into the world, ſecure, like one of Homer's heroes, in armour given him by all the gods. I would not have ſaid thus much of myſelf, for, I thank God, I am as free from vanity as ever any author was, and what I have ſaid every author thinks, but that, as yet, I have nobody elſe to ſay it for me, and it was abſolutely neceſſary that the public ſhould not be ignorant of ſo important a truth. The firſt impreſſion is often deciſive; and the generality of mankind chuſe to take an opinion ready-made, even from the party intereſted, rather than be at the trouble of forming one of their own. In a very little time, the unanimous voice of my readers will, I dare ſay, render any farther intimations of this kind unneceſſary.

As I foreſee that this paper will occaſion many queſtions, I ſhall here give the anſwers beforehand to ſuch of them as occur to me, that the curious may know what they have to expect for the future.

"What is this new paper, this conſtitutional jour-"nal?" ſays ſome ſolid politician, whoſe unerring judgment has never ſuffered him to ſtray out of the beaten road of facts and dates. "Has it matter "and found reasoning? or is it only a paper of wit "and fancy, for the amusement of the frivolous? Is "it whig or tory; for, or against, the court? I will "know a little more of it before I take it in." To this I answer and engage, that it shall have the most material of matter, and the most reasonable of reasoning. As to whig and tory, I know no real distinction between them; I look upon them as two brothers, who, in truth, mean the same thing, though they pursue it differently; and therefore, as Martia did in the like case, I declare myself for neither, yet for both. As to for, or against, the court, I only answer it shall be constitutional, and directed with regard to the court as Trajan desired his sword might be, for him, or against him, as he deserved it.

"Here is a new paper come out, I am told," says some vigorous minister. "It is treason to be sure, "but is it treason within or without the law? can I "get at it? I do not like the title on it, especially at "this time." With humble submission, I beg leave to assure his lordship, that I shall not write treason, because I never think treason. This royal family has not a more faithful and loyal subject in the kingdom than myself; and if I may borrow an expression I have long admired, it is under this royal family alone that I think we can live free, and that I hope we are determined to live free. His lordship shall most certainly never get at me, till it is criminal to be an Englishman; should that ever happen, indeed, he may possibly have the satisfaction of condemning

demning me to a wheel-barrow in the mines of the Hartz *.

"This Jeffrey Broadbottom, this conſtitutional "journal, is certainly levelled at us," ſays a conſcious ſullen apoſtate patriot to his fallen brethren in the Pandæmonium. "It is ten to one, but it is written "by ſome of our old friends, and then we ſhall have "all our former ſpeeches, pamphlets, and declara-"tions, turned upon us, and our paſt conduct ſet "over againſt our preſent. I wiſh we could buy it "off; as ſoon as ever I can find out the author I "will, for I have ſome reaſon to be pretty ſure that "there is no man who is not to be bought;" and then

Grinn'd horribly a ghaſtly ſmile.

Pray why do you think my paper is levelled at you? has your expiring conſcience in its laſt words told you ſo? and has the ſame authority informed you that I am to be bought? You are miſtaken in both. You may happen, indeed, ſometimes to hitch-in a paper, but you muſt be much more conſiderable than you are before you become the principal object of one; and you muſt ſtay till you are truſted with the diſpoſal of money, and till I love it as well as you do, two things which will never happen, ere you will be able to buy me.

"What is this new paper, this broad-bottom "Journal, I think they call it," ſays a fine woman in the genteel languor of her morning converſation with ſome fine gentleman of diſtinguiſhed taſte and politeneſs: "Is it like the Tatlers and Spectators? has

* Mines belonging to certain German dominions.

 "it

" it wit or humour? or is it only upon those odious " politics that one hears of all day long? in short, " will it do with one's tea in a morning?" " Not " with your tea," replies the fine gentleman, " but in- " comparably well with your ale, if you ever take " any; not that I have read it yet, but, to say the " truth, the title does not promise well. Jeffrey " Broadbottom and John Trott seem to be synony- " mous terms. I dare say, there is nothing of what " the French call *enjouement* in it; and I take it to " be a kind of heavy hot loaf, to stay the stomachs of " hungry politicians in a morning." Have a little patience with me, ye illustrious rulers of the *beau monde*, ye tremendous judges, whose decisions are the final decrees of fashion and taste. I know your importance too well not to engage your favour if possible: though I shall be often, what you never are, serious, I shall be sometimes, what you are always, trifling. My lazy and my idle hours shall be sacred to the amusement of yours; lighter subjects shall sometimes engage your attention, and unbend mine; and the events of the polite world shall fill up the intervals of the busy one.

The universal question will be, who is the author, or supposed author, of this paper? To which if I do not give an answer at present, I must beg leave to be excused; being determined at present, to shine like phosphorus in the dark, and scatter my light from the impenetrable recess of my own closet. I will, for a time at least, enjoy the sensible pleasure of unsought and unsuspected praise, and of hearing, wherever I go, my labors applauded, and severally ascribed to the most eminent wits and politicians of the age; as they certainly will be, till I think proper to declare myself, and vindicate the glory due to me alone.

Having thus given not only an account, but some samples, of what the public may expect from me hereafter, I shall conclude this paper with a friendly and disinterested piece of advice to such of my fellow-subjects as are desirous of information, instruction, or entertainment. Secure my paper in time, for the demand will soon be too great to be complied with; and those who take it in first shall, as in justice they ought, have the preference afterwards. Mr. Purser, my printer, assures me it is impossible to print off above one hundred and ninety-three thousand of these papers in a week; a very small proportion to the number of those who will be sollicitous to read them: for reckoning the people of this kingdom at eight millions, and deducting half that number for young children, blind people, and men of quality, who either cannot or do not chuse to read, there will remain four millions of reading souls, of whom three millions, eight hundred and seven thousand cannot have the satisfaction of reading this paper at the first hand, but must wait, with patience, for the future editions. I do not say this from any sordid view of interest, which I am infinitely above; for I most solemnly protest that I desire nothing for myself, and that the immense profits of this paper shall be all distributed among my friends, the printer, the publisher, compositor, press-men, flys, and devils, without quartering myself upon any one of them, or requiring any thing from them contrary to their former conduct, honor, or conscience.

JEFERY BROADBOTTOM.

XXIII.

THE WORLD*.

SATURDAY, May 3, 1753. N° 18.

THE following letter had appeared earlier in the world, if its length, or, what at present happens to be the same thing, its merit had not been so great. I have been trying to shorten it, without robbing it of its beauties; but, after many unsuccessful attempts, I find that the spirit of it is, as the human soul is imagined to be by some antient philosophers, *totus in toto, et totus in qualibet parte*. I have, therefore,

* This paper was set on foot by Mr. Moore, the ingenious author of the *Fables for the Female Sex*, and of the tragedy of the *Gamester*. He soon met with assistance from numerous correspondents, and, as he informs us in the dedication of one of his volumes to Soame Jenyns, esq; who was himself one of the writers in it, the *World* became *the only fashionable vehicle, in which men of rank and genius chose to convey their sentiments to the public*. Lord Chesterfield was one of these; but, as he sent his first paper to the publisher without any notice from whence it came, it underwent but a slight inspection, and was very near being excluded on account of its length. This neglect would have stopt any future communications; but fortunately lord Lyttelton happening to call at Mr. J. Dodsley's, this paper was shewn to him. He immediately knew the hand, and still more the manner of writing, of the noble author. Mr. Moore, being informed of this discovery, read the manuscript more attentively, discerned its beauties, and thought proper not only to publish it directly, but to introduce it with an apology for the delay, and a compliment to the author.

fore, changed the form of my paper, chusing rather to present my readers with an extraordinary half-sheet, than to keep from them any longer what was sent me for their instruction. At the same time, I must beg leave to say, that I shall never think myself obliged to repeat my complaisance, but to those of my correspondents, who, like the writer of this letter, can inform me of their grievances with all the elegance of wit.

" To Mr. FITZ-ADAM.

SIR,

I consider you as supplemental to the law of the land. I take your authority to begin, where the power of the law ends. The law is intended to stop the progress of crimes by punishing them; your paper seems calculated to check the course of follies by exposing them. May you be more successful in the latter than the law is in the former!

Upon this principle I shall lay my case plainly before you, and desire your publication of it as a warning to others. Though it may seem ridiculous to many of your readers, I can assure you, sir, that it is a very serious one to me, notwithstanding the ill-natured comfort which I might have, of thinking it of late a very common one.

I am a gentleman of a reasonable paternal estate in my county, and serve as knight of the shire for it. Having what is called a very good family-interest, my election incumbered my estate with a mortgage of only five thousand pounds; which I have not been able to clear, being obliged, by a good place which I have got ſince, to live in town, and in all the beſt company, nine months in the year. I married ſuitable to my circumſtances. My wife wanted neither fortune, beauty, nor underſtanding. Diſcretion and good humor on her part, joined to good-nature and good-manners on mine, made us live comfortably together for eighteen years. One ſon and one daughter were our only children. We complied with cuſtom in the education of both. My daughter learned ſome French and ſome dancing; and my ſon paſſed nine years at Weſtminſter-ſchool, in learning the words of two languages, long ſince dead, and not yet above half revived. When I took him away from ſchool, I reſolved to ſend him directly abroad, having been at Oxford myſelf. My wife approved of my deſign; but tacked a propoſal of her own to it, which ſhe urged with ſome earneſtneſs. "My "dear," ſaid ſhe, "I think you do very right to ſend "George abroad; for I love a foreign education, "though I ſhall not ſee the poor boy a great while; "but, ſince we are to part for ſo long a time, why "ſhould we not take that opportunity of carrying "him ourſelves as far as Paris? The journey is no- "thing, very little farther than to our own houſe in "the north; we ſhall ſave money by it, for every "thing is very cheap in France; it will form the "girl, who is of a right age for it; and a couple of "months, with a good French, and dancing, maſter, "will perfect her in both, and give her an air and "manner that will help her off in theſe days, when "huſbands are not plenty, eſpecially for girls with

"only

"only five thouſand pounds to their fortunes. Se-
"veral of my acquaintance, who have lately taken
"trips to Paris, have told me, that to be ſure we
"ſhould take this opportunity of going there. Be-
"ſides, my dear, as neither you nor I have ever
"been abroad, this little jaunt will amuſe and even
"improve us; for it is the eaſieſt thing in the world
"to get into all the beſt company at Paris."

My wife had no ſooner ended her ſpeech, which I eaſily perceived to be the reſult of meditation, than my daughter exerted all her little eloquence in ſeconding her mother's motion. "Ay, dear papa," ſaid ſhe, "let us go with brother to Paris; it will be "the charmingeſt thing in the world; we ſhall ſee all "the neweſt faſhions there; I ſhall learn to dance of "Marſeille *; in ſhort, I ſhall be quite another crea-"ture after it. You ſee how my couſin Kitty was "improved by going to Paris laſt year; I hardly "knew her again when ſhe came back; do, dear "papa, let us go."

The abſurdity of the propoſal ſtruck me at firſt; and I foreſaw a thouſand inconveniencies in it, though not half ſo many as I have ſince felt. However, knowing that direct contradiction, though ſupported by the beſt arguments, was not the likelieſt method to convert a female diſputant, I ſeemed a little to doubt, and contented myſelf with ſaying, "that I "was not, at firſt ſight at leaſt, ſenſible of the many "advantages which they had enumerated, but that, "on the contrary, I apprehended a great deal of trou-

* Marcel, the moſt famous dancing-maſter, at that time, at Paris. He is often mentioned in lord Cheſterfield's letters to his ſon.

"ble in the journey, and many inconveniencies in "consequence of it; that I had not observed many "men of my age considerably improved by their "travels, but that I had lately seen many women of "hers become very ridiculous by theirs; and that "for my daughter, as she had not a fine fortune, I "saw no necessity of her being a fine lady." Here the girl interrupted me, with saying, "For that very "reason, papa, I should be a fine lady. Being in "fashion is often as good as being a fortune; and I "have known air, dress, and accomplishments, stand "many a woman in stead of a fortune." "Nay, to "be sure," added my wife, "the girl is in the right "in that; and if with her figure she gets a certain "air and manner, I cannot see why she may not rea-"sonably hope to be as advantageously married, as "lady Betty Townly, or the two miss Bellairs, who "had none of them such good fortunes." I found by all this, that the attack upon me was a concerted one, and that both my wife and daughter were strongly infected with that migrating distemper, which has of late been so epidemical in this kingdom, and which annually carries such numbers of our private families to Paris, to expose themselves there as English, and here, after their return, as French; insomuch that I am assured that the French call those swarms of English, which now in a manner overrun France, a second incursion of the Goths and Vandals.

I endeavoured, as well as I could, to avert this impending folly by delays and gentle persuasions, but in vain; the attacks upon me were daily repeated, and ſometimes enforced by tears. At laſt I yielded, from mere good-nature, to the joint importunities of a wife and daughter whom I loved; not to mention the love of eaſe and domeſtic quiet, which is, much oftener than we care to own, the true motive of many things that we either do or omit.

My conſent being thus extorted, our ſetting out was preſſed. The journey wanted no preparations; we ſhould find every thing in France. My daughter, who ſpoke ſome French, and my ſon's governor, who was a Swiſs, were to be our interpreters upon the road; and when we came to Paris, a French ſervant or two would make all eaſy.

But, as if providence had a mind to puniſh our folly, our whole journey was a ſeries of diſtreſſes. We had not ſailed a league from Dover, before a violent ſtorm aroſe, in which we had like to have been loſt. Nothing could equal our fears but our ſickneſs, which perhaps leſſened them: at laſt we got into Calais, where the inexorable cuſtom-houſe officers took away half the few things which we had carried with us. We hired ſome chaiſes, which proved to be old and ſhattered ones, and broke down with us at leaſt every ten miles. Twice we were overturned, and ſome of us hurt, though there are no bad roads in France. At length, the ſixth day, we got to Paris, where our banker had provided a very good lodging for us; that is, very good rooms, very well furniſhed, and very dirty. Here the great ſcene opens. My wife and daughter, who had been a good deal diſheartened by our diſtreſſes, recovered their ſpirits, and grew extremely impatient for a conſultation of the neceſſary trades-people; when luckily our banker and his lady, informed of our arrival, came to make us a viſit. He graciouſly brought me five thouſand livres, which he aſſured me was not more than what would be neceſſary for our firſt ſetting out, as he called it; while his wife was pointing out to mine the moſt compendious method of ſpending three times as much. I told him, that I hoped that ſum would be very near ſufficient for the whole time; to which he anſwered coolly, "No, ſir, nor ſix times that "ſum, if you propoſe, as to be ſure you do, to ap-"pear here *bonnêtement*." This, I confeſs, ſtartled me a good deal; and I called out to my wife, "Do you "hear that, child?" She replied, unmoved, "Yes, "my dear, but now that we are here, there is no "help for it; it is but once, upon an extraordinary "occaſion, and one would not care to appear among "ſtrangers like ſcrubs." I made no anſwer to this ſolid reaſoning, but reſolved within myſelf to ſhorten our ſtay, and leſſen our follies, as much as I could. My banker, after having charged himſelf with the care of procuring me a *caroſſe de remiſe* and a *valet de place* for the next day, which in plain Engliſh is a hired coach and a footman, invited us to paſs all the next day at his houſe, where he aſſured us that we ſhould not meet with bad company. He was to carry me and my ſon before dinner to ſee the public buildings; and his lady was to call upon my wife and daughter to carry them to the genteeleſt ſhops, in order to fit them out to appear *bonnêtement*. The next morning I amuſed myſelf very well with ſeeing, while my wife and daughter amuſed themſelves ſtill better

better by preparing themſelves for being ſeen, till we met at dinner at our banker's; who, by way of ſample of the excellent company to which he was to introduce us, preſented to us an Iriſh abbé, and an Iriſh captain of Clare's; two attainted Scotch fugitives, and a young Scotch ſurgeon who ſtudied midwifry at the *Hôtel Dieu.* It is true, he lamented that ſir Harbottle Bumper and ſir Clotworthy Guzzle-down with their families, whom he had invited to meet us, happened unfortunately to have been engaged to go and drink brandy at Nueilly. Though this company ſounds but indifferently, and though we ſhould have been very ſorry to have kept it in London, I can aſſure you, ſir, that it was the beſt we kept the whole time we were at Paris.

I will omit many circumſtances which gave me uneaſineſs, though they would probably afford ſome entertainment to your readers, that I may haſten to the moſt material ones.

In about three days, the ſeveral mechanics, who were charged with the care of diſguiſing my wife and daughter, brought home their reſpective parts of this transformation, in order that they might appear *honnêtement.* More than the whole morning was employed in this operation, for we did not ſit down to dinner till near five o'clock. When my wife and daughter came at laſt into the eating-room, where I had waited for them at leaſt two hours, I was ſo ſtruck with their transformation, that I could neither conceal nor expreſs my aſtoniſhment. " Now, my dear," ſaid my wife, " we can appear a little like chriſtians." " And " ſtrollers too," replied I; " for ſuch have I ſeen,

" at

" at Southwark-fair, the respectable Sysigambis, and " the lovely Parisatis. This cannot surely be serious!" " Very serious, depend upon it, my dear," said my wife; " and pray, by the way, what may there be ridi- " culous in it? No such Sysigambis neither," continued she; " Betty is but sixteen, and you know I " had her at four-and-twenty." As I found that the name of Sysigambis, carrying an idea of age along with it, was offensive to my wife, I waved the parallel; and, addressing myself in common to my wife and daughter, I told them, " I perceived that there was a " painter now at Paris, who colored much higher " than Rigault, though he did not paint near so like; " for that I could hardly have guessed them to be the " pictures of themselves." To this they both answered at once, " That red was not paint; that no " colour in the world was *fard* but white, of which " they protested they had none." " But how do " you like my *pompon*, papa!" continued my daughter: " is it not a charming one? I think it is pret- " tier than mamma's." " It may, child, for any " thing that I know; because I do not know what " part of all this frippery thy *pompon* is." " It is " this, papa," replied the girl, putting up her hand to her head, and shewing me, in the middle of her hair, a complication of shreds and rags of velvets, feathers and ribbands, stuck with false stones of a thousand colors, and placed awry. " But what hast thou done " to thy hair, child!" said I; " is it blue? is that " painted too by the same eminent hand, that co- " lored thy cheeks?" " Indeed, papa," answered the girl, " as I told you before, there is no painting in

" the

"the caſe; but what gives my hair that bluiſh caſt is "the grey powder, which has always that effect upon "dark-colored hair, and ſets off the complexion "wonderfully." "Grey powder, child!" ſaid I, with ſome ſurprize: "grey hairs I knew were ve-"nerable; but till this moment I never knew that "they were genteel." "Extremely ſo, with ſome "complexions," ſaid my wife; "but it does not ſuit "with mine, and I never uſe it." "You are much "in the right, my dear," replied I, "not to play with "edge-tools. Leave it to the girl." This, which perhaps was too haſtily ſaid, and ſeemed to be a ſecond part of the Syſigambis, was not kindly taken; my wife was ſilent all dinner-time, and, I vainly hoped, aſhamed. My daughter, drunk with dreſs and ſix-teen, kept up the converſation to herſelf, till the long-wiſhed-for moment of the opera came, which ſepa-rated us, and left me time to reflect upon the ex-travagances, which I had already ſeen, and upon the ſtill greater, which I had but too much reaſon to dread.

From this period, to the time of our return to England, every day produced ſome new and ſhining folly, and ſome improper expence. Would to God that they had ended as they began, with our journey! but unfortunately we have imported them all. I no longer underſtand, or am underſtood, in my family. I hear of nothing but *le bon ton.* A French valet de chambre, who I am told is an excellent ſervant and fit for every thing, is brought over to curl my wife's and my daughter's hair, to *mount a deſſert,* as they call it, and occaſionally to *announce viſits.*

A very

A very ſlatternly, dirty, but at the ſame time a very genteel, French maid is appropriated to the uſe of my daughter. My meat too is as much diſguiſed in the dreſſing by a French cook, as my wife and my daughter are by their red, their pompons, their ſcraps of dirty gauze, flimſy ſattins, and black callicoes; not to mention their affected broken Engliſh, and mangled French, which jumbled together compoſe their preſent language. My French and Engliſh ſervants quarrel daily, and fight, for want of words to abuſe one another. My wife is become ridiculous, by being tranſlated into French; and the verſion of my daughter will, I dare ſay, hinder many a worthy Engliſh gentleman from attempting to read her. My expence, and conſequently my debt, increaſes; and I am made more unhappy by follies, than moſt other people are by crimes.

Should you think fit to publiſh this my caſe, together with ſome obſervations of your own upon it, I hope it may prove a uſeful Pharos, to deter private Engliſh families from the coaſts of France.

I am, SIR,

Your very humble ſervant,

R. D."

My correſpondent has ſaid enough to caution Engliſh gentlemen againſt carrying their wives and daughters to Paris; but I ſhall add a few words of my own, to diſſuade the ladies themſelves from any inclination to ſuch a vagary. In the firſt place, I aſſure them, that of all French ragouts there is none, to which an Engliſhman has ſo little appetite, as an Engliſh lady ſerved

ſerved up to him *à la Françoiſe*. Next I beg leave to inform them, that the French taſte in beauty is ſo different from ours, that a pretty Engliſh woman at Paris, inſtead of meeting with that admiration which her vanity hopes for, is conſidered only as a handſome corpſe; and if, to put a little life into her, ſome of her compaſſionate friends there ſhould perſuade her to lay on a great deal of *rouge*, in Engliſh called paint, ſhe muſt continue to wear it to extreme old age; unleſs ſhe prefers a ſpot of real yellow, the certain conſequence of paint, to an artificial one of red. And, laſtly, I propoſe it to their conſideration, whether the delicacy of an Engliſh lady's mind may not partake of the nature of ſome high-flavoured wines, which will not admit of being carried abroad, though, under right management, they are admirable at home.

XXIV.

THE WORLD.

THURSDAY, June 14, 1753. Nº 24.

I SHALL not at preſent enter into the great queſtion between the antients and the moderns; much leſs ſhall I preſume to decide upon a point of that importance, which has been the ſubject of debate among the learned from the days of Horace down to ours. To make my court to the learned, I will lament the gradual decay of human nature, for theſe laſt ſixteen centuries; but at the ſame time I will do justice to my contemporaries, and give them their due share of praise, where they have either struck out new inventions, or improved, and brought old ones to perfection. Some of them I shall now mention.

The most zealous and partial advocate for the antients will not, I believe, pretend to dispute the infinite superiority of the moderns in the art of healing. Hippocrates, Celsus, and Galen, had no specifics. They rather endeavoured to relieve, than pretended to cure. As for the astonishing cures of Æsculapius, I do not put them into the account; they are to be ascribed to his power, not to his skill: he was a god, and divinity was his NOSTRUM. But how prodigiously have my ingenious contemporaries extended the bounds of medicine! What nostrums, what specifics, have they not discovered! Collectively considered, they insure not only perfect health, but, by a necessary consequence, immortality; insomuch that I am astonished, when I still read in the weekly bills the great number of people, who chuse to die of such and such distempers, for every one of which there are infallible and specific cures, not only advertised, but attested, in all the news-papers.

When the lower sort of Irish, in the most uncivilized parts of Ireland, attend the funeral of a deceased friend or neighbour, before they give the last parting howl, they expostulate with the dead body, and reproach him with having died, notwithstanding that he had an excellent wife, a milch cow, seven fine children, and a competency of potatoes. Now though all these, particularly the excellent wife, are very good things in a state of perfect health, they cannot, as I apprehend, be looked upon as preventive either of ſickneſs or of death; but with how much more reaſon may we expoſtulate with, and cenſure, thoſe of our contemporaries, who, either from obſtinacy or incredulity, die in this great metropolis, or indeed in this kingdom, when they may prevent or cure, at a trifling expence, not only all diſtempers, but even old age and death itſelf! The RENOVATING ELIXIR *infallibly reſtores priſtine youth and vigor, be the patient ever ſo old and decayed*, and that without loſs of time or buſineſs; whereas the ſame operation among the antients was both tedious and painful, as it required a thorough boiling of the patient.

The moſt inflammatory and intrepid fevers fly at the firſt diſcharge of Dr. James's powder; and a drop or pill of the celebrated Mr. Ward corrects all the malignity of Pandora's box.

Ought not every man of great birth and eſtate, who for many years has been afflicted with the POSTEROMANIA, or rage of having poſterity, a diſtemper very common among perſons of that ſort, ought he not, I ſay, to be aſhamed of having no iſſue male to perpetuate his illuſtrious name and title, when, for ſo ſmall a ſum as three-and-ſix-pence, he and his lady might be ſupplied with a ſufficient quantity of the VIVIFYING DROPS, which infallibly cure imbecillity in men, and barrenneſs in women, though of never ſo long ſtanding?

Another very great diſcovery of the moderns, in the art of healing, is the infallible cure of the king's-evil, though never ſo inveterate, by only the touch of a lawful king, the right heir of Adam; for that is effentially neceffary. The antients were unacquainted with this ineftimable fecret, and even Solomon the fon of David, the wifeft of kings, knew nothing of the matter. But our Britifh Solomon, king James the firft, a fon of David alfo, was no ftranger to it, and practifed it with fuccefs. This fact is fufficiently proved by experience; but if it wanted any corroborating teftimony, we have that of the ingenious Mr. Carte, who, in his incomparable hiftory of England, afferts, and that in a marginal note too *, which is always more material than the text, that he knew SOMEBODY, who was radically cured of a moft obftinate king's-evil, by the touch of SOMEBODY. As our fagacious hiftorian does not even intimate that this SOMEBODY took any thing of the other SOMEBODY for the cure, it were to be wifhed that he had named this SOMEBODY, and his place of abode, "for the "benefit of the poor †," who are now reduced, and at fome expence, to have recourfe to Mr. Vickers the clergyman. Befides, I fairly confefs myfelf to be perfonally interefted in this enquiry, fince this SOMEBODY muft neceffarily be the right heir of Adam, and confequently I muft have the honor of being related to him.

Our laborious neighbours and kinfmen, the Germans, are not without their inventions and happy

* This unlucky note (which Mr. Carte was over-perfuaded by fome of his friends to infert) eventually deftroyed the credit of a hiftory of which great expectations had been formed.

† Thus the great dean of St. Patrick's gave the world a fingular fatire, in 1713, under the title of "Mr. Collins's difcourfe of free-"thinking; put into Englifh, by way of abftract, *for the ufe of the* "*poor*;" re-printed in the Supplement to his Works, 1776.

difcoveries

difcoveries in the art of medicine; for they laugh at a wound through the heart, if they can but apply their powder of fympathy—not to the wound itfelf, but to the fword or bullet that made it.

Having now, at leaft in my own opinion, fully proved the fuperiority of the moderns over the antients in the art of healing, I fhall proceed to fome other particulars, in which my contemporaries will as juftly claim, and I hope be allowed, the preference.

The ingenious Mr. Warburton, in his *Divine Legation of Mofes*, very juftly obferves, that hieroglyphics were the beginning of letters, but at the fame time he very candidly allows, that it was a very troublefome and uncertain method of communicating one's ideas; as it depended in a great meafure on the writer's fkill in drawing, an art little known in thofe days; and as a ftroke too much or too little, too high or too low, might be of the moft dangerous confequence in religion, bufinefs, or love. Cadmus removed this difficulty by his invention of unequivocal letters, but then he removed it too much; for thefe letters or marks, being the fame throughout, and fixed alphabetically, foon became generally known, and prevented that fecrecy, which in many cafes was to be wifhed for. This inconvenience fuggefted to the antients the invention of cryptography and fteganography, or a myfterious and unintelligible way of writing, by the help of which none but correfponding parties, who had the key, could decypher the matter. But human induftry foon refined upon this too; the art of decyphering was difcovered, and the fkill of the decypherer baffled all the labor of the cypherer.

The ſecrecy of all literary correſpondence became precarious; and neither buſineſs nor love could any longer be ſafely truſted to paper. Such for a conſiderable time was the unhappy ſtate of letters, till the BEAU MONDE, an inventive race of people, found out a new kind of cryptography, or ſteganography, unknown to the antients, and free from ſome of their inconveniencies. Lovers in general made uſe of it, controverſial writers commonly, and miniſters of ſtate ſometimes, in the moſt important diſpatches. It was writing in ſuch an unintelligible manner, and with ſuch obſcurity, that the correſponding parties themſelves neither underſtood, nor even gueſſed at, each other's meaning; which was a moſt effectual ſecurity againſt all the accidents, to which letters are liable by being either miſlaid or intercepted. But this method too, though long purſued, was alſo attended with ſome inconveniencies. It frequently produced miſtakes, by ſcattering falſe lights upon that friendly darkneſs, ſo propitious to buſineſs and love. But our inventive neighbours, the French, have very lately removed all theſe inconveniencies, by a happy diſcovery of a new kind of paper, as pleaſing to the eye, and as conducive to the diſpatch, the clearneſs, and at the ſame time the ſecrecy, of all literary correſpondence. My worthy friend Mr. Dodſley lately brought me a ſample of it, upon which, if I miſtake not, he will make very conſiderable improvements, as my countrymen often do upon the inventions of other nations. This ſheet of paper I conjectured to be the ground-work and principal material of a tender and paſſionate letter from a fine gentleman to a fine lady;

though

though in truth it might very well be the whole letter itself. At the top of the first page was delineated a lady, with very red cheeks and a very large hoop, in the fashionable attitude of knotting, and of making a very genteel French curtesy. This evidently appears to stand for MADAM, and saves the time and trouble of writing it. At the bottom of the third page, was painted a very fine well-dressed gentleman, with his hat under his left arm, and his right hand upon his heart, bowing most respectfully low; which single figure, by an admirable piece of brachygraphy; or short-hand, plainly conveys this deep sense, and stands instead of these many words, "I have the honor to be, with the tenderest and warmest sentiments, madam, your most inviolably attached, "faithful humble servant." The margin of the paper, which was about half an inch broad, was very properly decorated with all the emblems of triumphant beauty and tender suffering passion. Groups of lilies, roses, pearls, corals, suns, and stars, were intermixed with chains, bearded shafts, and bleeding hearts. Such a sheet of paper, I confess, seems to me to be a compleat letter; and I would advise all fine gentlemen, whose time I know is precious, to avail themselves of this admirable invention: it will save them a great deal of time, and perhaps some thought; and I cannot help thinking, that, were they even to take the trouble of filling up the paper with the tenderest sentiments of their hearts, or the most shining flights of their fancy, they would add no energy or delicacy to those types and symbols of the lady's conquest, and their own captivity and sufferings.

These blank letters, if I may call them so, when they convey so much, will mock the jealous curiosity of husbands and fathers, who will in vain hold them to the fire, to elicit the supposed juice of lemon, and upon whom they may afterwards pass for a piece of innocent pleasantry.

The dullest of my readers must, I am sure, by this time be aware, that the utility of this invention extends, *mutatis mutandis*, to whatever can be the subject of letters, and with much less trouble, and much more secrecy, propriety, and elegancy, than the old way of writing.

A painter of but moderate skill and fancy may, in a very short time, have reams of ready-painted paper by him, to supply the demands of the statesman, the divine, and the lover. And I think it my duty to inform the public, that my good friend Mr. Dodsley, who has long complained of the decay of trade, and who loves, with a prudent regard to his own interest, to encourage every useful invention, is at this time learning to paint with most unwearied diligence and application: and I make no doubt, but that, in a very little time, he will be able to furnish all sorts of persons with the very best ready-made goods of that kind. I warned him indeed against providing any for the two learned professions of the law and physic, which I apprehend would lie upon his hands: one of them being already in possession, to speak in their own style, of a more brachygraphical, cryptographical, and steganographical secret, in writing their WARRANTS; and the other not willingly admitting brevity in any shape. Otherwise, what in-

numerable

numerable ſkins of parchment and lines of writing might be ſaved in a marriage-ſettlement, for inſtance, if the firſt fourteen or fifteen ſons, the ſuppoſed future iſſue, LAWFULLY TO BE BEGOTTEN of that happy marriage, and upon whom the ſettlement is ſucceſſively made, were to be painted every one a ſize leſs than the other upon one ſkin of parchment, inſtead of being enumerated upon one hundred, according to propriety of birth and ſeniority of age; and moreover the elder, by an happy *pleonaſmus*, always to take before, and be preferred to, the younger! but this uſeful alteration is more to be wiſhed than expected, for reaſons which I do not at preſent think proper to mention.

I am ſenſible that the government may poſſibly object, that I am ſuggeſting to its enemies a method of carrying on their treaſonable correſpondences, with much more ſecrecy than formerly. But, as my intentions are honeſt, I ſhould be very ſorry to have my loyalty ſuſpected; and when I conſider the zeal, and at the ſame time the ingenuity, of the Jacobites, I am convinced that their letters in this new method will be ſo charged with groves of oaken boughs, white roſes and thiſtles interwoven, that their meaning will not be obſcure, and conſequently no danger will ariſe to the government from this new and excellent invention.

XXV.

XXV.

THE WORLD.

THURSDAY, June 21, 1753. N° 25.

I HAVE the pleaſure of informing my fair correſpondent, that her petition contained in the following letter is granted. I wiſh I could as eaſily reſtore to her what ſhe has loſt. But to a mind like hers, ſo elevated! ſo harmonized! time and the conſciouſneſs of ſo much purity of intention will bring relief. It muſt always afford her matter of the moſt pleaſing reflection, that her ſoul had no participation with her material part in that particular act, which ſhe appears to mention with ſo tender regret. But it is not my intention to anticipate her ſtory, by endeavouring to conſole her. Her letter, I hope, will caution all young ladies of equal virtue with herſelf againſt that exceſs of complaiſance, with which they are ſometimes too willing to entertain their lovers.

" To Mr. FITZ-ADAM.

SIR,

I HAVE not the leaſt ill-will to your friend Mr. Dodſley, whom I never ſaw in my life; but I addreſs myſelf to your equity and good-nature, for a ſmall ſhare only of your favour and recommendation in that new and valuable branch of trade, to which you have informed the public he is now applying himſelf, and

and which I hope you will not think it reaſonable that he ſhould monopolize. I mean that admirable ſhort and ſecret method of communicating one's ideas, by ingenious emblems and repreſentations of the pencil, inſtead of the vulgar and old method of letters by the pen. Give me leave, ſir, to ſtate my caſe and my qualifications to you: I am ſure you will decide with juſtice.

I am the daughter of a clergyman, who, having had a very good living, gave me a good education, and left me no fortune. I had naturally a turn to reading and drawing: my father encouraged and aſſiſted me in the one, allowed me a maſter to inſtruct me in the other, and I made an uncommon progreſs in them both. My heart was tender, and my ſentiments were delicate; perhaps too much ſo for my rank in life. This diſpoſition led me to ſtudy chiefly thoſe treaſures of divine honor, ſpotleſs virtue, and refined ſentiment, the voluminous romances of the laſt century: ſentiments, from which, I thank heaven, I have never deviated. From a ſympathizing ſoftneſs of ſoul, how often have I wept over thoſe affecting diſtreſſes! how have I ſhared the pangs of the chaſte and lovely Mariamne upon the death of the tender, the faithful Tiridates! and how has my indignation been excited, at the unfaithful and ungenerous hiſtorical miſrepreſentations of the gallant firſt Brutus, who was undoubtedly the tendereſt lover that ever lived! My drawings took the ſame elegant turn with my reading. I painted all the moſt moving and tender ſtories of charming Ovid's Metamorphoſes; not without ſometimes mingling my tears with my colors. I pre-

ſented

ſented ſome fans of my own painting to ſome ladies in the neighbourhood, who were pleaſed to commend both the execution and the deſigns. The latter I always took care ſhould be moving, and at the ſame time irreproachably pure; and I found means even to repreſent, with unblemiſhed delicacy, the unhappy paſſion of the unfortunate Paſiphaë. With this turn of mind, this ſoftneſs of ſoul, it will be ſuppoſed that I loved. I did ſo, ſir; tenderly and truly I loved. Why ſhould I diſown a paſſion, which, when clarified as mine was from the impure dregs of ſenſuality, is the nobleſt and moſt generous ſentiment of the human breaſt? O! that the falſe heart of the dear deceiver, whoſe perfidious vows betrayed mine, had been but as pure! The traitor was quartered, with his troop of dragoons, in the town where I lived. His perſon was a happy compound of the manly ſtrength of a hero, and all the ſofter graces of a lover; and I thought that I diſcovered in him, at firſt ſight, all the courage and all the tenderneſs of Oroondates. My figure, which was not bad, it ſeems, pleaſed him as much. He ſought and obtained my acquaintance. Soon by his eyes, and ſoon after by his words, he declared his paſſion to me. My bluſhes, my confuſion, and my ſilence, too plainly ſpoke mine. Good gods! how tender were his words! how languiſhingly ſoft his eyes! with what ardor did he preſs my hand; a trifling liberty, which one cannot decently refuſe, and for which refuſal there is no precedent! Sometimes he addreſſed me in the moving words of Varanes, ſometimes in the tender accents of Caſtalio, and ſometimes in the warmer language of Juba; for he was a very

good

good ſcholar. In ſhort, ſir, a month was not paſt before he preſſed for what he called a proof of my paſſion. I trembled at the very thought, and reproached him with the indelicacy of it. He perſiſted; and I, in compliance with cuſtom only, hinted previous marriage: he urged love, and I was not vulgar enough to refuſe to the man I tenderly loved the proof he required of my paſſion. I yielded, it is true; but it was to ſentiment, not to deſire. A few months gave me reaſon to ſuſpect that his paſſion was not quite ſo pure: and within the year, the perfidious wretch convinced me that it had been merely ſenſual: for, upon the removal of his troop to other quarters, he took a cold leave of me, and contented himſelf with ſaying, that in the courſe of quarters he hoped to have the pleaſure, ſome time or other, of ſeeing me again. You, Mr. Fitz-Adam, if you have any elegancy of ſoul, as I dare ſay you have, can better gueſs than I can expreſs the agonies I felt, and the tears I ſhed upon this occaſion: but all in vain; vain as the thouſand tender letters which I have written to him ſince, and to which I have received no anſwer. As all this paſſed within the courſe of ten months, I had but one child; which dear pledge of my firſt and only love I now maintain, at the expence of more than half of what I have to ſubſiſt upon myſelf.

Having now, as I hope, prepared your compaſſion, and proved my qualification, I proceed to the prayer of my petition; which is, that you will be pleaſed to recommend me to the public, with all that authority which you have ſo juſtly acquired, for a ſhare of this new and beneficial branch of trade; I mean no farther

 than

than the juſt bounds to which the female province may extend. Let Mr. Dodſley engroſs all the reſt, with my beſt wiſhes. Though I ſay it, I believe nobody has a clearer notion of the theory of delicate ſentiments than I have; and I have already a conſiderable ſtock in hand of theſe allegorical and emblematical paintings, applicable to almoſt every ſituation in which a woman of ſenſe, virtue, and delicacy, can find herſelf. I indulged my fancy in painting them, according to the various diſpoſitions of mind which my various fortunes produced. I think I may ſay without vanity, that I have made conſiderable improvements in the celebrated map of the realms of love in Clelia. I have adorned the banks of the gentle and cryſtalline Tender, with ſeveral new villages and groves; and added expreſſion to the pleaſing melancholic groves of ſighs and tender cares. I have whole quires, painted in my happier moments, of hearts united and crowned, fluttering Cupids, wanton zephyrs, conſtant and tender doves, myrtle bowers, banks of jeſſamine and tuberoſe, and ſhady groves. Theſe will require very little filling up, if any, from ladies who are in the tranſported ſituation of growing loves. For the forſaken and complaining fair, with whom, alas! I too fatally ſympathize, I have tender willows drooping over murmuring brooks, and gloomy walks of mournful cypreſs and ſolemn yew. In ſhort, ſir, I either have by me, or will forthwith provide, whatever can convey the moſt perfect ideas of elegant friendſhip, or pure, refined, and ſentimental paſſion. But I think it neceſſary to give notice, that if any ladies would expreſs any indelicate ideas of love, or require any types or emblems of ſenſual joy, they muſt not apply to,

SIR,

Your moſt obedient humble ſervant,

PARTHENISSA."

XXVI.

THE WORLD.

SATURDAY, July 19, 1753. N° 29.

SIR,

I TROUBLED you ſome time ago with an account of my diſtreſs, ariſing from the female part of my family. I told you that, by an unfortunate trip to Paris, my wife and daughter had run ſtark French, and I wiſh I could tell you now that they were perfectly recovered: but all I can ſay is, that the violence of the ſymptoms ſeems to abate, in proportion as the cloaths that inflamed them wear out.

My preſent misfortune flows from a direct contrary cauſe, and affects me much more ſenſibly. The little whims, affectations, and delicacies of ladies, may be both ridiculous and diſagreeable, eſpecially to thoſe who are obliged to be at once the witneſſes and the martyrs of them; but they are not evils to be compared with the obſtinate wrong-headedneſs, the idle and illiberal turn, of an only ſon, which is unfortunately my caſe.

I ac-

I acquainted you, that in the education of my ſon I had conformed to the common cuſtom of this country, perhaps I conformed to it too much and too ſoon; and that I carried him to Paris, from whence, after ſix months ſtay, he was to go upon his travels, and take the uſual tour of Italy and Germany. I thought it very neceſſary for a young man, though not for a young lady, to be well acquainted with the languages, the manners, the characters, and the conſtitutions, of other countries; the want of which I experienced and lamented in myſelf. In order to enable him to keep good company, I allowed him more than I could conveniently afford; and I truſted him to the care of a Swiſs governor, a gentleman of ſome learning, good-ſenſe, good-nature, and good-manners. But how cruelly I am diſappointed in all theſe hopes, what follows will inform you.

During his ſtay at Paris, he only frequented the worſt Engliſh company there, with whom he was unhappily engaged in two or three ſcrapes, which the credit and the good-nature of the Engliſh ambaſſador helped him out of. He hired a low Iriſh wench, whom he drove about in a hired chaiſe, to the great honor of himſelf, his family, and his country. He did not learn one word of French, and never ſpoke to Frenchman or Frenchwoman, excepting ſome vulgar and injurious epithets, which he beſtowed upon them in very plain Engliſh. His governor very honeſtly informed me of this conduct, which he tried in vain to reform, and adviſed their removal to Italy, which accordingly I immediately ordered. His

behaviour

behaviour there wil appear in the trueſt light to you, by his own and his governor's laſt letters to me, of which I here give you faithful copies.

"Rome, May the 3d, 1753.

"SIR,

"In the ſix weeks that I paſſed at Florence, and "the week I ſtayed at Genoa, I never had time to "write to you, being wholly taken up with ſeeing "things, of which the moſt remarkable is the ſteeple "of Piſa: it is the oddeſt thing I ever ſaw in my "life, it ſtands all awry; I wonder it does not tum- "ble down. I met with a great many of my coun- "trywomen, and we live together very ſociably. I "have been here now a month, and will give you "an account of my way of life. Here are a great "many agreeable Engliſh gentlemen; we are about "nine or ten as ſmart bucks as any in England. "We conſtantly breakfaſt together, and then either "go and ſee ſights, or drive about the outlets of "Rome in chaiſes; but the horſes are very bad, and "the chaiſes do not follow well. We meet before "dinner at the Engliſh coffee-houſe; where there is "a very good billiard-table, and very good com- "pany. From thence we go and dine together by "turns at each other's lodgings. Then, after a "chearful glaſs of claret, for we have made a ſhift "to get ſome here, we go to the coffee houſe again; "from thence to ſupper; and ſo to bed. I do not "believe that theſe Romans are a bit like the old "Romans; they are a parcel of thin-gutted, ſnivel- "ing, cringing dogs, and I verily believe that our "set could thresh forty of them. We never go "among them; it would not be worth while: be-"sides, we none of us speak Italian, and none of "those signors speak English; which shews what "sort of fellows they are. We saw the pope go by "the other day in a procession, but we resolved to "assert the honor of old England; so we neither "bowed, nor pulled off our hats, to the old rogue. "Provisions and liquor are but bad here; and, to "say the truth, I have not had one thorough good "meal's meat since I left England. No longer ago "than last Sunday, we wanted to have a good plumb-"pudding; but we found the materials difficult to "provide, and were obliged to get an English foot-"man to make it. Pray, sir, let me come home; "for I cannot find that one is a jot the better for "seeing all these outlandish places and people. But "if you will not let me come back, for God's sake, "sir, take away the impertinent *mounseer* you sent "with me. He is a considerable expence to you, "and of no manner of service to me. All the Eng-"lish here laugh at him, he is such a prig. He "thinks himself a fine gentleman, and is always "plaguing me to go into foreign companies, to learn "foreign languages, and to get foreign manners; as "if I were not to live and die in old England, and "as if good English acquaintance would not be "much more useful to me than outlandish ones. "Dear sir, grant me this request, and you shall ever "find me

"Your most dutiful son,

"G. D."

The

The following is a very honeſt and ſenſible letter, which I received at the ſame time from my ſon's governor.

"Rome, May the 3d, 1753.

"SIR,

"I think myſelf obliged in conſcience to inform "you, that the money you are pleaſed to allow me, "for my attendance upon your ſon, is abſolutely "thrown away; ſince I find, by melancholy expe-"rience, that I can be of no manner of uſe to him. "I have tried all poſſible methods to prevail with "him to anſwer, in ſome degree at leaſt, your good "intentions in ſending him abroad; but all in vain: "and, in return for my endeavours, I am either "laughed at or inſulted. Sometimes I am called a "beggarly French dog, and bid to go back to my "own country and eat my frogs; and ſometimes I "am *mounſeer ragout*, and told that I think myſelf a "very fine gentleman. I daily repreſent to him, "that, by ſending him abroad, you meant that he "ſhould learn the languages, the manners, and cha-"racters, of different countries; and that he ſhould "add to the claſſical education which you had given "him at home, a knowledge of the world, and the "genteel eaſy manners of a man of faſhion, which "can only be acquired by frequenting the beſt com-"panies abroad. To which he only anſwers me "with a ſneer of contempt, and ſays, "ſo be like-"ye, ha!" I would have connived at the common "vices of youth, if they had been attended with the "least degree of decency or refinement; but I must "not conceal from you, that your son's are of the "lowest and most degrading kind, and avowed in "the most public and indecent manner. I have never "been able to persuade him to deliver the letters of "recommendation which you procured him; he says, "he does not desire to keep such company. I ad-"vised him to take an Italian master; which he "flatly refused, saying that he should have time "enough to learn Italian, when he went back to "England. But he has taken, of himself, a music "master to teach him to play upon the German "flute, upon which he throws away two or three "hours every day. We spend a great deal of money, "without doing you or ourselves any honor by it; "though your son, like the generality of his coun-"trymen, values himself upon the expence, and "looks upon all foreigners, who are not able to make "so considerable a one, as a parcel of beggars and "scoundrels, speaks of them, and, if he spoke to "them, would treat them, as such.

"If I might presume to advise you, sir, it should "be to order us home forthwith. I can assure you "that your son's morals and manners will be in "much less danger under your own inspection at "home, than they can be under mine abroad; and "I defy him to keep worse English company "in England than he now keeps here. But, what-"ever you may think fit to determine concern-"ing him, I must humbly insist upon my own "dismission, and upon leave to assure you in person "of "of the reſpect with which I have the honor "to be,

"SIR,

"Your, &c."

I have complied with my ſon's requeſt, in conſequence of his governor's advice, and have ordered him to come home immediately. But what ſhall I do with him here, where he is but too likely to be encouraged and countenanced in theſe illiberal and ungentleman-like manners? My caſe is ſurely moſt ſingularly unfortunate; to be plagued on one ſide by the polite and elegant foreign follies of my wife and daughter, and on the other by the unconforming obſtinacy, the low vulgar exceſſes, and the porter-like manners, of my ſon.

Perhaps my fortune may ſuggeſt to you ſome thoughts upon the methods of education in general, which, conveyed to the public through your paper, may prove of public uſe. It is in that view ſingly that you have had this ſecond trouble from,

SIR,

Your moſt humble ſervant and conſtant reader,

R. D.

I allow the caſe of my worthy correſpondent to be compaſſionate, but I cannot poſſibly allow it to be ſingular. The public places daily prove the contrary too plainly. I confeſs I oftener pity than blame the errors of youth, when I reflect upon the fundamental errors generally committed by their parents in their education. Many totally neglect, and many miſtake it. The antients began the education of their children, by forming their hearts and their manners. They taught them the duty of men and of citizens; we teach them the languages of the antients, and leave their morals and manners to ſhift for themſelves.

As for the modern ſpecies of human bucks, I impute their brutality to the negligence or the fondneſs of their parents. It is obſerved in parks, among their betters, the real bucks, that the moſt troubleſome and miſchievous are thoſe who were bred up tame, fondled, and fed out of the hand, when fawns. They abuſe, when grown up, the indulgence they met with in their youth; and their familiarity grows troubleſome and dangerous with their horns.

XXVII.

THE WORLD.

SATURDAY, Dec. 7, 1753. N° 49.

THOUGH I am an old fellow, I am neither four nor ſilly enough yet, to be a ſnarling *laudator temporis acti*, and to hate or deſpiſe the preſent age becauſe it is the preſent. I cannot, like many of my cotemporaries, rail at the wonderful degeneracy and corruption of theſe times, nor, by ſneering compliments to the ingenious, the ſagacious moderns, intimate that they have not common ſenſe. I really do not think that the preſent age is marked out by

any

any new and diſtinguiſhed vices and follies, unknown to former ages. On the contrary, I am apt to ſuſpect that human nature was always very like what it is at this day; and that men, from the time of my great progenitors down to this moment, have always had in them the ſame ſeeds of virtue and vice, wiſdom and folly, of which only the modes have varied, from climate, education, and a thouſand other conſpiring cauſes.

Perhaps this uncommon good-humour and indulgence of mine to my cotemporaries may be owing to the natural benignity of my conſtitution, in which I can diſcover no particles of envy or ill-nature, even to my rivals, both in fame and profit, the weekly writers; or perhaps to the ſuperiority of my parts, which every body muſt acknowledge, and which places me infinitely above the mean ſentiments of envy and jealouſy. But, whatever may be the true cauſe, which probably neither my readers nor I ſhall ever diſcover with preciſion, this at leaſt is certain, that the preſent age has not only the honor and pleaſure of being extremely well with me, but, if I dare ſay ſo, better than any that I have yet either heard or read of. Both vices and virtues are ſmoothed and ſoftened by manners, and though they exiſt as they ever have done, yet the former are become leſs barbarous, and the latter leſs rough; inſomuch that I am as glad as Mr. Voltaire can be, that I have the good fortune to live in this age, independently of that intereſted conſideration, that it is rather better to be ſtill alive, than only to have lived.

This my benevolence to my countrymen and cotemporaries ought to be esteemed still the more meritorious in me, when I shall make it appear that no man's merit has been less attended to or rewarded than mine: and nothing produces ill-humor, rancour, and malevolence so much, as neglected and unrewarded merit.

The utility of my weekly labors is evident, and their effects, wherever they are read, prodigious. They are equally calculated, I may say it without vanity, to form the heart, improve the understanding, and please the fancy. Notwithstanding all which, the ungrateful public does not take above three thousand of them a week, though, according to Mr. Maitland's calculation of the number of inhabitants in this great metropolis, they ought to take two hundred thousand of them, supposing only five persons, and one paper to each family; and allowing seven millions of souls in the rest of the kingdom, I may modestly say, that one million more of them ought to be taken and circulated in the country. The profit arising from the sale of twelve hundred thousand papers would be some encouragement to me to continue these my labors, for the benefit of mankind.

I have not yet had the least intimation from the ministers, that they have any thoughts of calling me to their assistance, and giving me some considerable employment of honor and profit; and, having had no such intimations, I am justly apprehensive that they have no such intentions: such intimations being always long previous to the performance, often to the intentions.

Nor

Nor have I been invited, as I confeſs I expected to be, by any conſiderable borough or county, to repreſent them in the next parliament, and to defend their liberties, and the Chriſtian religion, againſt the miniſters and the Jews. But I think I can account for this ſeeming ſlight, without mortification to my vanity and ſelf-love; my name being a pentateuch name, which, in theſe ſuſpicious and doubtful times, ſavours too ſtrongly of Judaiſm; though, upon the faith of a Chriſtian, I have not the leaſt tendency to it; and I muſt do Mrs. Fitz-Adam, who I own has ſome influence over me, the juſtice to ſay, that ſhe has the utmoſt horror for thoſe ſanguinary rites and ceremonies.

Notwithſtanding all this ill uſage, for every man may be ſaid to be ill uſed who is not rewarded according to his own eſtimation of his own merit, which I feel and lament, I cannot however call the preſent age names, and brand it with degeneracy; nature, as I have already obſerved, being always the ſame, modes only varying. With modes, the ſignification of words alſo varies, and, in the courſe of thoſe variations, convey ideas very different from thoſe which they were originally intended to expreſs. I could give numberleſs inſtances of this kind, but at preſent I ſhall content myſelf with this ſingle one.

The word HONOR, in its proper ſignification, doubtleſs implies the united ſentiments of virtue, truth, and juſtice, carried by a generous mind beyond thoſe mean moral obligations, which the laws require, or can puniſh the violation of. A TRUE MAN OF HONOR will not content himſelf with the literal

teral discharge of the duties of a man and a citizen; he raises and dignifies them into magnanimity. He gives where he may with justice refuse, he forgives where he may with justice resent, and his whole conduct is directed by the noble sentiments of his own unvitiated heart; surer and more scrupulous guides than the laws of the land, which, being calculated for the generality of mankind, must necessarily be more a restraint upon vices in general, than an invitation and reward of particular virtues. But these extensive and compound notions of HONOR have been long contracted, and reduced to the single one of personal courage. Among the Romans, HONOR meant no more than contempt of dangers and death in the service, whether just or unjust, of their country. Their successors and conquerors, the Goths and Vandals, who did not deal much in complex ideas, simplified those of HONOR, and reduced them to this plain and single one, of fighting for fighting's sake, upon any, or all, no matter what, occasions.

Our present mode of HONOR is something more compounded, as will appear by the true character which I shall now give of a fashionable MAN OF HONOR.

A Gentleman *, which is now the genteel synonymous term for a MAN OF HONOR, must, like his Gothic ancestors, be ready for, and rather desirous of, single combat. And if by a proper degree of wrong-

* A gentleman is every man, who with a tolerable suit of cloaths, a sword by his side, and a watch and snuff-box in his pockets, asserts himself to be a gentleman, swears with energy that he will be treated as such, and that he will cut the throat of any man who presumes to say the contrary.

headedneſs he provokes it, he is only ſo much the more jealous of his HONOR, and more of a GENTLEMAN.

He may lie with impunity, if he is neither detected nor accuſed of it: for it is not the lie he tells, but the lie he is told of, that diſhonors him. In that caſe he demonſtrates his veracity by his ſword or his piſtol, and either kills or is killed with the greateſt HONOR.

He may abuſe and ſtarve his own wife, daughters, or ſiſters, and he may ſeduce thoſe of other men, particularly his friends, with inviolate HONOR, becauſe, as ſir John Brute very juſtly obſerves, *he wears a ſword.*

By the laws of HONOR, he is not obliged to pay his ſervants or his tradeſmen; for, as they are a pack of ſcoundrels, they cannot without inſolence demand their due of a gentleman: but he muſt punctually pay his gaming-debts to the ſharpers who have cheated him; for thoſe debts are really debts of HONOR.

He lies under one diſagreeable reſtraint; for he muſt not cheat at play, unleſs in a horſe-match: but then he may with great HONOR defraud in an office, or betray a truſt.

In public affairs, he may, not only with HONOR, but even with ſome degree of LUSTRE, be in the ſame ſeſſion a turbulent patriot, oppoſing the beſt meaſures, and a ſervile courtier, promoting the worſt; provided a very lucrative conſideration be known to be the motive of his converſion: for in that caſe the point of HONOR turns ſingly upon the *quantum.*

From

From these premises, which the more they are considered the truer they will be found, it appears that there are but two things which a man of the nicest HONOR may not do, which are, declining single combat, and cheating at play. Strange! that VIRTUE should be so difficult; and HONOR, its superior, so easy to attain to!

The uninformed herd of mankind are governed by words and names, which they implicitly receive without either knowing or asking their meaning. Even the philosophical and religious controversies, for the last three or four hundred years, have turned much more upon words and names, unascertained and misunderstood, than upon things fairly stated. The polite world, to save time and trouble, receive, adapt, and use words, in the signification of the day; not having leisure nor inclination to examine and analyse them: and thus, often misled by sounds, and not always secured by sense, they are hurried into fatal errors, which they do not give their understandings fair play enough to prevent.

In explaining words, therefore, and bringing them back to their true signification, one may sometimes happen to expose and explode those errors, which the abuse of them both occasions and protects. May that be the good fortune of this day's paper! How many unthinking and unhappy men really take themselves to be MEN of HONOR, upon these mistaken ideas of that word! And how fatal to others, especially to the young and unexperienced, is their example and success in the world! I could heartily wish that some good dramatic poet would exhibit at full length

length and in lively colors, upon the ſtage, this modiſh character of a MAN of HONOR, of which I have but ſlightly and haſtily chalked the outlines. Upon ſuch a ſubject, I am apt to think that a good poet might be more uſeful than a good preacher, as perhaps his audiences would be more numerous, and his matter more attended to. Beſides,

"Segnius irritant animos, demiſſa per aurem
"Quam quæ ſunt oculis ſubjecta fidelibus, et quæ
"Ipſe ſibi tradit ſpectator *."

P. S. To prevent miſtakes, I muſt obſerve that there is a great difference between a MAN of HONOR, and a PERSON of HONOR. By PERSONS of HONOR were meant, in the latter end of the laſt century, bad authors and poets of noble birth, who were but juſt not fools enough to prefix their names in great letters to the prologues, epilogues, and ſometimes even the plays, with which they entertained the public. But now that our nobility are too generous to interfere in the trade of us poor profeſſed authors, or to eclipſe our performances by the diſtinguiſhed and ſuperior excellency and luſtre of theirs; the meaning at preſent of a PERSON of HONOR is reduced to the SIMPLE idea of a PERSON of ILLUSTRIOUS BIRTH.

* Horat. Art. Poet.

—— What we hear
More ſlowly moves the heart than what we ſee.
DUNCOMBE's *tranſlation.*

XXVIII.

XXVIII.

THE WORLD.

THURSDAY, Sept. 19, 1754. N° 90.

AN old friend and fellow-ſtudent of mine at the univerſity, called upon me the other morning, and found me reading Plato's Sympoſion. I laid down my book to receive him, which, after the firſt uſual compliments, he took up, ſaying, "You "will give me leave to ſee what was the object of "your ſtudies." "Nothing leſs than the divine "Plato," ſaid I, "that amiable philoſopher—" "with "whom," interrupted my friend, "Cicero declares "that he would rather be in the wrong, than in the "right with any other." "I cannot," replied I, "carry my veneration for him to that degree of en-"thuſiaſm; but yet, wherever I underſtand him, for "I confeſs I do not every where, I prefer him to "all the antient philoſophers. His Sympoſion more "particularly engages and entertains me, as I ſee "there the manners and characters of the moſt emi-"nent men, of the politeſt times, of the politeſt "city of Greece. And, with all due reſpect to the "moderns, I much queſtion whether an account of "a modern Sympoſion, though written by the ableſt "hand, could be read with ſo much pleaſure and "improvement." "I do not know that," replied my friend; "for, though I revere the antients as "much as you poſſibly can, and look upon the mo-"derns as pigmies, when compared to thoſe giants, "yet

" yet if we come up to or near them in any thing, " it is in the elegance and delicacy of our convivial " intercourſe."

I was the more ſurprized at this doubt of my friend's, becauſe I knew that he implicitly ſubſcribed to, and ſuperſtitiouſly maintained, all the articles of the claſſical faith. I therefore aſked him, whether he was ſerious? He anſwered me " that he was: " that, in his mind, Plato ſpun out that ſilly affair " of love too fine and too long; and that, if I would " but let him introduce me to the club of which he " was an unworthy member, he believed I ſhould at " leaſt entertain the ſame doubt, or perhaps even " decide in favour of the moderns." I thanked my friend for his kindneſs, but added that, in whatever ſociety he was an unworthy member, I ſhould be ſtill a more unworthy gueſt; that, moreover, my retired and domeſtic turn of life was as inconſiſtent with the engagements of a club, as my natural taciturnity among ſtrangers would be miſplaced in the midſt of all that feſtal mirth and gaiety. " You miſtake me," anſwered my friend; " every member of our club " has the privilege of bringing one friend along with " him, who is by no means thereby to become a " member of it; and as for your taciturnity, we have " ſome ſilent members, who, by the way, are none " of our worſt. Silent people never ſpoil company; " but, on the contrary, by being good hearers, en- " courage good ſpeakers." " But I have another " difficulty," anſwered I, " and that I doubt a very " ſolid one, which is, that I drink nothing but wa- " ter." " So much the worſe for you," replied my friend,

friend, who, by the bye, loves his bottle moſt academically; "you will pay for the claret you do not "drink. We uſe no compulſion; every one drinks "as little as he pleaſes—" "Which I preſume," interrupted I, "is as much as he can." "That is "juſt as it happens," ſaid he: "ſometimes, it is "true, we make pretty good ſittings, but for my "own part, I chuſe to go home always before ele-"ven: for, take my word for it, it is the ſitting-up "late, and not the drink, that deſtroys the conſti-"tution." As I found that my friend would have taken a refuſal ill, I told him that for this once I would certainly attend him to the club, but deſired him to give me previouſly the outlines of the characters of the ſitting members, that I might know how to behave myſelf properly. "Your precau-"tion," ſaid he, "is a prudent one; and I will "make you ſo well acquainted with them before-"hand, that you ſhall not ſeem a ſtranger when "among them. You muſt know then, that our "club conſiſts of at leaſt forty members when com-"pleat. Of theſe, many are now in the country; "and, beſides, we have ſome vacancies, which can-"not be filled up till next winter. Palſies and apo-"plexies have of late, I do not know why, been "pretty rife among us, and carried off a good many. "It is not above a week ago, that poor Tom Toaſt-"well fell on a ſudden under the table, as we "thought only a little in drink, but he was carried "home, and never ſpoke more. Thoſe whom you "will probably meet with to-day are, firſt of all, "lord Feeble, a nobleman of admirable ſenſe, a true

" fine gentleman, and, for a man of quality, a pretty " claſſic. He has lived rather faſt formerly, and " impaired his conſtitution by ſitting up late, and " drinking your thin ſharp wines. He is ſtill what " you call nervous, which makes him a little low-" ſpirited and reſerved at firſt; but he grows very " affable and chearful, as ſoon as he has warmed his " ſtomach with about a bottle of good claret.

" Sir Tunbelly Guzzle is a very worthy north-" country baronet of a good eſtate, and one who was " beforehand in the world, till, being twice choſen " knight of the ſhire, and having in conſequence got " a pretty employment at court, he ran out conſider-" ably. He has left off houſe-keeping, and is now " upon a retrieving ſcheme. He is the heartieſt, " honeſteſt fellow living; and though he is a man " of very few words, I can aſſure you he does not " want ſenſe. He had an univerſity education, and " has a good notion of the claſſics. The poor man " is confined half the year at leaſt with the gout, " and has beſides an inveterate ſcurvy, which I can-" not account for: no man can live more regularly, " he eats nothing but plain meat, and very little of " that; he drinks no thin wines, and never ſits up " late, for he has his full doſe by eleven.

" Colonel Culverin is a brave old experienced of-" ficer, though but a lieutenant-colonel of foot. Be-" tween you and me, he has had great injuſtice done " him, and is now commanded by many, who were " not born when he came firſt into the army. He " has ſerved in Ireland, Minorca, and Gibraltar, and " would have been in all the late battles in Flanders, "had the regiment been ordered there. It is a "pleasure to hear him talk of war. He is the best-"natured man alive, but a little too jealous of his "honor, and too apt to be in a passion; but that is "soon over, and then he is sorry for it. I fear he "is dropsical, which I impute to his drinking your "champains and burgundies. He got that ill habit "abroad.

"Sir George Plyant is well born, has a genteel "fortune, keeps the very best company, and is to "be sure one of the best-bred men alive: he is so "good-natured, that he seems to have no will of "his own. He will drink as little or as much as "you please, and no matter of what. He has been "a mighty man with the ladies formerly, and loves "the crack of the whip still. He is our news-"monger; for, being a gentleman of the privy-"chamber, he goes to court every day, and conse-"quently knows pretty well what is going forward "there. Poor gentleman! I fear we shall not keep "him long; for he seems far gone in a consump-"tion, though the doctors say it is only a nervous "atrophy.

"Will Sitfast is the best-natured fellow living, "and an excellent companion, though he seldom "speaks; but he is no flincher, and sits every man's "hand out at the club. He is a very good scholar, "and can write very pretty Latin verses. I doubt "he is in a declining way; for a paralitical stroke "has lately twitched up one side of his mouth so, "that he is now obliged to take his wine diagonally.

"However,

"However, he keeps up his ſpirits bravely, and "never ſhams his glaſs.

"Doctor Carbuncle is an honeſt, jolly, merry par- "ſon, well affected to the government, and much "of a gentleman. He is the life of our club, in- "ſtead of being the leaſt reſtraint upon it. He is an "admirable ſcholar, and I really believe has all "Horace by heart; I know he has him always in his "pocket. His red face, inflamed noſe, and ſwelled "legs, make him generally thought a hard drinker "by thoſe who do not know him; but I muſt do "him the juſtice to ſay, that I never ſaw him diſ- "guiſed with liquor in my life. It is true, he is a "very large man, and can hold a great deal, which "makes the colonel call him pleaſantly enough *a* "*veſſel of election.*

"The laſt and leaſt," concluded my friend, "is "your humble ſervant ſuch as I am; and, if you "pleaſe, we will go and walk in the park till din- "ner-time." I agreed, and we ſet out together. But here the reader will perhaps expect that I ſhould let him walk on a little, while I give his character. We were of the ſame year of St. John's college in Cambridge: he was a younger brother of a good family, was bred to the church, and had juſt got a fellowſhip in the college, when, his elder brother dying, he ſucceeded to an eaſy fortune, and reſolved to make himſelf eaſy with it, that is, to do nothing. As he had reſided long in college, he had contracted all the habits and prejudices, the lazineſs, the ſoaking, the pride, and the pedantry of the cloyſter, which after a certain time are never to be rubbed off.

He confidered the critical knowledge of the Greek and Latin words as the utmoft effort of the human underftanding, and a glafs of good wine in good company as the higheft pitch of human felicity. Accordingly he paffes his mornings in reading the claffics, moft of which he has long had by heart, and his evenings in drinking his glafs of good wine, which, by frequent filling, amounts at leaft to two, and often to three bottles a day. I muft not omit mentioning that my friend is tormented with the ftone, which misfortune he imputes to his having once drunk water for a month, by the prefcription of the late doctor Cheyne, and by no means to at leaft two quarts of claret a day, for thefe laft thirty years. To return to my friend: "I am very much "miftaken," faid he, as we were walking in the park, "if you do not thank me for procuring you "this day's entertainment; for a fet of worthier gen-"tlemen, to be fure, never lived." "I make no "doubt of it," faid I, "and am therefore the more "concerned, when I reflect, that this club of worthy "gentlemen might, by your own account, be not im-"properly called an hofpital of incurables, as there "is not one among them, who does not labor under "fome chronical and mortal diftemper." "I fee what "you would be at," anfwered my friend; "you "would infinuate that it is all owing to wine: but "let me affure you, Mr. Fitz-Adam, that wine, ef-"pecially claret, if neat and good, can hurt no man." I did not reply to this aphorifm of my friend's, which I knew would draw on too long a difcuffion, efpecially as we were juft going into the club-room, where I took it for granted that it was one of the great conſtitutional principles. The account of this modern Sympoſion ſhall be the ſubject of my next paper.

XXIX.

THE WORLD.

SATURDAY, Sept. 26, 1754. N° 91.

MY friend preſented me to the company, in what he thought the moſt obliging manner; but which, I confeſs, put me a little out of countenance. "Give me leave, gentlemen," ſaid he, "to preſent "to you my old friend Mr. Fitz-Adam, the inge- "nious author of the World." The word *author* inſtantly excited the attention of the whole company, and drew all their eyes upon me: for people, who are not apt to write themſelves, have a ſtrange curioſity to ſee a live author. The gentlemen received me in common with thoſe geſtures that intimate welcome; and I on my part reſpectfully muttered ſome of thoſe nothings, which ſtand inſtead of the ſomething one ſhould ſay, and perhaps do full as well.

The weather being hot, the gentlemen were refreſhing themſelves before dinner, with what they called *a cool tankard*; in which they ſucceſſively drank to me. When it came to my turn, I thought I could not decently decline drinking the gentlemen's healths, which I did aggregately: but how was I ſurprized, when upon the first taste I discovered that this cooling and refreshing draught was composed of the strongest mountain wine, lowered indeed with a very little lemon and water, but then heightened again by a quantity of those comfortable aromatics, nutmeg and ginger! Dinner, which had been called for more than once with some impatience, was at last brought up, upon the colonel's threatening perdition to the master and all the waiters of the house, if it was delayed two minutes longer. We sat down without ceremony; and we were no sooner sat down, than every body, except myself, drank every body's health, which made a tumultuous kind of noise. I observed with surprize, that the common quantity of wine was put into glasses of an immense size and weight; but my surprize ceased when I saw the tremulous hands that took them, and for which I supposed they were intended as ballast. But even this precaution did not protect the nose of doctor Carbuncle from a severe shock, in his attempt to hit his mouth. The colonel, who observed this accident, cried out pleasantly, "Why, "doctor, I find you are but a bad engineer. While "you aim at your mouth, you will never hit it, take "my word for it. A floating battery, to hit the "mark, must be pointed something above, or below "it. If you would hit your mouth, direct your four-"pounder at your forehead, or your chin." The doctor good-humoredly thanked the colonel for the hint, and promised him to communicate it to his friends at Oxford, where he owned, that he had seen many a good glass of port spilt for want of it. Sir Tunbelly almost smiled, sir George laughed, and

the

the whole company, ſome how or other, applauded this elegant piece of raillery. But alas, things ſoon took a leſs pleaſant turn; for an enormous buttock of boiled ſalt beef, which had ſucceeded the ſoupe, proved not to be ſufficiently corned for ſir Tunbelly, who had beſpoke it, and at the ſame time lord Feeble took a diſlike to the claret, which he affirmed not to be the ſame which they had drank the day before; it had not "ſilkineſs, went rough "off the tongue," and his lordſhip ſhrewdly ſuſpected that it was mixed with "Benecarlo, or ſome of thoſe "black wines." This was a common cauſe, and excited univerſal attention. The whole company taſted it ſeriouſly, and every one found a different fault with it. The maſter of the houſe was immediately ſent for up, examined, and treated as a criminal. Sir Tunbelly reproached him with the freſhneſs of the beef, while at the ſame time all the others fell upon him for the badneſs of his wine, telling him that it was not fit uſage for ſuch good cuſtomers as they were, and, in fine, threatening him with a migration of the club to ſome other houſe. The criminal laid the blame of the beef's not being corned enough upon his cook, whom he promiſed to turn away, and atteſted heaven and earth, that the wine was the very ſame which they had all approved of the day before, and, as he had a ſoul to be ſaved, was true Chateau Margoux. "Chateau devil!" ſaid the colonel with warmth, "it is your d—d rough chaos* "wine." Will Sitfaſt, who thought himſelf obliged to articulate upon this occaſion, ſaid, he was not

* Cahors.

ſure it was a mixed wine, but that indeed it drank *down*. "If that is all," interrupted the doctor, "let us even drink it *up* then; or, if that will not do, "ſince we cannot have the true *Falernum*, let us take "up for once with the *vile Sabinum*. What ſay you, "gentlemen, to good honeſt port, which I am con-"vinced is a much wholeſomer ſtomach wine?" My friend, who in his heart loves port better than any other wine in the world, willingly ſeconded the doctor's motion, and ſpoke very favourably of your *Portingal* wines in general, if neat. Upon this, ſome was immediately brought up, which I obſerved my friend and the doctor ſtuck to the whole evening. I could not help aſking the doctor, if he really preferred port to lighter wines? To which he anſwered, "You know, Mr. Fitz-Adam, that uſe is ſecond na-"ture, and port is in a manner mother's milk to me; "for it is what my *Alma Mater* ſuckles all her nu-"merous progeny with." I ſilently aſſented to the doctor's account, which I was convinced was a true one, and then attended to the judicious animadverſions of the other gentlemen upon the claret, which were ſtill continued, though at the ſame time they continued to drink it. I hinted my ſurprize at this to ſir Tunbelly, who gravely anſwered me, and in a moving way, "Why what can we do?" "Not "drink it," replied I, "ſince it is not good." "But "what will you have us do? and how ſhall we paſs "the evening?" rejoined the baronet. "One cannot "go home at five o'clock." "That depends upon "a great deal of uſe," ſaid I. "It may be ſo, to a "certain degree," ſaid the doctor. "But give me

"leave

" leave to aſk you, Mr. Fitz-Adam, you, who drink " nothing but water, and live much at home, how " do you keep up your ſpirits?" " Why, doctor," ſaid I, " as I never lowered my ſpirits by ſtrong li- " quors, I do not want to raiſe them." Here we were interrupted by the colonel's raiſing his voice and indignation againſt the burgundy and the champain, ſwearing that the former was ropy, and the latter upon the fret, and not without ſome ſuſpicion of cyder and ſugar-candy; notwithſtanding which, he drank, in a bumper of it, " Confuſion to the town " of Briſtol and the bottle-act." It was a ſhame, he ſaid, that gentlemen could have no good burgundies and champains, for the ſake of ſome increaſe of the revenue, the manufacture of glaſs-bottles, and ſuch ſort of ſtuff. Sir George confirmed the ſame, adding that it was ſcandalous; and the whole company agreed, that the new parliament would certainly repeal ſo abſurd an act the very firſt ſeſſion; but, if they did not, they hoped they would receive inſtructions to that purpoſe from their conſtituents. " To " be ſure," ſaid the colonel. " What a d—d rout " they made about the repeal of the Jew-bill, for " which nobody cared one farthing! But, by the " way," continued he, " I think every body has done " eating, and therefore had not we better have the " dinner taken away, and the wine ſet upon the " table?" To this the company gave an unanimous aye. While this was doing, I aſked my friend, with ſeeming ſeriouſneſs, whether no part of the dinner was to be ſerved up again, when the wine ſhould be ſet upon the table? He ſeemed ſurprized at my

queſtion,

question, and asked me if I was hungry? To which I answered, no; but asked him in my turn if he was dry? To which he also answered, no. "Then pray," replied I, "why not as well eat without being hungry, "as drink without being dry?" My friend was so stunned with this, that he attempted no reply, but stared at me with as much astonishment, as he would have done at my great ancestor Adam, in his primitive state of nature.

The cloth was now taken away, and the bottles, glasses, and dishclouts, put upon the table, when Will Sitfast, who I found was a perpetual toast maker, took the chair, of course, as the man of application to business. He began the king's health in a bumper, which circulated in the same manner, not without some nice examinations of the chairman as to daylight. The bottle standing by me, I was called upon by the chairman, who added, that though a water-drinker, he hoped I would not refuse that health in wine. I begged to be excused, and told him that I never drank his majesty's health at all, though no one of his subjects wished it more heartily than I did; that hitherto it had not appeared to me, that there could be the least relation between the wine I drank, and the king's state of health, and that, till I was convinced that impairing my own health would improve his Majesty's, I was resolved to preserve the use of my faculties and my limbs, to employ both in his service if he could ever have occasion for them. I had foreseen the consequences of this refusal, and, though my friend had answered for my principles, I easily discovered an air of suspicion

in

in the countenances of the company, and I overheard the colonel whiſper to lord Feeble, "This author is "a very odd dog!"

My friend was aſhamed of me; but however, to help me off as well as he could, he ſaid to me aloud, "Mr. Fitz-Adam, this is one of thoſe ſingularities "which you have contracted by living ſo much "alone." From this moment, the company gave me up to my oddneſſes, and took no farther notice of me. I leaned ſilently upon the table, waiting for, though, to ſay the truth, without expecting, ſome of that feſtal gaiety, that urbanity, and that elegant mirth, of which my friend had promiſed ſo large a ſhare; inſtead of all which, the converſation ran chiefly into narrative, and grew duller and duller with every bottle. Lord Feeble recounted his former atchievements in love and wine; the colonel complained, though with dignity, of hardſhips and injuſtice; ſir George hinted at ſome important diſcoveries, which he had made that day at court, but cautiouſly avoided naming names; ſir Tunbelly ſlept between glaſs and glaſs; the doctor and my friend talked over college matters, and quoted Latin; and our worthy preſident applied himſelf wholly to buſineſs, never ſpeaking but to order, as, "Sir, the "bottle ſtands with you; ſir, you are to name a toaſt; "that has been drunk already; here, more claret!" &c. In the height of all this convivial pleaſantry, which I plainly ſaw was come to its zenith, I ſtole away at about nine o'clock, and went home; where reflections upon the entertainment of the day crowded into my mind, and may perhaps be the ſubject of ſome future paper.

XXX.

XXX.

THE WORLD.

SATURDAY, Oct. 3, 1754. N° 92.

THE entertainment, I do not ſay the diverſion, which I mentioned in my laſt paper, tumbled my imagination to ſuch a degree, and ſuggeſted ſuch a variety of indiſtinct ideas to my mind, that, notwithſtanding all the pains I took to ſort and digeſt, I could not reduce, them to method. I ſhall therefore throw them out in this paper without order, and juſt as they occurred to me.

When I conſidered that, perhaps, two millions of my fellow-ſubjects paſſed two parts in three of their lives in the very ſame manner in which the worthy members of my friend's club paſſed theirs, I was at a loſs to diſcover that attractive, irreſiſtible, and inviſible charm, for I confeſs I ſaw none, to which they ſo deliberately and aſſiduouſly ſacrificed their time, their health, and their reaſon; till, dipping accidentally into monſieur Paſcal, I read, upon the ſubject of hunting, the following paſſage. "What, un-"leſs to drown thought," ſays that excellent writer, "can make men throw away ſo much time upon a "ſilly animal, which they may buy much cheaper in "the market? It hinders us from looking into our-"ſelves, which is a view we cannot bear." That this is often one motive, and ſometimes the only one, of hunting, I can eaſily believe. But then it muſt be allowed too, that if the jolly ſportſman, who thus vigorouſly

vigorously runs away from himself, does not break his neck in his flight, he improves his health, at least, by his exercise. But what other motive can possibly be assigned for the soaker's daily and seriously swallowing his own destruction, except that of "drowning thought, and hindering him from looking into himself, which is a view he cannot bear?"

Unhappy the man who cannot willingly and frequently converse with himself; but miserable in the highest degree is the man who dares not! In one of these predicaments must that man be, who soaks and sleeps away his whole life. Either tired of himself for want of any reflections at all, or dreading himself for fear of the most tormenting ones, he flies, for refuge from his folly or his guilt, to the company of his fellow-sufferers, and to the intoxication of strong liquors.

Archbishop Tillotson asserts, and very truly, that no man can plead, in defence of swearing, that he was born of a swearing constitution. I believe the same thing may with equal truth be affirmed of drinking. No man is born a drinker. Drinking is an acquired, not a natural, vice. The child, when he first tastes strong liquors, rejects them with evident signs of disgust, but is insensibly brought first to bear, and then perhaps to like, them, by the folly of his parents, who promise them as an encouragement, and give them as a reward.

When the coroner's inquest examines the body of one of those unhappy wretches, who drown themselves in a pond or river, with commonly a provision of lead in their pockets to make the work the surer, the

the verdict is either *felo de se*, or lunatic. Is it then the water, or the suddenness of the plunge, that constitutes either the madness or the guilt of the act? is there any difference between a water and a wine suicide? If there be, it is evidently in favour of the former, which is never so deliberate and premeditated as the latter. The soaker jogs on with a gentler pace indeed, but to as sure and certain destruction, and, as a proof of his intention, would, I believe, upon examination, be generally found to have a good deal of lead about him too. He cannot alledge in his defence, that he has not warning, since he daily sees, in the chronical distempers of all his fellow-soakers, the fatal effects of that slow poison which he so greedily guzzles; for I defy all those honest gentlemen, that is, all the hard drinkers in England, a numerous body I doubt, to produce one single instance of a soaker, whose health and faculties are not visibly impaired by drinking. Some indeed, born much stronger than others, hold it out longer, and are absurdly quoted as living proofs even of the salutary effects of drinking; but though they have not yet any of the most distinguished characteristics of their profession about them, though they have not yet lost one half of themselves by a *hemiplegia*, nor the use of all their limbs by the gout, though they are but moderately mangy, and though the impending dropsy may not yet appear, I will venture to affirm, that the health they boast of is at best but an awkward state between sickness and health: if they are not actually sick, they are not actively well, and you will always find some complaint or other inadvertently dropped

from

from the triumphant ſoaker, within half an hour after he has aſſured you that he is *neither ſick nor ſorry.* My wife, who is a little ſuperſtitious, and perhaps too apt to point out and interpret judgements, otherwiſe an excellent woman, firmly believes, that the dropſy, of which moſt ſoakers finally die, is a manifeſt and juſt judgement upon them; the wine they ſo much loved being turned into water, and themſelves drowned at laſt in the element they ſo much abhorred.

A rational and ſober man, invited by the wit and gaiety of good company, and hurried away by an uncommon flow of ſpirits, may happen to drink too much, and perhaps accidentally to get drunk; but then theſe ſallies will be ſhort, and not frequent; whereas the ſoaker is an utter ſtranger to wit and mirth, and no friend to either.

His buſineſs is ſerious, and he applies himſelf ſeriouſly to it; he ſteadily purſues the numbing, ſtupifying, and petrifying, not the animating and exhilarating, qualities of the wine. Gallons of the Nepenthé would be loſt upon him. The more he drinks, the duller he grows; his politics become more obſcure, and his narratives more tedious and leſs intelligible; till at laſt *maudlin*, he employs what little articulation he has left, in relating his doleful tale to an inſenſible audience. I fear my countrymen have been too long noted for this manner of drinking, ſince a very old and eminent French hiſtorian *, ſpeaking of the Engliſh, who were then in poſſeſſion of Aquitain, the promiſed land of claret, ſays, *Ils ſe*

* Froiſſard.

*ſaouleren*t

ſaoulerent grandement, et ſe divertirent moult triſtement à la mode de leur païs.

A very ſkilful ſurgeon of my acquaintance aſſured me, that, having opened the body of a SOAKER, who died of an apoplexy, he had found all the finer tubes and veſſels plugged up with the tartar of the wine he had ſwallowed, ſo as to render the circulation of the blood abſolutely impoſſible, and the folds of the ſtomach ſo ſtiffened with it, that it could not perform its functions. He compared the body of the deceaſed to a ſiphon, ſo choaked up with the tartar and dregs of the wine that had run through it, as to be impervious. I adopted this image, which ſeemed to me a juſt one, and I ſhall for the future typify the SOAKER by the ſiphon, ſuction being equally the buſineſs of both.

An object, viewed at once, and in its full extent, will ſometimes ſtrike the mind, when the ſeveral parts and gradations of it, ſeparately ſeen, would be but little attended to. I ſhall therefore here preſent the ſociety of ſiphons with a calculation, of which they cannot diſpute the truth, and will not, I believe, deny the moderation; and yet perhaps they will be ſurprized when they ſee the groſs ſums of the wine they ſuck, of the money they pay for it, and of the time they loſe, in the courſe of ſeven years only.

I reckon that I put a ſtaunch ſiphon very low, when I put him only at two bottles a day, one with another. This in ſeven years amounts to four thouſand four hundred and ten bottles *, which makes twenty hogſheads and ſeventy bottles.

* This calculation is defective, the number of bottles drank in that time amounting to 5110.

Supposing this quantity to cost only four shillings a bottle, which I take to be the lowest price of claret, the sum amounts to eight hundred and eighty-two pounds.

Allowing every siphon but six hours a day to suck his two bottles in, which is a short allowance, that time amounts to six hundred and thirty-eight days, eighteen hours; one full quarter of his life, for the above-mentioned seven years. Can any rational being coolly consider these three gross sums, of wine, and consequently distempers swallowed, of money lavished, and time lost, without shame, regret, and a resolution of reformation?

I am well aware that the numerous society of siphons will say, like sir Tunbelly, "What would "this fellow have us do?" To which I am at no loss for an answer. Do any thing else. Preserve and improve that reason, which was given you to be your guide through this world, and to a better. Attend to, and discharge, your religious, your moral, and your social duties. These are occupations worthy of a rational being, they will agreeably and usefully employ your time, and will banish from your breasts that tiresome listlessness, or those tormenting thoughts, from which you endeavour, though in vain, to fly. Is your retrospect uncomfortable? Exert yourselves in time to make your prospect better; and let the former serve as a back-ground to the latter. Cultivate and improve your minds, according to your several educations and capacities. There are several useful books suited to them all. True religion and virtue give a chearful and happy turn to the mind, admit of all true pleasures, and even procure the truest.

Cantabrigius drinks nothing but water, and rides more miles in a year than the keenest sportsman, and with almost equal velocity. The former keeps his head clear, the latter his body in health. It is not from himself that he runs, but to his acquaintance, a synonymous term for his friends. Internally safe, he seeks no sanctuary from himself, no intoxication for his mind. His penetration makes him discover and divert himself with the follies of mankind, which his wit enables him to expose with the truest ridicule, though always without personal offence. Chearful abroad, because happy at home; and thus happy, because virtuous!

XXXI.

THE WORLD.

THURSDAY, Nov. 14, 1754. N° 98.

IT gives me great pleasure that I am able, in this day's paper, to congratulate the polite part of my fellow-subjects of both sexes, upon the splendid revival of that most rational entertainment, an Italian opera. Of late years it had seemed to sicken, so that I greatly feared that the unsuccessful efforts, which it made from time to time, were its convulsive and expiring pangs. But it now appears, and indeed much to the honor of this country, that we have still

too

too many protectors and protectresses of the liberal arts, to suffer that of music, the most liberal of them all, to sink for want of due encouragement.

I am sensible that Italian operas have frequently been the objects of the ridicule of many of our greatest wits; and, viewed in one light only, perhaps not without some reason. But, as I consider all public diversions singly with regard to the effects which they may have upon the morals and manners of the public, I confess I respect the Italian operas, as the most innocent of any.

The severe monsieur Boileau justly condemns the French operas, the morals of which he calls,

"——— Morale lubrique
"Que Lully rechauffa des sons de sa musique *."

But then it must be considered that French operas are always in French, and consequently may be understood by many French people, and that they are fine dramatic tragedies, adorned with all the graces of poetry and harmony of sounds, and may probably inspire too tender, if not voluptuous, sentiments. Can the Italian opera be accused of any thing of this kind? Certainly not. Were what is called the poetry of it intelligible in itself, it would not be understood by one in fifty of a British audience: but I believe that even an Italian of common candor will confess, that he does not understand one word of it. It is not the intention of the thing; for, should the ingenious author of the words, by mistake, put any

* Boileau Sat. x. l. 141, 142.
Lessons of licentiousness, which Lully (the founder of the French operas) animated with the sounds of his music.

meaning into them, he would, to a certain degree, check and cramp the genius of the compoſer of the muſic, who perhaps might think himſelf obliged to adapt his ſounds to the ſenſe: whereas now he is at liberty to ſcatter indiſcriminately, among the kings, queens, heroes, and heroines, his ADAGIOS, his ALLEGROS, his PATHETICS, his CHROMATICS, and his JIGGS. It would alſo have been a reſtraint upon the actors and actreſſes, who might poſſibly have attempted to form their action upon the meaning of their parts; but as it is, if they do but ſeem, by turns, to be angry and ſorry in the two firſt acts, and very merry in the laſt ſcene of the laſt, they are ſure to meet with the deſerved applauſe.

Signior Metaſtaſio attempted ſome time ago a very dangerous innovation. He tried gently to throw ſome ſenſe into his operas; but it did not take: the conſequences were obvious; and nobody knew where they would ſtop.

The whole ſkill and judgment of the poet now conſiſts in ſelecting about a hundred words, for the opera vocabulary does not exceed that number, that terminate in liquids and vowels, and rhyme to each other. Theſe words excite ideas in the hearer, though they were not the reſult of any in the poet. Thus the word *tortorella*, ſtretched out to a quaver of a quarter of an hour, excites in us the ideas of tender and faithful love; but if it is ſucceeded by *navicella*, that ſoothing idea gives way to the boiſterous and horrid one of a ſkiff, that is, a heart, toſſed by the winds and waves upon the main ocean of love. The handcuffs and fetters in which the hero com-

monly

monly appears, at the end of the ſecond, or beginning of the third act, indicate captivity; and when properly jingled to a pathetic piece of recitativo upon *queſti ceppi*, are really very moving, and inſpire a love of liberty. Can any thing be more innocent, or more moral, than this muſical pantomime, in which there is not one indecent word or action, but where, on the contrary, the moſt generous ſentiments are, however imperfectly, pointed out and inculcated?

I was once indeed afraid, that the licentiouſneſs of the times had infected even the opera: for in that of Alexander, the hero going into the heroine's apartment, found her taking a nap in an eaſy-chair. Tempted by ſo much beauty, and invited by ſo favourable an opportunity, he gently approached, and *ſtole a pair of gloves.* I confeſs, I dreaded the conſequences of this bold ſtep; and the more ſo, as it was taken by the celebrated ſignior Seneſino. But all went off very well; for the hero contented himſelf with giving the good company a ſong, in which he declared the lips he had juſt kiſſed were a couple of rubies.

Another good effect of the Italian operas is, that they contribute extremely to the keeping of good hours; the whole audience, though paſſionately fond of muſic, being ſo tired before they are half, and ſo ſleepy before they are quite, done, that they make the beſt of their way home, too drowſy to enter upon freſh ſpirits that night.

Having thus reſcued theſe excellent muſical dramas from the unjuſt ridicule, which ſome people of vulgar and illiberal taſtes have endeavoured to throw upon

 them,

them, I muſt proceed, and do juſtice to the virtuoſos and virtuoſas who perform them. But, I believe, it will be neceſſary for me to premiſe, for the ſake of many of my Engliſh readers, that VIRTÙ among the modern Italians ſignifies nothing leſs than what VIRTUS did among the antient ones, or what VIRTUE ſignifies among us; on the contrary, I might ſay that it ſignifies almoſt every thing elſe. Conſequently thoſe reſpectable titles of virtuoſo and virtuoſa have not the leaſt relation to the moral characters of the parties. They mean only that thoſe perſons, endowed ſome by nature, and ſome by art, with good voices, have from their infancy devoted their time and labor to the various combinations of ſeven notes: a ſtudy that muſt unqueſtionably have formed their minds, enlarged their notions, and have rendered them moſt agreeable and inſtructive companions; and as ſuch, I obſerve that they are juſtly ſolicited, received, and cheriſhed, by people of the firſt diſtinction.

As theſe illuſtrious perſonages come over here with no ſordid view of profit, but merely *per far piacer a la nobilita Ingleſe*, that is, to oblige the Engliſh nobility, they are exceedingly good and condeſcending to ſuch of the ſaid Engliſh nobility, and even gentry, as are deſirous to contract an intimacy with them. They will, for a word's ſpeaking, dine, ſup, or paſs the whole day, with people of a certain condition, and perhaps ſing or play, if civilly requeſted. Nay, I have known many of them ſo good as to paſs two or three months of the ſummer at the country ſeats of ſome of their noble friends, and thereby mitigate the horrors of the country and manſion-houſe, to my lady and

and her daughters. I have been aſſured by many of their chief patrons and patroneſſes, that they are all *the beſt creatures in the world*; and from the time of ſignor Cavaliero Nicolini down to this day, I have conſtantly heard the ſeveral great performers, ſuch as Farinelli, Careſtini, Monticelli, Gaſſarielli, as well as the ſignore Cuzzoni, Fauſtina, &c. much more praiſed for their affability, the gentleneſs of their manners, and all the good qualities of the head and heart, than for either their muſical ſkill or execution. I have even known theſe their ſocial virtues lay their protectors and protectreſſes under great difficulties, how to reward ſuch diſtinguiſhed merit. But benefit-nights luckily came in to their aſſiſtance, and gave them an opportunity of inſinuating, with all due regard, into the hands of the performer, in lieu of a ticket, a conſiderable bank-bill, a gold ſnuff-box, a diamond ring, or ſome ſuch trifle. It is to be hoped, that the illuſtrious ſignor Farinelli has not yet forgot the many inſtances he experienced of Britiſh munificence: for it is certain that many private families *ſtill remember them.*

All this is very well; and I greatly approve of it, as I am of tolerating and naturalizing principles. But however, as the beſt things may admit of improvement by certain modifications, I ſhall now ſuggeſt two; the one of a public, the other of a private, nature. I would by all means welcome theſe reſpectable gueſts, but I would by no means part with them, as is too ſoon and too often the caſe.

Some of them, when they have got ten or fifteen thouſand pounds here, unkindly withdraw themſelves, and purchaſe eſtates in land in their own countries; and others are ſeduced from us, by the preſſing invitations of ſome great potentate to come over to ſuperintend his pleaſures, and to take a ſhare in his counſels. This is not only a great loſs to their particular friends, the nobility and gentry, but to the nation in general, by turning the balance of our muſical commerce conſiderably againſt us. I would therefore humbly propoſe, that immediately upon the arrival of theſe valuable ſtrangers, a writ of *ne exeat regnum* ſhould be iſſued to keep them here. The other modification, which I beg leave to hint at only, it being of a private nature, is, that no virtuoſo, whoſe voice is below a *contralto*, ſhall be taken to the country-ſeat of any family whatſoever; much leſs any ſtrapping fiddler, baſſoon, or baſs viol, who does not even pretend to ſing, or, if he does, ſings a rough tenor or a tremendous baſs. The conſequences may be ſerious, but at leaſt the appearances are not edifying.

XXXII.

THE WORLD.

THURSDAY, NOV. 28, 1754. Nº 100.

I HEARD the other day, with great pleaſure, from my worthy friend Mr. Dodſley, that Mr. Johnſon's Engliſh dictionary, with a grammar and hiſtory of our language prefixed, will be publiſhed this winter, in two large volumes in folio.

I had

I had long lamented, that we had no lawful ſtandard of our language ſet up, for thoſe to repair to, who might chuſe to ſpeak and write it grammatically and correctly: and I have as long wiſhed that either ſome one perſon of diſtinguiſhed abilities would undertake the work ſingly, or that a certain number of gentlemen would form themſelves, or be formed by the government, into a ſociety for that purpoſe. The late ingenious doctor Swift propoſed a plan of this nature to his friend, as he thought him, the lord treaſurer Oxford, but without ſucceſs; preciſion and perſpicuity not being in general the favourite objects of miniſters, and perhaps ſtill leſs ſo of that miniſter than any other.

Many people have imagined, that ſo extenſive a work would have been beſt formed by numbers of perſons, who ſhould have taken their ſeveral departments, of examining, ſifting, winnowing (I borrow this image from the Italian *Cruſca*), purifying, and finally fixing our language, by incorporating their reſpective funds into one joint ſtock. But, whether this opinion be true or falſe, I think the public in general, and the republic of letters in particular, greatly obliged to Mr. Johnſon, for having undertaken and executed ſo great and deſireable a work. Perfection is not to be expected from man; but, if we are to judge by the various works of Mr. Johnſon, already publiſhed, we have good reaſon to believe, that he will bring this as near to perfection, as any one man could do. The plan of it, which he publiſhed ſome years ago, ſeems to me to be a proof of it. Nothing can be more rationally imagined,

imagined, or more accurately and elegantly expressed. I therefore recommend the previous perusal of it to all those, who intend to buy the dictionary, and who, I suppose, are all those who can afford it.

The celebrated dictionaries of the Florentine and French academies owe their present size and perfection to very small beginnings. Some private gentlemen at Florence, and some at Paris, had met at each other's houses, to talk over and consider their respective languages: upon which they published some short essays, which essays were the embryos of those perfect productions, that now do so much honor to the two nations. Even Spain, which seems not to be the soil where, of late at least, letters have either prospered or been cultivated, has produced a dictionary, and a good one too, of the Spanish language, in six large volumes in folio.

I cannot help thinking it a sort of disgrace to our nation, that hitherto we have had no such standard of our language; our dictionaries at present being more properly, what our neighbours the Dutch and the Germans call theirs, word-books, than dictionaries in the superior sense of that title. All words, good and bad, are there jumbled indiscriminately together, insomuch that the injudicious reader may speak, and write, as inelegantly, improperly, and vulgarly, as he pleases, by and with the authority of one or other of our word-books.

It must be owned that our language is at present in a state of anarchy; and hitherto, perhaps, it may not have been the worse for it. During our free and open trade, many words and expressions have been

been imported, adopted, and naturalized, from other languages, which have greatly enriched our own. Let it ſtill preſerve what real ſtrength and beauty it may have borrowed from others; but let it not, like the Tarpeian maid, be overwhelmed and cruſhed by unneceſſary foreign ornaments. The time for diſcrimination ſeems to be now come. Toleration, adoption, and naturalization, have run their lengths. Good order and authority are now neceſſary. But where ſhall we find them, and at the ſame time the obedience due to them? We muſt have recourſe to the old Roman expedient in times of confuſion, and chuſe a dictator. Upon this principle, I give my vote for Mr. Johnſon to fill that great and arduous poſt. And I hereby declare, that I make a total ſurrender of all my rights and privileges in the Engliſh language, as a free-born Britiſh ſubject, to the ſaid Mr. Johnſon, during the term of his dictatorſhip. Nay more; I will not only obey him, like an old Roman, as my dictator, but, like a modern Roman, I will implicitly believe in him as my pope, and hold him to be infallible while in the chair; but no longer. More than this he cannot well require; for I preſume that obedience can never be expected, when there is neither terror to enforce, nor intereſt to invite it.

I confeſs that I have ſo much honeſt Engliſh pride, or perhaps prejudice, about me, as to think myſelf more conſiderable for whatever contributes to the honor, the advantage, or the ornament, of my native country. I have therefore a ſenſible pleaſure in reflecting upon the rapid progreſs, which our language

has

has lately made, and ſtill continues to make, all over Europe. It is frequently ſpoken, and almoſt univerſally underſtood, in Holland; it is kindly entertained as a relation in the moſt civilized parts of Germany; and it is ſtudied as a learned language, though yet little ſpoke, by all thoſe in France and Italy, who either have, or pretend to have, any learning.

The ſpreading the French language over moſt parts of Europe, to the degree of making it almoſt an univerſal one, was always reckoned among the glories of the reign of Lewis the fourteenth. But be it remembered, that the ſucceſs of his arms firſt opened the way to it; though at the ſame time it muſt be owned, that a great number of moſt excellent authors, who flouriſhed in his time, added ſtrength and velocity to its progreſs. Whereas our language has made its way ſingly by its own weight and merit, under the conduct of thoſe leaders, Shakeſpear, Bacon, Milton, Locke, Newton, Swift, Pope, Addiſon, &c. A nobler ſort of conqueſt, and a far more glorious triumph, ſince graced by none but willing captives!

Theſe authors, though for the moſt part but indifferently tranſlated into foreign languages, gave other nations a ſample of the Britiſh genius. The copies, imperfect as they were, pleaſed and excited a general deſire of ſeeing the originals; and both our authors and our language ſoon became claſſical.

But a grammar, a dictionary, and a hiſtory of our language, through its ſeveral ſtages, were ſtill wanting at home, and importunately called for from abroad. Mr. Johnſon's labors will now, and, I dare ſay, very fully,

fully, ſupply that want, and greatly contribute to the farther ſpreading of our language in other countries. Learners were diſcouraged by finding no ſtandard to reſort to, and conſequently thought it incapable of any. They will be undeceived and encouraged.

There are many hints and conſiderations relative to our language, which I ſhould have taken the liberty of ſuggeſting to Mr. Johnſon, had I not been convinced that they have equally occurred to him: but there is one, and a very material one it is, to which perhaps he may not have given all the neceſſary attention. I mean the genteeler part of our language, which owes both its riſe and progreſs to my fair countrywomen, whoſe natural turn is more to the copiouſneſs, than to the correction of diction. I would not adviſe him to be raſh enough to proſcribe any of thoſe happy redundancies, and luxuriancies of expreſſion, with which they have enriched our language. They willingly inflict fetters, but very unwillingly ſubmit to wear them. In this caſe the taſk will be ſo difficult, that I deſign, as a common friend, to propoſe in ſome future paper, the means which appear to me the moſt likely to reconcile matters.

P. S. I hope that none of my courteous readers will upon this occaſion be ſo uncourteous, as to ſuſpect me of being a hired and intereſted puff of this work; for I moſt ſolemnly proteſt, that neither Mr. Johnſon, nor any perſon employed by him, nor any bookſeller or bookſellers concerned in the ſucceſs of it, have ever offered me the uſual compliment of a pair of gloves or a bottle of wine: nor has even

Mr.

Mr. Dodſley, though my publiſher, and, as I am informed, deeply intereſted in the ſale of this dictionary, ſo much as invited me to take a bit of mutton with him.

XXXIII.

THE WORLD.

SATURDAY, Dec. 5, 1754. N° 101.

WHEN I intimated in my laſt paper ſome diſtruſt of Mr. Johnſon's complaiſance to the fairer part of his readers, it was becauſe I had a greater opinion of his impartiality and ſeverity as a judge, than of his gallantry as a fine gentleman. And indeed I am well aware of the difficulties he would have to encounter, if he attempted to reconcile the polite with the grammatical part of our language. Should he, by an act of power, baniſh and attaint many of the favourite words and expreſſions, with which the ladies have ſo profuſely enriched our language, he would excite the indignation of the moſt formidable, becauſe the moſt lovely, part of his readers: his dictionary would be condemned as a ſyſtem of tyranny, and he himſelf, like the laſt Tarquin, run the riſque of being depoſed. So popular and ſo powerful is the female cauſe! On the other hand, ſhould he, by an act of grace, admit, legitimate, and incorporate into our language, thoſe words and expreſſions, which, haſtily begot, owe

owe their birth to the incontinency of female eloquence; what severe censures might he not justly apprehend from the learned part of his readers, who do not understand complaisances of that nature!

For my own part, as I am always inclined to plead the cause of my fair fellow-subjects, I shall now take the liberty of laying before Mr. Johnson those arguments, which upon this occasion may be urged in their favour, as introductory to the compromise which I shall humbly offer and conclude with.

Language is indisputably the more immediate province of the fair sex: there they shine, there they excel. The torrents of their eloquence, especially in the vituperative way, stun all opposition, and bear away, in one promiscuous heap, nouns, verbs, moods, and tenses. If words are wanting, which indeed happens but seldom, indignation instantly makes new ones; and I have often known four or five syllables, that never met one another before, hastily and fortuitously jumbled into some word of mighty import.

Nor is the tender part of our language less obliged to that soft and amiable sex; their love being at least as productive as their indignation. Should they lament in an involuntary retirement the absence of the adored object, they give new murmurs to the brook, new sounds to the echo, and new notes to the plaintive Philomela. But when this happy copiousness flows, as it often does, into gentle numbers, good gods! how is the poetical diction enriched, and the poetical licence extended! Even in common conversation, I never see a pretty mouth opening to speak, but I expect, and am seldom disappointed, some

ſome new improvement of our language. I remember many expreſſive words coined in that fair mint. I aſſiſted at the birth of that moſt ſignificant word FLIRTATION, which dropped from the moſt beautiful mouth in the world, and which has ſince received the ſanction of our moſt accurate Laureat in one of his comedies. Some inattentive and undiſcerning people have, I know, taken it to be a term ſynonymous with coquetry; but I lay hold of this opportunity to undeceive them, and eventually to inform Mr. Johnſon, that flirtation is ſhort of coquetry, and intimates only the firſt hints of approximation, which ſubſequent coquetry may reduce to thoſe preliminary articles, that commonly end in a definitive treaty.

I was alſo a witneſs to the riſe and progreſs of that moſt important verb, TO FUZZ; which, if not of legitimate birth, is at leaſt of fair extraction. As I am not ſure that it has yet made its way into Mr. Johnſon's literary retirement, I think myſelf obliged to inform him that it is at preſent the moſt uſeful and the moſt uſed word in our language; ſince it means no leſs than dealing twice together with the ſame pack of cards, for luck's ſake, at whiſt.

Not contented with enriching our language by words abſolutely new, my fair countrywomen have gone ſtill farther, and improved it by the application and extenſion of old ones to various and very different ſignifications. They take a word and change it, like a guinea into ſhillings for pocket-money, to be employed in the ſeveral occaſional purpoſes of the day. For inſtance, the adjective *vaſt* and its adverb *vaſtly* mean any thing, and are the faſhionable words of of the most fashionable people. A fine woman, under this head I comprehend all fine gentlemen too, not knowing in truth where to place them properly, is *vastly* obliged, or *vastly* offended, *vastly* glad, or *vastly* sorry. Large objects are *vastly* great, small ones are *vastly* little; and I had lately the pleasure to hear a fine woman pronounce, by a happy metonymy, a very small gold snuff-box that was produced in company to be *vastly* pretty, because it was *vastly* little. Mr. Johnson will do well to consider seriously to what degree he will restrain the various and extensive significations of this great word.

Another very material point still remains to be considered; I mean the orthography of our language, which is at present very various and unsettled.

We have at present two very different orthographies, the *pedantic*, and the *polite*; the one founded upon certain dry crabbed rules of etymology and grammar, the other singly upon the justness and delicacy of the ear. I am thoroughly persuaded that Mr. Johnson will endeavour to establish the former; and I perfectly agree with him, provided it can be quietly brought about. Spelling, as well as music, is better performed by book, than merely by the ear, which may be variously affected by the same sounds. I therefore most earnestly recommend to my fair countrywomen, and to their faithful or faithless servants, the fine gentlemen of this realm, to surrender, as well for their own private as for the public utility, all their natural rights and privileges of mis-spelling, which they have so long enjoyed, and so vigorously exerted. I have really known very fatal consequences attend that loose and uncertain practice of auricular orthography; of which I shall produce two instances as a sufficient warning.

A very fine gentleman wrote a very harmless innocent letter to a very fine lady, giving an account of some trifling commissions, which he had executed according to her orders. This letter, though directed to the lady, was, by the mistake of a servant, delivered to, and opened by, her husband; who, finding all his attempts to understand it unsuccessful, took it for granted that it was a concerted cypher, under which a criminal correspondence, not much to his own honor or advantage, was secretly carried on. With the letter in his hand, and rage in his heart, he went immediately to his wife, and reproached her in the most injurious terms with her supposed infidelity. The lady, conscious of her own innocence, calmly requested to see the grounds of so unjust an accusation; and, being accustomed to the auricular orthography, made shift to read to her incensed husband the most inoffensive letter that ever was written. The husband was undeceived, or at least wise enough to seem so; for in such cases one must not peremptorily decide. However, as sudden impressions are generally pretty strong, he has been observed to be more suspicious ever since.

The other accident had much worse consequences. Matters were happily brought, between a fine gentleman and a fine lady, to the decisive period of an appointment at a third place. *The place where* is always the lover's business, *the time when* the lady's. Accordingly an impatient and rapturous letter from the lover signified to the lady the house and street

where;

where; to which a tender anſwer from the lady aſſented, and appointed the time *when*. But unfortunately, from the uncertainty of the lover's auricular orthography, the lady miſtook both houſe and ſtreet, was conveyed in a hackney-chair to a wrong one, and in the hurry and agitation, which ladies are ſometimes in upon theſe occaſions, ruſhed into a houſe where ſhe happened to be known, and her intentions conſequently diſcovered. In the mean time the lover paſſed three or four hours at the right place, in the alternate agonies of impatient and diſappointed love, tender fear, and anxious jealouſy.

Such examples really make one tremble; and will, I am convinced, determine my fair fellow-ſubjects and their adherents to adopt, and ſcrupulouſly conform to, Mr. Johnſon's rules of true orthography by book. In return to this conceſſion, I ſeriouſly adviſe him to publiſh, by way of appendix to his great work, a genteel Neological dictionary, containing thoſe polite, though perhaps not ſtrictly grammatical, words and phraſes, commonly uſed, and ſometimes underſtood, by the *beau monde*. By ſuch an act of toleration, who knows but he may, in time, bring them within the pale of the Engliſh language? The beſt Latin dictionaries have commonly a ſhort ſupplemental one annexed, of the obſolete and barbarous Latin words, which pedants ſometimes borrow to ſhew their erudition. Surely then my countrywomen, the enrichers, the patroneſſes, and the harmonizers of our language, deſerve greater indulgence. I muſt alſo hint to Mr. Johnſon, that ſuch a ſmall ſupplemental dictionary will contribute infinitely to

 the

the ſale of the great one; and I make no queſtion but that, under the protection of that little work, the great one will be received in the genteeleſt houſes: We ſhall frequently meet with it in ladies dreſſing-rooms, lying upon the harpſichord, together with the knotting-bag, and ſignor Di-Giardino's incomparable concertos; and even ſometimes in the powder-rooms of our young nobility, upon the ſame ſhelf with their German flute, their powder-maſk, and their four-horſe-whip.

XXXIV.

THE WORLD.

THURSDAY, January 2, 1755. N° 105.

AS I am deſirous of beginning the new year well, I ſhall devote this paper to the ſervice of my fair countrywomen, for whom I have ſo tender a concern, that I examine into their conduct with a kind of parental vigilance and affection. I ſincerely wiſh to approve, but at the ſame time am determined to admoniſh and reprimand whenever, for their ſakes, I may think it neceſſary. I will not, as far as in me lies, ſuffer the errors of their minds to diſgrace thoſe beautiful dwellings in which they are lodged; nor will I, on the other hand, ſilently and quietly allow the affectation and abuſe of their perſons, to reflect contempt and ridicule upon their underſtandings.

Native, artleſs beauty has long been the peculiar diſtinction of my fair fellow-ſubjects. Our poets have long ſung their genuine lilies and roſes, and our painters have long endeavoured, though in vain, to imitate them: beautiful nature mocked all their art. But I am now informed by perſons of unqueſtioned truth and ſagacity, and indeed I have obſerved but too many inſtances of it myſelf, that a great number of thoſe ineſtimable originals, by a ſtrange inverſion of things, give the lie to their poets, and ſervilely copy their painters; degrading and diſguiſing themſelves into worſe copies of bad copies of themſelves. It is even whiſpered about town of that excellent artiſt, Mr. Liotard *, that he lately refuſed a fine woman to draw her picture, alledging that he never copied any body's works but his own and GOD ALMIGHTY's.

I have taken great pains to inform myſelf of the growth and extent of this heinous crime of ſelf-painting, I had almoſt given it a harder name, and I am ſorry to ſay, that I have found it to be extremely epidemical. The preſent ſtate of it, in its ſeveral degrees, appears to be this.

The inferior claſs of women, who always ape their betters, make uſe of a ſort of rough caſt, little ſuperior to the common lath and plaiſter, which comes very cheap, and can be afforded out of the caſual profits of the evening.

The claſs immediately above theſe, paint occaſionally, either in ſize or oil, which, at ſixpence *per* foot ſquare, comes within a moderate weekly allowance.

* A celebrated limner in crayons, very faithful to nature; who after having travelled in ſeveral parts of the world, and received great encouragement in England, is now retired to his own country Geneva.

The generality of women of fashion make use of a superfine stucco, or plaister of Paris highly glazed, which does not require a daily renewal, and will, with some slight occasional repairs, last as long as their curls, and stand a pretty strong collision.

As for the transcendent and divine powder, with an exquisite varnish superinduced to fix it, it is by no means common, but is reserved for the ladies not only of the first rank, but of the most considerable fortunes; it being so very costly, that few pin-monies can keep a face in it, as a face of condition ought to be kept. Perhaps the same number of pearls *whole*, might be more acceptable to some lovers, than in powder upon the lady's face.

I would now fain undeceive my fair countrywomen of an error, which, gross as it is, they too fondly entertain. They flatter themselves that this artificial is not discoverable, or distinguishable, from native, white. But I beg leave to assure them, that, however well-prepared the color may be, or however skilful the hand that lays it on, it is immediately discovered by the eye at a considerable distance, and by the nose upon a nearer approach; and I over-heard the other day at the coffee-house captain Phelim McManus complaining, that when warm upon the face it had the most nauseous taste imaginable. Thus offensive to three of the senses, it is not, probably, very inviting to a fourth.

Talking upon this subject lately with a friend, he said, that, in his opinion, a woman who painted white gave the public a pledge of her chastity, by fortifying it with a wall, which she must be sure that no man would desire either to batter or scale. But, I confess, I did not agree with him as to the motive, though I did as to the consequences; which are, I believe, in general, that they lose both *operam et oleum.* I have observed that many of the sagacious landlords of this great metropolis, who lett lodgings, do, at the beginning of the winter, new vamp, paint and stucco the fronts of their houses, in order to catch the eyes of passengers, and engage lodgers. Now, to say the truth, I cannot help suspecting that this is rather the real motive of my fair countrywomen, when they thus incrust themselves. But alas! those outward repairs will never tempt people to inquire within. The cases are greatly different; in the former they both adorn and preserve, in the latter they disgust and destroy.

In order therefore to put an effectual stop to this enormity, and save, as far as I am able, the native carnations, the eyes, the teeth, the breath, and the reputations, of my beautiful fellow-subjects; I here give notice, that, if, within one kalendar month from the date hereof, I allow that time for the consumption of stock in hand, I shall receive any authentic testimonies, and I have my spies abroad, of this sophistication and adulteration of the fairest works of nature, I am resolved to publish at full-length the names of the delinquents. This may perhaps at first sight seem a bold measure, and actions of scandal and defamation may be thought of: but I go upon safe ground; for, before I took this resolution, I was determined to know all the worst possible consequences of it to myself, and therefore consulted one of the most eminent council in England, an old acquaintance and friend of mine, whose opinion I shall here most faithfully relate.

When I had stated my case to him as clearly as I was able, he stroaked his chin for some time, picked his nose, and hemmed thrice, in order to give me his very best opinion. "By publishing the names at full-"length in your paper, I humbly conceive," said he, "that you avoid all the troublesome consequences of "*innuendos*. But the present question, if I appre-"hend it aright, seems to be, whether you may there-"by be liable to any other action, or actions, which, "for brevity sake, I will not here enumerate. Now, "by what occurs to me off-hand, and without con-"sulting my books, I humbly apprehend that no "action will lie against you: but, on the contrary, I "do conceive, and indeed take upon me to affirm, "that you may proceed against these criminals, for "such I will be bold to call them, either by action "or indictment; the crime being of a public and a "heinous nature. Here is not only the *suppressio* "*veri*, which is highly penal, but the *crimen falsi* too. "An *action popular*, or of *qui tam*, would certainly "lie; but however I should certainly prefer an in-"dictment upon the statutes of forgery, 2 Geo. II. "cap. 25. and 7 Geo. II. cap. 22: for forgery, I "maintain it, it is. The fact, as you well know, will "be tried by a jury, of whom one moiety will doubt-"less be plaisterers; so that it will unquestionably "be found." Here my council paused for some time, and hemmed pretty often; however, I remained silent, observing plainly by his countenance that he had

had not finiſhed, but was thinking on. In a little time he reſumed his diſcourſe, and ſaid, "All things "conſidered, Mr. Fitz-Adam, I would adviſe you to "bring your indictment upon the *Black Act*, 9 Geo. I. "cap. 22. which is a very fine penal ſtatute." I confeſs I could not check the ſudden impulſe of ſurprize, which this occaſioned in me, and interrupting him perhaps too haſtily, "What, ſir," ſaid I, "indict a wo- "man upon the *Black Act* for *painting white?*" Here my council, interrupting me in his turn, ſaid with ſome warmth, "Mr. Fitz-Adam, Mr. Fitz-Adam, "you, like too many others, have not ſufficiently con- "ſidered all the beauty, good ſenſe, and ſolid reaſon- "ing, of the law. The law, ſir, let me tell you, abhors "all refinements, ſubtleties, and quibblings upon "words. What is black or white to the law? Do "you imagine that the law views colors by the rule of "optics? No, God forbid it ſhould. The law "makes black white, or white black, according to "the rules of juſtice. The law conſiders the mean- "ing, the intention, the *quo animo* of all actions, not "their external modes. Here a woman diſguiſes her "face with white, as the Waltham people did with "black, and with the ſame fraudulent and felonious "intention. Though the color be different, the guilt "is the ſame in the intendment of the law. It is "felony without benefit of clergy, and the puniſhment "is death." As I perceived that my friend had now done, I aſked his pardon for the improper interruption I had given him, owned myſelf convinced, and offered him a fee, which he took by habit, but ſoon re-

turned,

turned, by reflecting upon our long acquaintance and friendſhip.

This, I hope, will be ſufficient to make ſuch of my fair countrywomen as are conſcious of their guilt, ſeriouſly conſider their danger; though perhaps, from my natural lenity, I ſhall not proceed againſt them with the utmoſt rigor of the law, nor follow the example of the ingenious author of our laſt muſical drama, who ſtrings up a whole row of Penelope's maids of honor. I ſhall therefore content myſelf with publiſhing the names of the delinquents as abovementioned; but others may poſſibly not have the ſame indulgence; and the law is open for all.

I ſhall conclude this paper with a word or two of ſerious advice to all my readers, of all ſorts and ſexes. Let us follow nature, our honeſt and faithful guide, and be upon our guard againſt the flattering deluſions of art. Nature may be helped and improved, but will not be forced or changed. All attempts in direct oppoſition to her are attended with ridicule, many with guilt. The woman, to whom nature has denied beauty, in vain endeavours to make it by art; as the man, to whom nature has denied wit, becomes ridiculous by the affectation of it: they both defeat their own purpoſes, and are in the caſe of the valetudinarian, who creates or increaſes his diſtempers by his remedies, and dies of his immoderate deſire to live.

XXXV.

THE WORLD.

THURSDAY, Feb. 13, 1755. N° 111.

IT is very well known that religion and politics are perfectly underſtood by every body, as they require neither ſtudy nor experience. All people therefore decide peremptorily, though often variouſly, upon both.

All ſects, ſeverally ſure of being in the right, intimate, at leaſt, if not denounce, damnation to thoſe who differ from them, in points ſo clear, ſo plain, and ſo obvious. On the other hand, the infidel, not leſs an enthuſiaſt than any of them, though upon his own principles he cannot damn, becauſe he knows to demonſtration that there is no future ſtate, would very gladly hang, as hypocrites or fools, the whole body of believers.

In politics, the ſects are as various and as warm: and what ſeems very extraordinary, is, that thoſe who have ſtudied them the moſt, and experienced them the longeſt, always know them the leaſt. Every adminiſtration is in the wrong, though they have the clue and ſecret of buſineſs in their hands; and not leſs than ſix millions of their fellow-ſubjects, for I only except very young children, are willing and able to diſcover, cenſure, reform, and correct, their errors, and put them in the right way.

Theſe conſiderations, among many others, determined me originally not to meddle with religion or or politics, in which I could not inſtruct, and upon which I thought it not decent to trifle.

Entertainment alone muſt be the object of an humble weekly author of a ſheet and a half. A certain degree of bulk is abſolutely neceſſary for a certain degree of dignity, either in man or book. A ſyſtem of ethics, to be reſpected as it ought, requires at leaſt a quarto; and even moral eſſays cannot decently, and with utility, appear in leſs than a thick octavo. But ſhould I, in my ignoble ſtate of a fugitive ſheet and a half, preſume with a grave face to cenſure folly, or with an angry one to laſh vice, the porter of every well-bred family in town would have orders to deny me; and I ſhould forfeit my place at the breakfaſt-table, where now, to my great honor and emolument, I am pretty generally ſerved up. But if, by the introduction of that wit and humor, which I believe my enemies muſt allow me, I can without offence to the politer part of my readers ſlide in any uſeful moral, I will not neglect the opportunity: for I will be witty whenever I can, and inſtructive whenever I dare; and when my ſcattered leaves ſhall, like the Sibyls, come to be collected, I believe, I may without vanity aſſert, that they will be, at leaſt, as good oracles.

But in this deſign too I am aware of difficulties, little inferior to thoſe which diſcouraged me from meddling with religion and politics: for every body has wit and humour, and many have more of both than they, or at leaſt their friends, know what to do with. As they are gifts of nature, not to be acquired by art, who is there that thinks himſelf ſo diſinherited

inherited by nature as not to have ſome ſhare of them? Nay, thoſe, if ſuch there are, who are modeſt enough to think themſelves cut off with a ſhilling, huſband that twelve-pence with care, and frugally ſpend their penny upon occaſion, as ſly wags, and dry jokers.

In this univerſal profuſion, this prodigious plenty of wit and humour, I cannot help diſtruſting a little the ſucceſs, though by no means the merit, of my own: for I have interior conviction, that no man in England has ſo much. But taſtes are various, and the market is glutted. However, I ſhould hope that my candid readers will have the ſame regard for my opinion, which they have for moſt of the opinions they entertain; that is, that they will take it upon truſt, eſpecially as they have it *from the gentleman's own mouth.*

The better to take my meaſures for the future, I have endeavoured to trace the progreſs and reception of my paper through the ſeveral claſſes of its readers.

In families of condition, it is firſt received by the porter, who, yawning, juſt caſts his half-open eyes upon it, for it comes out ſo early as between ten and eleven; but, finding neither the politics nor the caſualties of the week in it, throws it aſide, and takes up in its ſtead a daily news-paper, in which all thoſe matters are related with truth and perſpicuity.

From thence it is ſent up to Mrs. Betty, to lay upon the breakfaſt-table. She receives it in pretty much the ſame manner, finds it deficient in point of news, and lays it down in exchange for the Daily-

Advertiſer,

Advertiser, where ſhe turns with impatience to the advertiſements, to ſee what invitations are thrown out by ſingle gentlemen of undoubted characters, to agreeable young women of unblemiſhed reputations, to become either their wives or their companions. And, by a prudent forecaſt, ſhe particularly attends to the premiums ſo frequently offered for a fine wholeſome breaſt of milk.

When it is introduced into my lady's dreſſing-room, it undergoes a ſeverer examination: for, if my lord and lady ever meet, it is then and there. The youngeſt, probably, of the young ladies is appointed to read it aloud, to uſe her to read at ſight. If my lord, who is a judge of wit, as well as of property, in the laſt reſort, gives a favourable nod, and ſays, *it is well enough to-day*, my lady, who does not care to contradict him in trifles, pronounces it to be *charming*. But if unfortunately my lord, with an air of diſtaſte, calls it *poor ſtuff*, my lady diſcovers it to be *horridly ſtupid*. The young family are unanimouſly of opinion, that the name of Adam Fitz-Adam is a very comical one, and enquire into the meaning of the globe in the frontiſpiece; by which, if any body could tell them, they might get a pretty notion of geography.

In families of an inferior claſs, I meet with a fuller, though perhaps not a more favourable, trial. My merits and demerits are freely diſcuſſed. Some think me too grave, others trifling. The miſtreſs of the houſe, though ſhe deteſts ſcandal, wiſhes, for example's ſake only, that I would draw the characters, and expoſe the intrigues, of the fine folks.

The

The maſter wonders that I do not give the miniſters a rap; and concludes that I receive huſh-money. But all agree in ſaying facetiouſly and pleaſantly enough, that the WORLD does not inform them how the WORLD goes. This is followed by many other *bons mots*, equally ingenious, alluding to the title of my paper, and worth at leaſt the two-pence a week that it coſts.

In the city, for my paper has made its way to that end of the town upon the ſuppoſition of its being a faſhionable one in this, I am received and conſidered in a different light. All my general reflexions upon the vices or the follies of the age are, by the ladies, ſuppoſed to be levelled at particular perſons, or at leaſt diſcovered to be very applicable to ſuch and ſuch of the QUALITY. They are alſo thought to be very pat to ſeveral of their own neighbours and acquaintance; and ſhrewd hints of the kind greatly embelliſh the converſation of the evening. The graver and more frugal part of that opulent metropolis, who do not themſelves buy, but borrow my paper of thoſe who do, complain that, though there is generally room ſufficient at the end of the laſt page, I never inſert the price of ſtocks nor of goods at Bear-key. And they are every one of them aſtoniſhed how certain tranſactions of the court of aldermen on one hand, and of the common-council on the other, can poſſibly eſcape my animadverſion, ſince it is impoſſible that they can have eſcaped my knowledge.

Such are the cenſures and difficulties, to which a poor weekly author is expoſed. However, I have

the

the pleafure, and fomething more than the pleafure, of finding that two thoufand of my papers are circulated weekly. This number exceeds the largeft that was ever printed even of the Spectators, which in no other refpect do I pretend to equal. Such extraordinary fuccefs would be fufficient to flatter the vanity of a good author, and to turn the head of a bad one. But I prudently check and ftifle thofe growing fentiments in my own breaft, by reflecting upon the other circumftances that tend to my humiliation. I muft confefs that the prefent fafhion of curling the hair has proved exceedingly favourable to me: and perhaps the quality of my paper, as it happens to be peculiarly adapted to that purpofe, may contribute, more than its merit, to the fale of it. A head that has taken a right French turn, requires, as I am affured, fourfcore curls in diftinct papers, and thofe curls muft be renewed as often as the head is combed, which is perhaps once a month. Four of my papers are fufficient for that purpofe, and amount only to eight-pence, which is very little more than what the fame quantity of plain paper would coft. Taking it therefore all together, it feems not inconfiftent with good œconomy to purchafe it at fo fmall a price. This reflection might mortify me as an author; but, on the other hand, felf-love, which is ingenious in availing itfelf of the flighteft favourable circumftances, comforts me with the thought, that, of the prodigious number of daily and weekly papers that are now publifhed, mine is perhaps the only one that is ultimately applied to the head.

XXXVI.

THE WORLD.

SATURDAY, Feb. 20, 1755. N° 112.

A LATE noble author has moſt juſtly and elegantly defined cuſtom to be, "The reſult of "the paſſions and prejudices of many, and of the de-"ſigns of a few; the ape of reaſon, who uſurps her "ſeat, exerciſes her power, and is obeyed by man-"kind in her ſtead."

This definition enables us to account for the various abſurd and wicked cuſtoms which have ſeverally and ſucceſſively prevailed in all ages and countries, and alſo for thoſe which unfortunately prevail in this: for they may all be traced up to the paſſions and prejudices of the many, and the deſigns of a few.

It is certain, however, that there has not been a time, when the prerogative of human reaſon was more freely aſſerted, nor errors and prejudices more ably attacked and expoſed by the beſt writers, than now. But may not the principle of inquiry and detection be carried too far, or at leaſt made too general? And ſhould not a prudent diſcrimination of caſes be attended to?

A prejudice is by no means neceſſarily, though generally thought ſo, an error. On the contrary, it may be a moſt unqueſtioned truth, though it be ſtill a prejudice in thoſe who, without any examination, take it upon truſt, and entertain it by habit.

There are even ſome prejudices, founded upon error, which ought to be connived at, or perhaps encouraged; their effects being more beneficial to ſociety, than their detection can poſſibly be.

Human reaſon, even when improved by knowledge, and undiſturbed by the paſſions, is not an infallible, though it is our beſt, guide: but, unimproved by knowledge, and adulterated by paſſion, it becomes the moſt dangerous one; conſtituting obſtinate wrongheadedneſs, and dignifying, nay almoſt ſanctifying, error.

The bulk of mankind have neither leiſure nor knowledge ſufficient to reaſon right: why then ſhould they be taught to reaſon at all? Will not honeſt inſtinct prompt, and wholſome prejudices guide them, much better than half reaſoning?

The power of the magiſtrate to puniſh bad, and the authority of thoſe of ſuperior rank to ſet good examples, properly exerted, would probably be of more diffuſive advantage to ſociety, than the moſt learned, theological, philoſophical, moral and caſuiſtical diſſertations. As for inſtance.

An honeſt cobler in his ſtall thinks and calls himſelf a good honeſt proteſtant; and, if he lives at the city end of the town, probably goes to his pariſh-church on Sundays. Would it be honeſt, would it be wiſe, to ſay to this cobler, "Friend, you only think yourſelf a member of the church of England; but in reality you are not one, ſince you are only ſo from habit and prejudice, not from examination and reflection. But ſtudy the ableſt controverſial writers of the popiſh and reformed churches; read Bellarmine, Chillingworth, and Stillingfleet; and then you may juſtly call yourſelf, what in truth you are not now, a proteſtant."

Should our mender of ſhoes follow this advice, which I hope he would not, a uſeful cobler would most certainly be loſt, in a uſeleſs polemic, and a ſcurvy logician.

It would be juſt the ſame thing in morals. Our cobler received from his parents that beſt and ſhorteſt of all chriſtian and moral precepts, "Do as you would "be done by:" he adopted it without much examination, and ſcrupulouſly practiſed it in general, though with ſome few exceptions perhaps in his own trade. But ſhould ſome philoſopher, for the advancement of truth and knowledge, aſſure this cobler, "That his honeſty was mere prejudice and habit, be-"cauſe he had never ſufficiently conſidered the rela-"tion and fitneſs of things, nor contemplated the "beauty of virtue; but that, if he would carefully "ſtudy the Characteriſtics, the Moral Philoſopher, "and thirty or forty volumes more upon that ſubject, "he might then, and not till then, juſtly call him-"ſelf an honeſt man;" what would become of the honeſty of the cobler after this uſeful diſcovery, I do not know: but this I very well know, that he ſhould no longer be MY cobler.

I ſhall borrow him in two inſtances more, and then leave him to his honeſt, uſeful, homeſpun prejudices, which half-knowledge and leſs reaſoning will, I hope, never tempt him to lay aſide.

My cobler is alſo a politician. He reads the firſt news-papers he can get, deſirous to be informed of the ſtate of affairs in Europe, and of the ſtreet robberies in London. He has not, I preſume, analyſed the intereſts of the reſpective countries of Europe, nor deeply conſidered thoſe of his own: ſtill leſs is he ſyſtematically informed of the political duties of a

 citizen

citizen and a subject. But his heart and his habit supply those defects. He glows with zeal for the honor and prosperity of Old England; he will fight for it, if there be occasion, and drink to it perhaps a little too often, and too much. However, is it not to be wished that there were in this country six millions of such honest and zealous, though uninformed, citizens?

All these unreflected and unexamined opinions of our cobler, though prejudices in him, are in themselves undoubted and demonstrable truths, and ought therefore to be cherished even in their coarsest dress. But I shall now give an instance of a common prejudice in this country, which is the result of error, and which yet I believe no man in his senses would desire should be exposed or removed.

Our honest cobler is thoroughly convinced, as his forefathers were for many centuries, that one Englishman can beat three Frenchmen; and, in that persuasion, he would by no means decline the trial. Now, though in my own private opinion, deduced from physical principles, I am apt to believe that one Englishman could beat no more than two Frenchmen of equal strength and size with himself, I should however be very unwilling to undeceive him of that useful and sanguine error, which certainly made his countrymen triumph in the fields of Poictiers and Crecy.

But there are prejudices of a very different nature from these; prejudices not only founded on original error, but that gave birth and sanction to the most absurd, extravagant, impious, and immoral customs.

Honor,

Honor, that ſacred name, which ought to mean the ſpirit, the ſupererogation of virtue, is, by cuſtom, profaned, reduced, and ſhrunk to mean only a readineſs to fight a duel upon either a real or an imaginary affront, and not to cheat at play. No vices nor immoralities whatſoever blaſt this faſhionable character, but rather, on the contrary, dignify and adorn it: and what ſhould baniſh a man from all ſociety, recommends him in general to the beſt. He may, with great honor, ſtarve the tradeſmen, who by their induſtry ſupply not only his wants, but his luxury; he may debauch his friend's wife, daughter, or ſiſter; he may, in ſhort, unboundedly gratify every appetite, paſſion, and intereſt, and ſcatter deſolation round him, if he be but ready for ſingle combat, and a ſcrupulous obſerver of all the moral obligations of a gameſter.

Theſe are the prejudices for wit to ridicule, for ſatire to laſh, for the rigor of the law to puniſh, and (which would be the moſt effectual of all) for faſhion to diſcountenance and proſcribe. And theſe ſhall in their turns be the ſubjects of ſome future papers.

XXXVII.

THE WORLD.

SATURDAY, Feb. 27, 1755. N° 113.

THE cuſtom of DUELLING is moſt evidently "the "reſult of the paſſions of the many, and of the "deſigns of a few;" but here the definition ſtops;

ſince, far from being "the ape of reaſon," it prevails in open defiance of it. It is the manifeſt offspring of barbarity and folly, a monſtrous birth, and diſtinguiſhed by the moſt ſhocking and ridiculous marks of both its parents.

I would not willingly give offence to the politer part of my readers, whom I acknowledge to be my beſt cuſtomers, and therefore I will not ſo much as hint at the impiety of this practice; nor will I labor to ſhew how repugnant it is to inſtinct, reaſon, and every moral and ſocial obligation, even to the faſhionable fitneſs of things. Viewed on the criminal ſide, it excites horror; on the abſurd ſide, it is an inexhauſtible fund of ridicule. The guilt has been conſidered and expoſed by abler pens than mine, and indeed ought to be cenſured with more dignity than a fugitive weekly paper can pretend to: I ſhall therefore content myſelf with ridiculing the folly of it.

The antients moſt certainly have had very imperfect notions of HONOR, for they had none of DUELLING. One reads, it is true, of murders committed every now and then among the Greeks and Romans, prompted only by intereſt or revenge, and performed without the leaſt Attic politeneſs, or Roman urbanity. No letters of gentle invitation were ſent to any man to come and have his throat cut the next morning; and we may obſerve that Milo had not the common decency to give Clodius, the moſt profligate of men, the moſt dangerous of citizens, and his own inveterate enemy, an equal chance of deſtroying him.

This delicacy of ſentiment, this refinement of manners, was reſerved for the politer Goths, Viſigoths, Oſtrogoths,

Ostrogoths, Vandals, &c. to introduce, cultivate, and establish. I must confess that they have generally been considered as barbarous nations; and to be sure there are some circumstances which seem to favour that opinion. They made open war upon learning, and gave no quarter even to the monuments of arts and sciences. But then it must be owned, on the other hand, that upon those ruins they established the honorable and noble science of HOMICIDE, dignified, exalted, and ascertained TRUE HONOR, worshiped it as their deity, and sacrificed to it hecatombs of human victims.

In those happy days, HONOR, that is, single combat, was the great and unerring test of civil rights, moral actions, and sound doctrines. It was sanctified by the church, and the churchmen were occasionally allowed the honor and pleasure of it; for we read of many instances of DUELS between men and priests. Nay, it was, without appeal, the infallible test of female chastity. If a princess, or any lady of distinction, was suspected of a little incontinency, some brave champion, who was commonly privy to, or perhaps the author of it, stood forth in her defence, and asserted her innocence with the point of his sword or lance. If, by his activity, skill, strength and courage, he murdered the accuser, the lady was spotless; but, if her champion fell, her guilt was manifest. This heroic gallantry in defence of the fair, I presume, occasioned that association of ideas, otherwise seemingly unrelative to each other, of the BRAVE and the FAIR: for indeed in those days it behoved a lady, who had the least regard for her reputation, to chuse a lover of uncommon activity, strength, and courage. This notion, as I am well assured, still prevails in many reputable families about Covent-garden, where the BRAVE in the kitchen are always within call of the FAIR in the first or second floor.

By this summary method of proceeding, the quibbles, the delays, and the expence of the law were avoided, and the troublesome shackles of the gospel knocked off; HONOR ruling in their stead. To prove the utility and justice of this method, I cannot help mentioning a very extraordinary DUEL between a man of distinction and a dog, in the year 1371, in presence of king Charles the fifth of France. Both the relation and the print of this DUEL are to be found in father Monfaucon.

A gentleman of the court was supposed to have murdered another, who had been missing for some days. This suspicion arose from the mute testimony of the absent person's dog, a large Irish greyhound, who with uncommon rage attacked this supposed murderer wherever he met him. As he was a gentleman, and a man of very nice honor, though by the way he really had murdered the man, he could not bear lying under so dishonorable a suspicion, and therefore applied to the king for leave to justify his innocence by single combat with the said dog. The king, being a great lover of justice, granted his suit, ordered lists to be made ready, appointed the time, and named the weapons. The gentleman was to have an offensive club in his hand, the dog a defensive tub to resort to occasionally. The Irish grey-

hound

hound willingly met this fair inviter at the time and place appointed; for it has always been obſervable of that particular breed, that they have an uncommon alacrity at ſingle combat. They fought, the dog prevailed, and almoſt killed the honorable gentleman, who had then the honor to confeſs his guilt, and of being hanged for it in a few days.

When letters, arts, and ſciences, revived in Europe, the ſcience of HOMICIDE was farther cultivated and improved. If, on the one hand, it loſt a little of the extent of its juridiction; on the other, it acquired great preciſion, clearneſs, and beauty, by the care and pains of the very beſt Italian and Spaniſh authors, who reduced it into a regular body, and delighted the world with their admirable codes, digeſts, pandects, and reports, *della cavallereſca*, in ſome hundreds of volumes. Almoſt all poſſible caſes of HONOR were conſidered and ſtated; two-and-thirty different ſorts of lies were diſtinguiſhed, and the adequate ſatisfaction neceſſary for each, was with great ſolidity and preciſion aſcertained. A kick with a thin ſhoe was declared more injurious to honor, though not ſo painful to the part kicked, than a kick with a thick ſhoe; and, in ſhort, a thouſand other diſcoveries of the like nature, equally beneficial to ſociety, were communicated to the world in thoſe voluminous treaſures of HONOR.

In the preſent degenerate age, the fundamental laws of HONOR are exploded and ridiculed, and ſingle combat thought a very uncertain, and even unjuſt, deciſion of civil property, female chaſtity, and criminal accuſations; but I would humbly aſk, why?

Is not ſingle combat as juſt a deciſion of any other thing whatſoever, as it is of veracity, the caſe to which it is now in a manner confined? I am of opinion that there are more men in the world who lie and fight too, than there are who will lie and not fight; becauſe I believe there are more men in the world who have, than who want, courage. But, if fighting is the teſt of veracity, my readers of condition will, I hope, pardon me, when I ſay, that my future inquiries and reſearches after truth ſhall be altogether confined to the three regiments of guards.

There is one reaſon, indeed, which makes me ſuſpect that a DUEL may not always be the infallible criterion of veracity; and that is, that the combatants very rarely meet upon equal terms. I beg leave to ſtate a caſe, which may very probably, and not even unfrequently happen, and which yet is not provided for, nor even mentioned in the INSTITUTES OF HONOR.

A very lean, ſlender, active young fellow of great HONOR, weighing perhaps not quite twelve ſtone, and who has from his youth taken leſſons of HOMICIDE from a murder-maſter, has, or thinks he has, a point of honor to diſcuſs with an unweildy, fat, middle-aged gentleman, of nice HONOR likewiſe, weighing four-and-twenty ſtone, and who in his youth may not poſſibly have had the ſame commendable application to the noble ſcience of HOMICIDE. The lean gentleman ſends a very civil letter to the fat one, inviting him to come and be killed by him the next morning in Hyde-park. Should the fat gentleman accept this invitation, and waddle to the place appointed, he he goes to inevitable ſlaughter. Now, upon this ſtate of the caſe, might not the fat gentleman, conſiſtent with the rules of HONOR, return the following anſwer to the invitation of the lean one?

"SIR,

"I find by your letter that you do me the juſtice "to believe, that I have the true notions of honor "that become a gentleman; and I hope I ſhall never "give you reaſon to change your opinion. As I "entertain the ſame opinion of you, I muſt ſuppoſe "that you will not deſire that we ſhould meet upon "unequal terms, which muſt be the caſe were we to "meet to-morrow. At preſent I unfortunately weigh "four-and-twenty ſtone, and I gueſs that you do "not exceed twelve. From this circumſtance ſingly, "I am doubly the mark that you are; but, beſides "this, you are active, and I am unweildy. I there-"fore propoſe to you, that, from this day forwards, "we ſeverally endeavour by all poſſible means, you "to fatten, and I to waſte, till we can meet at the "medium of eighteen ſtone. I will loſe no time on "my part, being impatient to prove to you that I "am not quite unworthy of the good opinion which "you are pleaſed to expreſs of,

"SIR,

"Your very humble ſervant.

"*P. S.* I believe it may not be amiſs for us to "communicate to each other, from time to "time, our gradations of increaſe or decreaſe, "towards the deſired medium, in which, I pre-

"ſume,

"sume, two or three pounds more or less, on "either side, ought not to be considered."

This, among many more cases that I could mention, sufficiently proves, not only the expediency, but the necessity, of restoring, revising, and perhaps adding to, the practice, rules, and statutes, of single combat, as it flourished in the fifteenth and sixteenth centuries. I grant that it would probably make the common law useless; but little, trifling, and private interests ought not to stand in the way of great, public, and national advantages.

XXXVIII.

THE WORLD.

THURSDAY, March 6, 1755. N° 114.

THE notion of BIRTH, as it is commonly called and established by custom, is also the manifest result *of the prejudices of the many, and of the designs of a few*. It is the child of Pride and Folly, coupled together by that industrious pandar Self-love. It is surely the strongest instance, and the weakest prop, of human vanity. If it means any thing, it means a long lineal descent from a founder, whose industry or good fortune, whose merit, or perhaps whose guilt, has enabled his posterity to live useless to society, and to transmit to theirs their pride and their patrimony. However, this extravagant notion,

tion, this chimerical advantage, the effect of blind chance, where prudence and option cannot even pretend to have the least share, is that FLY which, by a kind of Egyptian superstition, custom all over Europe has deified, and at whose tawdry shrine good sense, good manners, and good nature, are daily sacrificed.

The vulgar distinction between people of BIRTH and people of NO BIRTH will probably puzzle the critics and antiquaries of the thirtieth or fortieth centuries, when, in their judicious or laborious researches into the customs and manners of these present times, they shall have reason to suppose, that in the sixteenth, seventeenth, and eighteenth centuries, the island of Great Britain was inhabited by two sorts of people, some BORN, but the much greater number UNBORN. The fact will appear so *incredible*, that it will certainly be *believed*; the only difficulty will be how to account for it; and that, as it commonly does, will engross the attention of the learned. The case of Cadmus's men will doubtless be urged as a case in point, to prove the possibility of the thing; and the truth of it will be confirmed by the records of the university of Oxford, where it will appear that an unborn person, called for that reason *Terræ Filius*, annually entertained that university with an oration in the theatre.

I therefore take with pleasure this opportunity of explaining and clearing up this difficulty to my remotest successors in the republic of letters, by giving them the true meaning of the several expressions of GREAT BIRTH, NOBLE BIRTH, and NO BIRTH AT ALL.

Great

Great and illuſtrious BIRTH is aſcertained and authenticated by a pedigree carefully preſerved in the family, which takes at leaſt an hour's time to unroll, and, when unrolled, diſcloſes twenty intermarriages of valiant and puiſſant Geoffreys and Hildebrands, with as many chaſte and pious Blaunches and Mauds, before the Conqueſt, not without here and there a daſh of the Plantagenets. But, if unfortunately the inſolent worms ſhould have devoured the pedigree as well as the perſons of the illuſtrious family, that defect may be ſupplied by the authentic records of the heralds office, that ineſtimable repoſitory of good ſenſe and uſeful knowledge. If this GREAT BIRTH is graced with a peerage, ſo much the better, but, if not, it is no great matter; for, being ſo ſolid a good in itſelf, it wants no borrowed advantages, and is unqueſtionably the moſt pleaſing ſentiment, that a truly generous mind is capable of feeling.

NOBLE BIRTH implies only a peerage in the family. Anceſtors are by no means neceſſary for this kind of birth; the patent is the midwife of it, and the very firſt deſcent is noble. The family arms, however modern, are dignified by the coronet and mantle; but the family livery is ſometimes, for very good reaſons, laid aſide.

BIRTH, ſingly, and without an epithet, extends, I cannot poſſibly ſay how far, but negatively it ſtops where uſeful arts and induſtry begin. Merchants, tradeſmen, yeomen, farmers, and ploughmen, are not BORN, or at leaſt in ſo mean a way as not to deſerve that name; and it is perhaps for that reaſon that their mothers are ſaid to be *delivered*, rather than

brought

brought to bed of them. But baronets, knights, and esquires, have the honor of being BORN.

I must confess that, before I got the key to this fashionable language, I was a good deal puzzled myself with the distinction between BIRTH and NO BIRTH; and, having no other guide than my own weak reason, I mistook the matter most grossly. I foolishly imagined that *well born*, meant born with a sound mind in a sound body; a healthy, strong constitution, joined to a good heart and a good understanding. But I never suspected that it could possibly mean the shrivelled, tasteless fruit of an old genealogical tree. I communicated my doubts, and applied for information, to my late worthy and curious friend the celebrated Mrs. Kennon, whose valuable collection of fossils and minerals, lately sold, sufficiently proves her skill and researches in the most recondite parts of nature. She, with that frankness and humanity which were natural to her, assured me that it was all vulgar error, in which however the nobility and gentry prided themselves, but that in truth she had never observed the children of the quality to be wholsomer and stronger than others, but rather the contrary; which difference she imputed to certain causes, which I shall not here specify. This natural, and, I dare say, to the best of her observation, true, account confirmed me in my former philosophical error. But still, not thoroughly satisfied with it, and thinking that there must be something more in what was so universally valued, I determined to get some farther information, by addressing myself to a person of vast, immense, prodigious BIRTH, and descended *atavis*

regibus,

regibus, with whom I have the honor of being acquainted. As he expatiates willingly upon that ſubject, it was very eaſy for me to ſet him a going upon it, inſomuch, that, upon ſome few doubts which I humbly ſuggeſted to him, he ſpoke to me in the following manner:

"I believe, Mr. Fitz-Adam, you are not, for nobody is, ignorant of the antiquity of my family, "which by authentic records I can trace to king Alfred, ſome of whoſe blood runs at this moment in "my veins, and I will not conceal from you that I "find infinite inward comfort and ſatisfaction in that "reflection. Let people of NO BIRTH laugh as much "as they pleaſe at theſe notions; they are not imaginary; they are real; they are ſolid; and whoever "is WELL BORN, is glad that he is ſo. A merchant, "a tradeſman, a yeoman, a farmer, and ſuch ſort of "people, may perhaps have common honeſty and "vulgar virtues; but, take my word for it, the more "refined and generous ſentiments of honor, courage, "and magnanimity, can only flow in antient and "noble blood. What ſhall animate a tradeſman or "mean-born man to any great and heroic virtues? "Shall it be the examples of his anceſtors? He has "none. Or ſhall it be that impure blood that rather "ſtagnates than circulates in his veins? No; ANTIENT BIRTH and NOBLE BLOOD are the only true "ſources of great virtues. This truth appears even "among brutes, who, we obſerve, never degenerate, "except in caſes of miſ-alliances with their inferiors. "Are not the pedigrees of horſes, cocks, &c. carefully preſerved, as the never-failing proofs of their

"ſwiftneſs

" swiftness and courage? I repeat it again, BIRTH is " an inestimable advantage, not to be adequately un- " derstood but by those who have it."

My friend was going on, and, to say the truth, growing dull; when I took the liberty of interrupting him, by acknowledging that the cogency of his arguments, and the self-evidence of his facts, had entirely removed all my doubts, and convinced me of the unspeakable advantages of ILLUSTRIOUS BIRTH, and unfortunately I added, that my own vanity was greatly flattered by it, in consequence of my being lineally descended from the first man. Upon this my friend looked grave, and seemed rather displeased; whether from a suspicion that I was jesting, or upon an apprehension that I meant to *out-descend* him, I cannot determine; for he contented himself with saying, " That is not a necessary consequence neither, Mr. " Fitz-Adam, since I have read somewhere or other " of pre-adamites, which opinion did not seem to " me an absurd one."

Here I took my leave of him, and went home full of reflections upon the astonishing power of self-love, that can extract comfort and pleasure from such groundless, absurd, and extravagant prejudices. In all other respects my friend is neither a fool nor a madman, and can talk very rationally upon any rational subject. But such is the inconsistency both of the human mind and the human heart, that one must not form a general judgement of either, from one glaring error, or one shining excellence.

XXXIX.

THE WORLD.

THURSDAY, April 17, 1755. N° 120.

MOST people complain of fortune, few of nature; and the kinder they think the latter has been to them, the more they murmur at what they call the injuſtice of the former.

Why have not I the riches, the rank, the power, of ſuch and ſuch, is the common expoſtulation with fortune: but why have not I the merit, the talents, the wit, or the beauty, of ſuch and ſuch others, is a reproach rarely or never made to nature.

The truth is, that nature, ſeldom profuſe, and ſeldom niggardly, has diſtributed her gifts more equally than ſhe is generally ſuppoſed to have done. Education and ſituation make the great difference. Culture improves, and occaſions elicit, natural talents. I make no doubt but that there are potentially, if I may uſe that pedantic word, many Bacons, Lockes, Newtons, Cæſars, Cromwells, and Marlboroughs, at the plough-tail, behind counters, and, perhaps, even among the nobility; but the ſoil muſt be cultivated, and the ſeaſons favourable, for the fruit to have all its ſpirit and flavor.

If ſometimes our common parent has been a little partial, and not kept the ſcales quite even; if one preponderates too much, we throw into the lighter a due counterpoiſe of vanity, which never fails to ſet all right. Hence it happens, that hardly any one man

would,

would, without reserve, and in every particular, change with any other.

Though all are thus satisfied with the dispensations of nature, how few listen to her voice! how few follow her as a guide! In vain she points out to us the plain and direct way to truth; vanity, fancy, affectation, and fashion, assume her shape, and wind us through fairy-ground to folly and error.

These deviations from nature are often attended by serious consequences, and always by ridiculous ones; for there is nothing truer than the trite observation, "that people are never ridiculous for being what "they really are, but for affecting what they really "are not." Affectation is the only source, and at the same time the only justifiable object, of ridicule. No man whatsoever, be his pretensions what they will, has a natural right to be ridiculous: it is an acquired right, and not to be acquired without some industry; which perhaps is the reason why so many people are so jealous and tenacious of it. Even some people's VICES are not their own, but affected and adopted, though at the same time unenjoyed, in hopes of shining in those fashionable societies, where the reputation of certain vices gives lustre. In these cases, the execution is commonly as awkward, as the design is absurd; and the ridicule equals the guilt.

This calls to my mind a thing, that really happened not many years ago. A young fellow of some rank and fortune, just let loose from the university, resolved, in order to make a figure in the world, to assume the shining character of, what he called, a rake. By way of learning the rudiments of his intended profeſſion, he frequented the theatres, where he was often drunk, and always noiſy. Being one night at the repreſentation of that moſt abſurd play, the *Libertine deſtroyed*, he was ſo charmed with the profligacy of the hero of the piece, that, to the edification of the audience, he ſwore many oaths that he would be the libertine *deſtroyed*. A diſcreet friend of his, who ſat by him, kindly repreſented to him, that to be the *libertine* was a laudable deſign, which he greatly approved of; but that to be the libertine *deſtroyed* ſeemed to him an unneceſſary part of his plan, and rather raſh. He perſiſted, however, in his firſt reſolution, and inſiſted upon being the libertine, and *deſtroyed*. Probably he was ſo; at leaſt the preſumption is in his favour. There are, I am perſuaded, ſo many caſes of this nature, that for my own part I would deſire no greater ſtep towards the reformation of manners for the next twenty years, than that our people ſhould have no vices but *their own*.

The blockhead who affects wiſdom, becauſe nature has given him dulneſs, becomes ridiculous only by his adopted character; whereas he might have ſtagnated unobſerved in his native mud, or perhaps have engroſſed deeds, collected ſhells, and ſtudied heraldry, or logic, with ſome ſucceſs.

The ſhining coxcomb aims at all, and decides finally upon every thing, becauſe nature has given him pertneſs. The degree of parts and animal ſpirits, neceſſary to conſtitute that character, if properly applied, might have made him uſeful in many parts of life; but his affectation and preſumption make him uſeleſs in moſt, and ridiculous in all.

The

The ſeptuagenary fine gentleman might probably, from his long experience and knowledge of the world, be eſteemed and reſpected in the ſeveral relations of domeſtic life, which, at his age, nature points out to him: he will moſt ridiculouſly ſpin out the rotten thread of his former gallantries. He dreſſes, languiſhes, ogles, as he did at five-and-twenty; and modeſtly intimates that he is not without a *bonne fortune*, which *bonne fortune* at laſt appears to be the proſtitute he had long kept, not to himſelf, whom he marries and owns, becauſe *the poor girl was ſo fond of him, and ſo deſirous to be made an honeſt woman.*

The ſexagenary widow remembers that ſhe was handſome, but forgets that it was thirty years ago, and thinks herſelf ſo, or at leaſt very *likeable*, ſtill. The pardonable affectations of her youth and beauty unpardonably continue, increaſe even with her years, and are doubly exerted in hopes of concealing the number. All the gaudy glittering parts of dreſs, which rather degraded than adorned her beauty in its bloom, now expoſe to the higheſt and juſteſt ridicule her ſhrivelled or her overgrown carcaſe. She totters or ſweats under the load of her jewels, embroideries, and brocades, which, like ſo many Egyptian hieroglyphics, ſerve only to authenticate the venerable antiquity of her auguſt mummy. Her eyes dimly twinkle tenderneſs, or leer deſire: their language, however inelegant, is intelligible, and the half-pay captain underſtands it. He addreſſes his vows to her vanity, which aſſures her they are ſincere. She pities him, and prefers him to credit, decency, and every ſocial

 duty.

duty. He tenderly prefers her, though not without ſome heſitation, to a jail.

Self-love, kept within due bounds, is a natural and uſeful ſentiment. It is, in truth, ſocial love too, as Mr. Pope has very juſtly obſerved: it is the ſpring of many good actions, and of no ridiculous ones. But ſelf-flattery is only the ape or caricatura of ſelf-love, and reſembles it no more than to heighten the ridicule. Like other flattery, it is the moſt profuſely beſtowed and greedily ſwallowed, where it is the leaſt deſerved. I will conclude this ſubject with the ſubſtance of a fable of the ingenious monſieur De La Motte, which ſeems not unapplicable to it.

Jupiter made a lottery in heaven, in which mortals, as well as gods, were allowed to have tickets. The prize was WISDOM; and Minerva got it. The mortals murmured, and accuſed the gods of foul play. Jupiter, to wipe off this aſperſion, declared another lottery, for mortals ſingly, and excluſively of the gods. The prize was FOLLY. They got it, and ſhared it among themſelves. All were ſatisfied. The loſs of WISDOM was neither regretted nor remembered; FOLLY ſupplied its place, and thoſe, who had the largeſt ſhare of it, thought themſelves the wiſeſt.

XL.

XL.

THE WORLD.

THURSDAY, Oct. 16, 1755. N° 146.

I HAVE so tender a regard for my fair country-women, that I most heartily congratulate them upon the approaching meeting of the parliament, which I consider, and I believe they do so too, as the general gaol-delivery of the several counties of the united kingdom.

That beautiful part of our species once engrossed my cares; they still share them: I have been exceedingly affected all the summer with the thoughts of their captivity, and have felt a sympathetic grief for them.

In truth, what can be more moving, than to imagine a fine woman, of the highest rank and fashion, torn from all the elegant and refined pleasures of the metropolis; hurried by a merciless husband into country captivity, and there exposed to the incursions of the neighbouring knights, squires, and parsons, their wives, sons, daughters, dogs, and horses? The metropolis was at once the seat of her empire, and the theatre of her joys. Exiled from thence, how great the fall! how dreadful the prison! Methinks I see her sitting in her dressing-room at the mansion-seat, sublimely sullen, like a dethroned eastern monarch. Some few books, scattered up and down, seem to imply that she finds no consolation in any. The unopened knotting-bag speaks her painful leisure.

Insensible to the proffered endearments of her tender infants, they are sent away for being so abominably noisy. Her dress is even neglected, and her complexion laid by. I am not ashamed to own my weakness, if it be one; for I confess that this image struck me so strongly, dwelt upon my mind so long, that it drew tears from my eyes.

The prorogation of the parliament last spring was the fatal fore-runner of this summer captivity. I was well aware of it, and had some thoughts of preparing a short treatise of consolation, which I would have presented to my fair countrywomen, in two or three weekly papers, to have accompanied them in their exile: but I must own that I found the attempt greatly above my strength; and an inadequate consolation only redoubles the grief, by reviving in the mind the cause of it. Thus at a loss, I searched, as every modest modern should do, the antients, in order to say in English whatever they had said in Latin or Greek upon the like occasion; but, far from finding any case in point, I could not find one in any degree like it. I particularly consulted Cicero, upon that exile which he bore so very indifferently himself; but, to my great surprize, could not meet with one single word of consolation, addressed or adapted to the fair and tender part of his species. To say the truth, that philosopher seems to have had either a contempt for, or an aversion to, the fair sex; for it is very observable, that, even in his essay upon old age, there is not one single period addressed directly and exclusively to them; whereas I humbly presume that an old woman wants at least as much, if not more, comfort,

comfort, than an old man. Far be it from me to offer them that refined ſtoical argument to prove that exile can be no misfortune, becauſe the exiled perſons can always carry their virtue along with them, if they pleaſe.

However, though I could adminiſter no adequate comfort to my fair fellow-ſubjects under their country captivity, my tender concern for them prompts me to offer them ſome advice upon their approaching liberty.

As there muſt have been, during this ſuſpenſion, I will not ſay only of pleaſure, but, in a manner, of exiſtence, a conſiderable ſaving in the article of pin-money, I earneſtly recommend to them, immediately upon their coming to town, to apply that ſinking fund to the diſcharge of debts already incurred, and not divert it to the current ſervice of the enſuing year. I would not be miſunderſtood; I mean only the payment of debts of honor, contracted at commerce, bragg, or faro; as they are apt to hang heavy upon the minds of women of ſentiment, and even to affect their countenances upon the approach of a creditor. As for ſhop-debts, to mercers, milliners, jewellers, French pedlars, and ſuch-like, it is no great matter whether they are paid or not; ſomehow or other thoſe people will ſhift for themſelves, or, at worſt, fall ultimately upon the huſband.

I will alſo adviſe thoſe fine women, who, by an unfortunate concurrence of odious circumſtances, have been obliged to begin an acquaintance with their huſbands and children in the country, not to break it off intirely in town, but, on the contrary, to allow a few minutes every day to the keeping it up; ſince a time may come, when perhaps they may like their company rather better than none at all.

As my fair fellow-ſubjects were always famous for their public ſpirit and love of their country, I hope they will, upon the preſent emergency of the war with France, diſtinguiſh themſelves by unequivocal proofs of patriotiſm. I flatter myſelf that they will, at their firſt appearance in town, publicly renounce thoſe French faſhions, which of late years have brought their principles, both with regard to religion and government, a little in queſtion. And therefore I exhort them to diſband their curls, comb their heads, wear white linen, and clean pocket-handkerchiefs, in open defiance of all the power of France. But, above all, I inſiſt upon their laying aſide that ſhameful piratical practice of hoiſting falſe colors upon their top gallant, in the miſtaken notion of captivating and enſlaving their countrymen. This they may the more eaſily do at firſt, ſince it is to be preſumed that, during their retirement, their faces have enjoyed uninterrupted reſt. Mercury and vermillion have made no depredation theſe ſix months; good air and good hours may perhaps have reſtored, to a certain degree at leaſt, their natural carnation: but at worſt, I will venture to aſſure them, that ſuch of their lovers, who may know them again in that ſtate of native artleſs beauty, will rejoice to find the communication opened again, and all the barriers of plaſter and ſtucco removed. Be it known to them, that there is not a man in England, who does not infinitely prefer the browneſt natural, to the whiteſt

artificial,

artificial, ſkin; and I have received numberleſs letters from men of the firſt faſhion, not only requeſting, but requiring me to proclaim this truth, with leave to publiſh their names, which however I declined: but, if I thought it could be of any uſe, I could eaſily preſent them with a round robin to that effect, of above a thouſand of the moſt reſpectable names. One of my correſpondents, a member of the Royal Society, illuſtrates his indignation at glazed faces, by an apt and well-known phyſical experiment. The ſhining glaſs tube, ſays he, when warmed by friction, attracts a feather, probably a white one, to cloſe contact; but the ſame feather, from the moment that it is taken off the tube, flies it with more velocity than it approached it with before. I make no application; but avert the omen, my dear countrywomen!

Another, who ſeems to have ſome knowledge of chemiſtry, has ſent me a receipt for a moſt excellent waſh, which he deſires me to publiſh, by way of *ſuccedaneum* to the various greazy, glutinous, and pernicious applications ſo much uſed of late. It is as follows.

Take of fair clear water *quantum ſufficit*; put it into a clean earthen or china baſon, then take a clean linen cloth, dip it in that water, and apply it to the face night and morning, or oftener, as occaſion may require.

I own, the ſimplicity and purity of this admirable lotion recommend it greatly to me, and engage me to recommend it to my fair countrywomen. It is free from all the inconveniencies and naſtineſs of all other preparations

preparations of art whatsoever. It does not stink, as all others do; it does not corrode the skin, as all others do; it does not destroy the eyes, nor rot the teeth, as all others do; and it does not communicate itself by collision, nor betray the transactions of a *tête à tête*, as most others do.

Having thus paid my tribute of grief to my lovely countrywomen during their captivity, and my tribute of congratulations upon their approaching liberty, I heartily wish them a good journey to London. May they soon enter, in joyful triumph, that metropolis, which six months ago they quitted with tears!

XLI.

THE WORLD.

THURSDAY *, Oct. 30, 1755. N° 148.

CIVILITY and GOOD-BREEDING are generally thought, and often used, as synonymous terms, but are by no means so.

* Lord Chesterfield, being at Bath, shewed one of his last Worlds to his friend general Irwine, who dined with him almost every day. The general, in the course of the conversation, mentioned good-breeding, as distinguished from mere civility, as a subject that deserved to be treated by him. His lordship at first declined it; but on his friend's insisting, and urging the singular propriety of its being undertaken by a man who was so perfect a master of the thing, he suddenly called for pen and ink, and wrote this excellent piece off hand, as he did all the others, without any rasure or interlineation. The paper, ever after, went by the name of general Irwine's paper.

GOOD-

Good-breeding neceſſarily implies civility; but civility does not reciprocally imply good-breeding. The former has its intrinſic weight and value, which the latter always adorns, and often doubles by its workmanſhip.

To ſacrifice one's own ſelf-love to other people's is a ſhort, but, I believe, a true definition of civility: to do it with eaſe, propriety, and grace, is good-breeding. The one is the reſult of good-nature; the other of good-ſenſe, joined to experience, obſervation, and attention.

A ploughman will be civil, if he is good-natured, but cannot be well-bred. A courtier will be well-bred, though perhaps without good-nature, if he has but good-ſenſe.

Flattery is the diſgrace of good-breeding, as brutality often is of truth and ſincerity. Good-breeding is the middle point between thoſe two odious extremes.

Ceremony is the ſuperſtition of good breeding, as well as of religion; but yet, being an out-work to both, ſhould not be abſolutely demoliſhed. It is always, to a certain degree, to be complied with, though deſpiſed by thoſe who think, becauſe admired and reſpected by thoſe who do not.

The moſt perfect degree of good-breeding, as I have already hinted, is only to be acquired by great knowledge of the world, and keeping the beſt company. It is not the object of mere ſpeculation, and cannot be exactly defined, as it conſiſts in a fitneſs, a propriety of words, actions, and even looks, adapted to the infinite variety and combinations of perſons,

places,

places, and things. It is a mode, not a ſubſtance: for what is GOOD-BREEDING at St. James's would paſs for foppery or banter in a remote village; and the home-ſpun CIVILITY of that village would be conſidered as brutality at court.

A cloyſtered pedant may form true notions of CIVILITY; but if, amidſt the cobwebs of his cell, he pretends to ſpin a ſpeculative ſyſtem of GOOD-BREEDING, he will not be leſs abſurd than his predeceſſor, who judiciouſly undertook to inſtruct Hannibal in the art of war. The moſt ridiculous and moſt awkward of men are, therefore, the ſpeculatively well-bred monks of all religions and all profeſſions.

GOOD-BREEDING, like charity, not only covers a multitude of faults, but, to a certain degree, ſupplies the want of ſome virtues. In the common intercourſe of life, it acts good-nature, and often does what good-nature will not always do; it keeps both wits and fools within thoſe bounds of decency, which the former are too apt to tranſgreſs, and which the latter never know.

Courts are unqueſtionably the ſeats of GOOD-BREEDING, and muſt neceſſarily be ſo; otherwiſe they would be the ſeats of violence and deſolation. There all the paſſions are in their higheſt ſtate of fermentation. All purſue what but few can obtain, and many ſeek what but one can enjoy. GOOD-BREEDING alone reſtrains their exceſſes. There, if enemies did not embrace, they would ſtab. There, ſmiles are often put on, to conceal tears. There, mutual ſervices are profeſſed, while mutual injuries are intended; and there, the guile of the ſerpent ſimulates the gentleneſs of the dove: all this, it is true, at the expence of ſincerity, but, upon the whole, to the advantage of ſocial intercourſe in general.

I would not be miſapprehended, and ſuppoſed to recommend GOOD-BREEDING, thus prophaned and proſtituted to the purpoſes of guilt and perfidy; but I think I may juſtly infer from it, to what a degree the accompliſhment of GOOD-BREEDING muſt adorn and enforce virtue and truth, when it can thus ſoften the outrages and deformity of vice and falſhood.

I am ſorry to be obliged to confeſs that my native country is not perhaps the ſeat of the moſt perfect GOOD-BREEDING, though I really believe that it yields to none in hearty and ſincere CIVILITY, as far as CIVILITY is, and to a certain degree it is, an inferior moral duty of doing as one would be done by. If France exceeds us in that particular, the incomparable author of *L'Eſprit des Loix* accounts for it very impartially, and I believe very truly. "If my "countrymen," ſays he, "are the beſt-bred people "in the world, it is only becauſe they are the vain- "eſt." It is certain that their GOOD-BREEDING and attentions, by flattering the vanity and ſelf-love of others, repay their own with intereſt. It is a general commerce, uſually carried on by a barter of attentions, and often without one grain of ſolid merit, by way of medium to make up the balance.

It were to be wiſhed that GOOD-BREEDING were in general thought a more eſſential part of the education of our youth, eſpecially of diſtinction, than at preſent it ſeems to be. It might even be ſubſtituted in the room of ſome academical ſtudies, that take up

a great

a great deal of time to very little purpose; or at least, it might usefully share some of those many hours, that are so frequently employed upon a coach-box, or in stables. Surely those who, by their rank and fortune, are called to adorn courts, ought at least not to disgrace them by their manners.

But I observe with concern, that it is the fashion for our youth of both sexes to brand GOOD-BREEDING with the name of ceremony and formality. As such, they ridicule and explode it, and adopt in its stead an offensive carelessness and inattention, to the diminution, I will venture to say, even of their own pleasures, if they know what true pleasures are.

Love and friendship necessarily produce, and justly authorize, familiarity; but then GOOD BREEDING must mark out its bounds, and say, thus far shalt thou go, and no farther; for I have known many a passion and many a friendship degraded, weakened, and at last, if I may use the expression, wholly slatterned away by an unguarded and illiberal familiarity. Nor is GOOD-BREEDING less the ornament and cement of common social life: it connects, it endears, and, at the same time that it indulges the just liberty, restrains that indecent licentiousness of conversation, which alienates and provokes. Great talents make a man famous, great merit makes him respected, and great learning makes him esteemed; but GOOD-BREEDING alone can make him be loved.

I recommend it in a more particular manner to my countrywomen, as the greatest ornament to such of them as have beauty, and the safest refuge for those who have not. It facilitates the victories, decorates the

the triumphs, and ſecures the conqueſts of beauty, or in ſome degree atones for the want of it. It almoſt deifies a fine woman, and procures reſpect at leaſt to thoſe who have not charms enough to be admired.

Upon the whole, though GOOD-BREEDING cannot, ſtrictly ſpeaking, be called a virtue, yet it is productive of ſo many good effects, that, in my opinion, it may juſtly be reckoned more than a mere accompliſhment.

XLII.

THE WORLD.

THURSDAY, NOV. 20, 1755. Nº 151.

I WAS lately ſubpœnaed, by a card, to a general aſſembly at lady Townly's, where I went ſo awkwardly early, that I found nobody but the five or ſix people who had dined there, and who, for want of hands enough for play, were reduced to the cruel neceſſity of converſing, till ſomething better ſhould offer. Lady Townly obſerved with concern and impatience, "that people of faſhion now came intolera-
" bly late, and in a glut at once, which laid the lady
" of the houſe under great difficulties, to make the
" parties properly." " That, no doubt," ſaid Manly,
" is to be lamented; and the more ſo, as it ſeems to
" give your ladyſhip ſome concern: but in the mean
" time, for want of ſomething better to do, I ſhould
" be glad to know the true meaning of a term that

" you have juſt made uſe of, *people of faſhion*. I con-
" feſs, I have never yet had a preciſe and clear idea
" of it; and I am ſure I cannot apply more properly
" for information, than to this company, which is
" moſt unqueſtionably compoſed of *people of faſhion*,
" whatever *people of faſhion* may be. I therefore beg
" to know the meaning of that term: what are they,
" who are they, and what conſtitutes, I had almoſt
" ſaid, anoints them, *people of faſhion?*"

Theſe queſtions, inſtead of receiving immediate anſwers, occaſioned a general ſilence of above a minute, which perhaps was the reſult of the whole company's having diſcovered, for the firſt time, that they had long and often made uſe of a term which they had never underſtood: for a little reflection frequently produces thoſe diſcoveries. Belinda firſt broke this ſilence, by ſaying, " One well knows who " are meant by *people of faſhion*, though one does " not juſt know how to deſcribe them: they are " thoſe that one generally lives with; they are peo-" ple of a certain ſort."—" They certainly are ſo," interrupted Manly; " but the point is of what ſort? " If you mean by people of a certain ſort, yourſelf, " which is commonly the meaning of thoſe who " make uſe of that expreſſion, you are indiſputably " in the right, as you have all the qualifications that " can, or, at leaſt, ought to conſtitute and adorn a " *woman of faſhion*. But, pray, muſt all *women of* " *faſhion* have all your accompliſhments? If ſo, the " myriads of them which I had imagined from what " I heard every day, and every where, will dwindle " into a handful." " Without having thoſe ac-

" compliſh-

" complishments which you so partially allow me," answered Belinda, " I still pretend to be a *woman of* " *fashion*; a character, which I cannot think requires " an uncommon share of talents or merit." " That " is the very point," replied Manly, " which I want " to come at; and therefore give me leave to question " you a little more particularly. You have some " advantages, which even your modesty will not al- " low you to disclaim, such as your birth and for- " tune: do they constitute you a *woman of fashion?*" As Belinda was going to answer, Bellair pertly interposed, and said, " Neither, to be sure, Mr. Manly: " if birth constituted *fashion*, we must look for it in " that inestimable treasure of useful knowledge, the " peerage of England; or, if wealth, we should find " the very best at the Bank, and at Garraway's." " Well then, Bellair," said Manly, " since you have " taken upon you to be Belinda's sponsor, let me " ask you two or three questions, which you can " more properly answer than she could. Is it her " beauty?" " By no means neither," replied Bellair; " for, at that rate, there might perhaps be a " *woman of fashion* with a gold chain about her neck " in the city, or, with a fat amber necklace in the " country: prodigies, as yet unheard-of and unseen." " Is it then her wit and good-breeding?" continued Manly. " Each contributes," answered Bellair; " but both would not be sufficient, without a certain " *je ne sçais quoi*, a something or other that I feel " better than I can explain."

Here Dorimant, who had sat all this time silent, but looked mischievous, said, " I could say some-

 " thing."

"thing."—"Ay, and ſomething very impertinent, "according to cuſtom," anſwered Belinda; "ſo "hold your tongue, I charge you." "You are ſin- "gularly charitable, Belinda," replied Dorimant, "in "being ſo ſure that I was going to be impertinent, "only becauſe I was going to ſpeak. Why this ſuſ- "picion of me?" "Why! becauſe I know you to be "an odious, abominable creature, upon all ſubjects "of this kind." This amicable quarrel was put an end to by Harriet, who, on a ſudden, and with her uſual vivacity, cried out, "I am ſure I have it now, "and can tell you exactly "what *people of faſhion* "are: they are juſt the reverſe of your *odd people.*" "Very poſſible, madam," anſwered Manly, "and "therefore I could wiſh that you would give your- "ſelf the trouble of defining *odd people*; and ſo, by "the rule of contraries, help us to a true notion of "*people of faſhion.*" "Ay, that I can very eaſily "do," ſaid Harriet. "In the firſt place, your *odd* "*people* are thoſe that one never lets in, unleſs one is "at home to the whole town." "A little more par- "ticular, dear Harriet," interrupted Manly. "So I "will," ſaid Harriet, "for I hate them all. There "are ſeveral ſorts of them. Your prudes, for in- "ſtance, who reſpect and value themſelves upon the "unblemiſhed purity of their characters; who rail at "the indecency of the times, cenſure the moſt in- "nocent freedoms, and ſuſpect the Lord knows "what, if they do but obſerve a cloſe and familiar "whiſper between a man and a woman, in a remote "corner of the room. There are, beſides, a ſober, "formal, ſort of married women, inſipid creatures, "who lead domeftic lives, and who can be merry, "as they think, at home, with their own and their "hufband's relations, particularly at Chriftmas. Like "turtles, they are true and tender to their lawful "mates, and breed like rabbets, to beggar and per- "petuate their families. Thefe are very *odd women*, "to be fure; but deliver me from your fevere and "auguft dowagers, who are the fcourges of *people of* "*fashion*, by infefting all public places, in order to "make their fpiteful remarks. One meets them "every where, and they feem to have the fecret of "multiplying themfelves into ten different places at "once. Their poor horfes, like thofe of the fun, go "round the world every day, baiting only at eleven "in the morning, and fix in the evening, at their "parifh-churches. They fpeak as movingly of their "*poor late lords*, as if they had ever cared for one "another; and, to do them honor, repeat fome of "the many filly things they ufed to fay. Laftly, "there are your maiden ladies of riper years, or- "phans of diftinction, who live together by twos and "threes, who club their ftocks for a neat little "houfe, a light-bodied coach, and a foot-boy—" "And," added Bellair, "quarrel every day about "the dividend." "True," faid Harriet, "they are "not the fweeteft-tempered creatures in the world; "but, after all, one muft forgive them fome malig- "nity, in confideration of their difappointments. "Well, have I now defcribed *odd people* to your fa- "tisfaction?" "Admirably," anfwered Manly; "and "fo well, that one can, to a great degree at leaft, "judge of their antipodes, *the people of fashion*. But

"ſtill there ſeems ſomething wanting; for the pre-
"ſent account, by the rule of contraries, ſtands only
"thus: that *women of faſhion* muſt not care for their
"huſbands, muſt not go to church, and muſt not
"have unblemiſhed, or at leaſt unſuſpected, reputa-
"tions. Now, though all theſe are very commend-
"able qualifications, it muſt be owned, they are
"but negative ones, and conſequently there muſt be
"ſome poſitive ones neceſſary to compleat ſo amia-
"ble a character." "I was going to add," interrupted Harriet, "which, by the way, was more
"than I engaged for, that *people of faſhion* were pro-
"perly thoſe who ſet the faſhions, and who gave the
"tone of dreſs, language, manners, and pleaſures,
"to the town." "I admit it," ſaid Manly; "but
"what I want ſtill to know is, who gave them power,
"or did they uſurp it? for, by the nature of that
"power, it does not ſeem to me to admit of a ſuc-
"ceſſion by hereditary and divine right." "Were
"I allowed to ſpeak," ſaid Dorimant, "perhaps I
"could both ſhorten and clear up this caſe. But I
"dare not, unleſs Belinda, to whom I profeſs im-
"plicit obedience, gives me leave." "Even let
"him ſpeak, Belinda," ſaid Harriet; "I know he
"will abuſe us, but we are uſed to him." "Well,
"ſay your ſay then," ſaid Belinda. "See what an
"impertinent ſneer he has already." Upon this,
Dorimant, addreſſing himſelf more particularly to
Belinda, and ſmiling, ſaid,

"Then think
"That he, who thus commanded dares to ſpeak,
"Unleſs commanded, would have died in ſilence."

"O, your

"O, your ſervant, ſir, ſaid Belinda;" that fit of hu-"mility will, I am ſure, not laſt long; but how-"ever go on." "I will, to anſwer Manly's queſ-"tion," ſaid Dorimant, "which, by the way, has "ſomething the air of a catechiſm. Who made "theſe *people of faſhion?* I give this ſhort and plain "anſwer; they made one another. The men, by "their attentions and credit, make the *women of* "*faſhion*; and the women, by either their ſuppoſed "or real favours, make the *men* ſuch. They are "mutually neceſſary to each other." "Impertinent "enough of all conſcience," ſaid Belinda. "So, "without the aſſiſtance of you faſhionable men, what "ſhould we poor women be?" "Why faith," re-plied Dorimant, "but *odd women*, I doubt; as we "ſhould be but odd fellows without your friendly "aid to faſhion us. In one word, a frequent and "reciprocal colliſion of the two ſexes is abſolutely "neceſſary, to give one that high poliſh which is "properly called *faſhion*." "Mr. Dorimant has, I "own," ſaid Manly, "opened new and important "matter; and my ſcattered and confuſed notions "ſeem now to take ſome form, and tend to a point. "But, as examples always beſt clear up abſtruſe mat-"ters, let us now propoſe ſome examples of both "ſorts, and take the opinions of the company upon "them. For inſtance, I will offer one to your con-"ſideration. Is Berynthia a *woman of faſhion* or "not?" The whole company readily, and almoſt at once, anſwered, "Doubtleſs ſhe is." "That may "be," ſaid Manly, "but why? For ſhe has neither "birth nor fortune, and but ſmall remains of beauty."

" All that is true, I confefs," faid Belinda; " but " fhe is well-dreft, well-bred, good-humoured, and " always ready to go with one any where." " Might " I prefume," faid Dorimant, " to add a title, and " perhaps the beft, to her claims of *fashion*, I fhould " fay that fhe was of Belville's creation, who is the " very fountain of honor of that fort. He dignified " her by his addreffes; and thofe who have the " good fortune to fhare his reputation"—" Have," faid Belinda with fome warmth, " the misfortune to " lofe their own." I told you," turning to Harriet, " what would happen if we allowed him to fpeak: " and juft fo it has happened; for the gentleman " has almoft in plain terms afferted, that a woman " cannot be a *woman of fashion* till fhe has loft her " reputation." " Fye, Belinda, how you wrong " me!" replied Dorimant. " Loft her reputation! " Such a thought never entered into my head; I " only meant miflaid it. With a very little care " fhe will find it again." " There you are in the " right," faid Bellair; " for it is moft certain that " the reputation of a *woman of fashion* fhould not be " too muddy." " True," replied Dorimant, " nor " too limpid neither; it muft not be mere rock-" water, cold and clear; it fhould fparkle a little." " Well," faid Harriet, " now that Berynthia is una-" nimoufly voted a *woman of fashion*, what think you " of Loveit? Is fhe, or is fhe not one?" " If fhe is " one," anfwered Dorimant, " I am very much mif-" taken if it is not of Mirabel's creation."—" By " *writ*, I believe," faid Bellair, " for I faw him give " her a letter one night at the opera." " But fhe

" has

"has other good claims too," added Dorimant. "Her fortune, though not large, is easy; and nobody fears certain applications from her. She has "a small house of her own, which she has fitted up "very prettily, and is often *at home*, not to crowds "indeed, but to people of the best fashion, from "twenty, occasionally down to two; and let me tell "you, that nothing makes a woman of Loveit's "sort better received abroad, than being often *at home*." "I own," said Bellair, "that I looked "upon her rather as a genteel led-captain, a post-"script to *women of fashion*." "Perhaps too some-"times the cover," answered Dorimant, "and if so, "an equal. You may joke as much as you please "upon poor Loveit, but she is the best-humoured "creature in the world; and I maintain her to be a "*woman of fashion*; for, in short, we all roll with "her, as the soldiers say." "I want to know," said Belinda, "what you will determine upon a character "very different from the two last, I mean lady Love-"less: is she a *woman of fashion?*" "Dear Belinda," answered Harriet hastily, "how could she possibly "come into your head?" "Very naturally," said Belinda; "she has birth, beauty, and fortune; she "is well-bred." "I own it," said Harriet; "but "still she is handsome without meaning, well-shaped "without air, genteel without graces, and well-drest "without taste. She is such an insipid creature, she "seldom comes about, but lives at home with her "lord, and so domestically tame, that she eats out "of his hand, and teaches her young ones to peck "out of her own. Odd, very odd, take my word

"for

"for it." "Ay, mere rock-water," ſaid Dorimant, "and, as I told you an hour ago, that will not do." "No, moſt certainly," added Bellair; "all that re-"ſerve, ſimplicity, and coldneſs, can never do. It "ſeems to me rather that the true compoſition of "*people of faſhion*, like that of Venice treacle, con-"ſiſts of an infinite number of fine ingredients, but "all of the warm kind." "Truce with your filthy "treacle," ſaid Harriet; "and ſince the converſa-"tion has hitherto chiefly turned upon us poor wo-"men, I think we have a right to inſiſt upon the "definition of you *men of faſhion*." "No doubt of "it," ſaid Dorimant; "nothing is more juſt, and "nothing more eaſy. Allowing ſome ſmall differ-"ence for modes and habits, the *men* and the *women* "*of faſhion* are in truth the counterparts of each "other: they fit like tallies, are made of the ſame "wood, and are cut out for one another."

As Dorimant was going on, probably to illuſtrate his aſſertion, a valet de chambre proclaimed in a ſolemn manner the arrival of the dutcheſs dowager of Mattadore and her three daughters, who were immediately followed by lord Formal, ſir Peter Plauſible, and divers others of both ſexes, and of equal importance. The lady of the houſe, with infinite ſkill and indefatigable pains, ſoon peopled the ſeveral card-tables, with the greateſt propriety, and to univerſal ſatisfaction; and the night concluded with ſlams, honors, beſt-games, pairs, pair-royals, and all other ſuch rational demonſtrations of joy.

For my own part, I made my eſcape as ſoon as I poſſibly could, with my head full of that moſt extraordinary

traordinary conversation, which I had just heard, and which, from having taken no part in it, I had attended to the more, and retained the better. I went straight home, and immediately reduced it into writing, as I here offer it for the present edification of my readers. But, as it has furnished me with great and new lights, I propose, as soon as possible, to give the public a new and compleat system of ethics, founded upon these principles of *people of fashion*; as, in my opinion, they are better calculated than many others, for the use and instruction of all private families.

XLIII.

THE WORLD.

THURSDAY, Aug. 12, 1756. N° 189.

WE are accused by the French, and perhaps but too justly, of having no word in our language, which answers to their word *police*, which therefore we have been obliged to adopt, not having, as they say, the thing.

It does not occur to me that we have any one word in our language, I hope not from the same reason, to express the ideas which they comprehend under their word *les mœurs*. *Manners* are too little, *morals* too much. I should define it thus; *a general exterior decency, fitness, and propriety of conduct, in the common intercourse of life.*

Cicero,

Cicero, in his Offices, makes uſe of the word *decorum* in this ſenſe, to expreſs what the Greeks ſignified by their word (I will not ſhock the eyes of my polite readers with Greek types) *to prepon*.

The thing however is unqueſtionably of importance, by whatever word it may be dignified or degraded, diſtinguiſhed or miſtaken; it ſhall therefore be the ſubject of this paper to explain and recommend it; and upon this occaſion I ſhall adopt the word *decorum*.

But, as I have ſome private reaſons for deſiring not to leſſen the ſale of theſe my lucubrations, I muſt premiſe, that, notwithſtanding this ſerious introduction, I am not going to preach either religious or moral duties. On the contrary, it is a ſcheme of intereſt which I mean to communicate, and which, if the ſuppoſed characteriſtic of the preſent age be true, muſt, I ſhould apprehend, be highly acceptable to the generality of my readers.

I take it for granted that the moſt ſenſible and informed part of mankind, I mean people of faſhion, purſue ſingly their own intereſts and pleaſures; that they deſire as far as poſſible to enjoy them excluſively, and to avail themſelves of the ſimplicity, the ignorance, and the prejudices, of the vulgar, who have neither the ſame ſtrength of mind, nor the ſame advantages of education. Now it is certain that nothing would more contribute to that deſirable end, than a ſtrict obſervance of this *decorum*, which, as I have already hinted, does not extend to religious or moral duties, does not prohibit the enjoyments of vice, but only throws a veil of decency between it

and

and the vulgar, conceals part of its native deformity, and prevents ſcandal, and bad example. It is a ſort of pepper-corn quit-rent paid to virtue, as an acknowledgment of its ſuperiority; but, according to our preſent conſtitution, is the eaſy price of freedom, not the tribute of vaſſalage.

Thoſe who would be reſpected by others, muſt firſt reſpect themſelves. A certain exterior purity and dignity of character commands reſpect, procures credit, and invites confidence; but the public exerciſe and oſtentation of vice has all the contrary effects.

The middle claſs of people in this country, though generally ſtraining to imitate their betters, have not yet ſhaken off the prejudices of their education; very many of them ſtill believe in a ſupreme being, in a future ſtate of rewards and puniſhments, and retain ſome coarſe, home-ſpun notions of moral good and evil. The rational ſyſtem of materialiſm has not yet reached them, and, in my opinion, it may be full as well it never ſhould; for, as I am not of levelling principles, I am for preſerving a due ſubordination from inferiors to ſuperiors, which an equality of profligacy muſt totally deſtroy.

A fair character is a more lucrative thing than people are generally aware of; and I am informed that an eminent money-ſcrivener has lately calculated with great accuracy the advantage of it, and that it has turned out a clear profit of thirteen and a half *per cent.* in the general tranſactions of life; which advantage, frequently repeated, as it muſt be in the courſe of the year, amounts to a very conſiderable object.

To proceed to a few inſtances. If the courtier would but wear the appearance of truth, promiſe leſs, and perform more, he would acquire ſuch a degree of truſt and confidence, as would enable him to ſtrike on a ſudden, and with ſucceſs, ſome ſplendid ſtroke of perfidy, to the infinite advantage of himſelf and his party.

A patriot, of all people, ſhould be a ſtrict obſerver of this *decorum*, if he would, as it is to be preſumed he would, bear a good price at the court market. The love of his dear country, well acted and little felt, will certainly get him into good keeping, and perhaps procure him a handſome ſettlement for life; but, if his proſtitution be flagrant, he is only made uſe of in caſes of the utmoſt neceſſity, and even then only by cullies. I muſt obſerve by the bye, that of late the market has been a little glutted with patriots, and conſequently they do not ſell quite ſo well.

Few maſters of families are, I ſhould preſume, deſirous to be robbed indiſcriminately by all their ſervants; and as ſervants in general are more afraid of the devil, and leſs of the gallows, than their maſters, it ſeems to be as imprudent as indecent to remove that wholſome fear, either by their examples, or their philoſophical diſſertations, exploding in their preſence, though ever ſo juſtly, all the idle notions of future puniſhments, or of moral good and evil. At preſent, honeſt faithful ſervants rob their maſters conſcientiouſly only in their reſpective ſtations: but take away thoſe checks and reſtraints which the prejudices of their education have laid them under, they will ſoon rob indiſcriminately, and out of their ſeveral de-

partments;

partments; which would probably create ſome little confuſion in families, eſpecially in numerous ones.

I cannot omit obſerving, that this *decorum* extends to the little trifling offices of common life; ſuch as ſeeming to take a tender and affectionate part in the health or fortune of your acquaintance, and a readineſs and alacrity to ſerve them in things of little conſequence to them, and of none at all to you. Theſe attentions bring-in good intereſt; the weak and the ignorant miſtake them for the real ſentiments of your heart, and give you their eſteem and friendſhip in return. The wiſe, indeed, pay you in your own coin, or by a truck of commodities of equal value, upon which, however, there is no loſs; ſo that, upon the whole, this commerce, ſkilfully carried on, is a very lucrative one.

In all my ſchemes for the general good of mankind, I have always a particular attention to the utility that may ariſe from them to my fair fellow-ſubjects, for whom I have the tendereſt and moſt unfeigned concern; and I lay hold of this opportunity, moſt earneſtly to recommend to them the ſtricteſt obſervance of this *decorum*. I will admit that a fine woman of a certain rank cannot have too many real vices; but, at the ſame time, I do inſiſt upon it, that it is eſſentially her intereſt, not to have the appearance of any one. This *decorum*, I confeſs, will conceal her conqueſts, and prevent her triumphs; but, on the other hand, if ſhe will be pleaſed to reflect that thoſe conqueſts are known, ſooner or later, always to end in her total defeat, ſhe will not upon an average find herſelf a loſer. There are indeed ſome huſbands of ſuch humane and hoſpitable diſpoſitions, that they ſeem determined to ſhare all their happineſs with their friends and acquaintance; ſo that, with regard to ſuch huſbands ſingly, this *decorum* were uſeleſs: but the far greater number are of a churliſh and uncommunicative diſpoſition, troubleſome upon bare ſuſpicions, and brutal upon proofs. Theſe are capable of inflicting upon the fair delinquent the pains and penalties of exile and impriſonment at the dreadful manſion-ſeat, notwithſtanding the moſt ſolemn proteſtations and oaths, backed with the moſt moving tears, that nothing really criminal has paſſed. But it muſt be owned that, of all negatives, that is much the hardeſt to be proved.

Though deep play be a very innocent and even commendable amuſement in itſelf, it is however, as things are yet conſtituted, a great breach, nay perpaps the higheſt violation poſſible, of the *decorum* in the fair ſex. If generally fortunate, it induces ſome ſuſpicion of dexterity; if unfortunate, of debt; and in this latter caſe, the ways and means for raiſing the ſupplies neceſſary for the current year are ſometimes ſuppoſed to be unwarrantable. But what is ſtill much more important, is, that the agonies of an ill run will disfigure the fineſt face in the world, and cauſe moſt ungraceful emotions. I have known a bad game, ſuddenly produced upon a good game, for a deep ſtake at bragg or commerce, almoſt make the vermillion turn pale, and elicit from lips, where the ſweets of Hybla dwelt, and where the loves and graces played, ſome murmured oaths, which, though minced and mitigated a little in their terminations, ſeemed to me, upon the whole, to be rather unbecoming.

Another ſingular advantage, which will ariſe to my fair countrywomen of diſtinction from the obſervance of this *decorum*, is, that they will never want ſome creditable led-captain to attend them at a minute's warning to operas, plays, Ranelagh, and Vauxhall; whereas I have known ſome women of extreme condition, who, by neglecting the *decorum*, had ſlatterned away their characters to ſuch a degree, as to be obliged upon thoſe emergencies to take up with mere toad-eaters of very equivocal rank and character, who by no means graced their entry into public places.

To the young unmarried ladies, I beg leave to repreſent, that this *decorum* will make a difference of at leaſt five-and-twenty if not fifty *per cent.* in their fortunes. The pretty men, who have commonly the honor of attending them, are not in general the marrying kind of men; they love them too much, or too little, know them too well, or not well enough, to think of marrying them. The huſband-like men are a ſet of aukward fellows with good eſtates, and who, not having got the better of vulgar prejudices, lay ſome ſtreſs upon the characters of their wives, and the legitimacy of the heirs to their eſtates and titles. Theſe are to be caught only by *les mœurs*; the hook muſt be baited with the *decorum*; the naked one will not do.

I muſt own that it ſeems too ſevere to deny young ladies the innocent amuſements of the preſent times, but I beg of them to recollect that I mean only with regard to outward appearances; and I ſhould preſume that *tête-à-têtes* with the pretty men might be contrived and brought about in places leſs public than Kenſington-gardens, the two parks, the high roads, or the ſtreets of London.

Having thus combined, as I flatter myſelf that I have, the ſolid enjoyments of vice, with the uſeful appearances of virtue, I think myſelf entitled to the thanks of my country in general, and to that juſt praiſe which Horace gives to the author, *qui miſcuit utile dulci*, or, in Engliſh, who joins the uſeful with the agreeable.

XLIV.

THE WORLD.

THURSDAY, Sept. 30, 1756. N° 196.

IT is a vulgar notion, and worthy of the vulgar, for it is both falſe and abſurd, that paſſionate people are the beſt-natured people in the world. *They are a little haſty, it is true; a trifle will put them in a fury; and, while they are in that fury, they neither know nor care what they ſay or do: but then, as ſoon as it is over, they are extremely ſorry and penitent for any injury or miſchief they did.* This panegyric of theſe choleric good-natured people, when examined and ſimplified, amounts in plain common ſenſe and Engliſh to this: that they are good-natured when they are not ill-natured; and that when, in their fits of rage, they have ſaid or done things that have brought

brought them to the gaol or the gallows, they are extremely ſorry for it. It is indeed highly probable that they are; but where is the reparation to thoſe whoſe reputations, limbs, or lives, they have either wounded or deſtroyed? This concern comes too late, and is only for themſelves. Self-love was the cauſe of the injury, and is the only motive of the repentance.

Had theſe furious people real good-nature, their firſt offence would be their laſt, and they would reſolve at all events never to relapſe. The moment they felt their choler riſing, they would enjoin themſelves an abſolute ſilence and inaction, and by that ſudden check rather expoſe themſelves to a momentary ridicule, which, by the way, would be followed by univerſal applauſe, than run the leaſt riſk of being irreparably miſchievous.

I know it is ſaid in their behalf, that this impulſe to wrath is conſtitutionally ſo ſudden and ſo ſtrong, that they cannot ſtifle it, even in its birth: but experience ſhews us, that this allegation is notoriouſly falſe; for we daily obſerve that theſe ſtormy perſons both can and do lay thoſe guſts of paſſion, when awed by reſpect, reſtrained by intereſt, or intimidated by fear. The moſt outrageous furioſo does not give a looſe to his anger in preſence of his ſovereign, or his miſtreſs; nor the expectant heir in preſence of the peeviſh dotard from whom he hopes for an inheritance. The ſoliciting courtier, though perhaps under the ſtrongeſt provocations from unjuſt delays and broken promiſes, calmly ſwallows his unavailing wrath, diſguiſes it even under ſmiles, and gently waits for more favourable moments: nor does the criminal fly in a passion at his judge or his jury.

There is then but one solid excuse to be alledged in favour of these people; and, if they will frankly urge it, I will candidly admit it, because it points out its own remedy. I mean, let them fairly confess themselves mad, as they most unquestionably are: for what plea can those that are frantic ten times a day, bring against shaving, bleeding, and a dark room, when so many much more harmless madmen are confined in their cells at Bedlam, for being mad only once in a moon? Nay, I have been assured by the late ingenious doctor Monro, that such of his patients who are really of a good-natured disposition, and who, in their lucid intervals, were allowed the liberty of walking about the hospital, would frequently, when they found the previous symptoms of their returning madness, voluntarily apply for confinement, conscious of the mischief which they might possibly do if at liberty. If those who pretend not to be mad, but who really are so, had the same fund of good-nature, they would make the same application to their friends, if they have any.

There is in the Menagiana a very pretty story of one of these angry gentlemen, which sets their extravagancy in a very ridiculous light.

Two gentlemen were riding together, one of whom, who was a choleric one, happened to be mounted on a high-mettled horse. The horse grew a little troublesome; at which the rider grew very angry, and whipped and spurred him with great fury; to which the horse, almost as wrongheaded as his master, re-

plied

plied with kicking and plunging. The companion, concerned for the danger, and ashamed of the folly of his friend, said to him cooly, "Be quiet, be quiet, "and shew yourself the wiser of the two."

This sort of madness, for I will call it by no other name, flows from various causes, of which I shall now enumerate the most general.

Light unballasted heads are very apt to be overset by every gust, or even breeze, of passion; they appretiate things wrong, and think every thing of importance, but what really is so: hence those frequent and sudden transitions from silly joy to sillier anger, according as the present silly humour is gratified or thwarted. This is the never-failing characteristic of the uneducated vulgar, who often in the same half-hour fight with fury, and shake hands with affection. Such heads give themselves no time to reason; and, if you attempt to reason with them, they think you rally them, and resent the affront. They are, in short, overgrown children, and continue so in the most advanced age. Far be it from me to insinuate, what some ill-bred authors have bluntly asserted, that this is in general the case of the fairest part of our species, whose great vivacity does not always allow them time to reason consequentially, but hurries them into testiness upon the least opposition to their will. But, at the same time, with all the partiality which I have for them, and nobody can have more than I have, I must confess that, in all their debates, I have much more admired the copiousness of their rhetoric, than the conclusiveness of their logic.

People of ſtrong animal ſpirits, warm conſtitutions, and a cold genius, a moſt unfortunate and ridiculous though common compound, are moſt iraſcible animals, and very dangerous in their wrath. They are active, puzzling, blundering, and petulantly enterprizing and perſevering. They are impatient of the leaſt contradiction, having neither arguments nor words to reply with; and the animal part of their compoſition burſts out into furious exploſions, which have often miſchievous conſequences. Nothing is too outrageous or criminal for them to ſay or do in theſe fits; but, as the beginning of their frenzy is eaſily diſcoverable, by their glaring eyes, inflamed countenances, and rapid motions, the company, as conſervators of the peace, which, by the way, every man is till the authority of a magiſtrate can be procured, ſhould forcibly ſeize theſe madmen, and confine them in the mean time in ſome dark cloſet, vault, or coal-hole.

Men of nice honor, without one grain of common honeſty, for ſuch there are, are wonderfully combuſtible. The honorable is to ſupport and protect the diſhoneſt part of their character. The conſciouſneſs of their guilt makes them both ſore and jealous.

There is another and very iraſcible ſort of human animals, whoſe madneſs proceeds from pride. Theſe are generally the people, who, having juſt fortunes ſufficient to live idle, and uſeleſs to ſociety, create themſelves gentlemen, and are ſcrupulouſly tender of the rank and dignity which they have not. They require the more reſpect, from being conſcious that they have no right to any. They conſtrue every

thing

thing into a ſlight, aſk explanations with heat, and miſunderſtand them with fury. "Who are you? "What are you? Do you know who you ſpeak to? "I will teach you to be ſilent to a gentleman," are their daily idioms of ſpeech, which frequently end in aſſault and battery, to the great emolument of the Round-houſe and Crown-office.

I have known many young fellows, who, at their firſt ſetting out into the world, or in the army, have ſimulated a paſſion which they did not feel, merely as an indication of *ſpirit*, which word is falſely looked upon as ſynonymous with courage. They dreſs and look fierce, ſwear enormouſly, and rage furiouſly, ſeduced by that popular word, *ſpirit*. But I beg leave to inform theſe miſtaken young gentlemen, whoſe error I compaſſionate, that the true ſpirit of a rational being conſiſts in cool and ſteady reſolution, which can only be the reſult of reflection and virtue.

I am very ſorry to be obliged to own, that there is not a more irritable part of the ſpecies, than my brother authors. Criticiſm, cenſure, or even the ſlighteſt diſapprobation of their immortal works, excite their moſt furious indignation. It is true, indeed, that they expreſs their reſentment in a manner leſs dangerous both to others and to themſelves. Like incenſed porcupines, they dart their quills at the objects of their wrath. The wounds given by theſe ſhafts are not mortal, and only painful in proportion to the diſtance from whence they fly. Thoſe which are diſcharged, as by much the greateſt numbers are, from great heights, ſuch as garrets or four-pair-of-ſtair rooms, are puffed away by the wind, and never hit the mark; but those which are let off from a first or second floor, are apt to occasion a little smarting, and sometimes festering, especially if the party wounded be unsound.

Our GREAT CREATOR has wisely given us passions, to rouze us into action, and to engage our gratitude to him by the pleasures they procure us; but, at the same time, he has kindly given us reason sufficient, if we will but give that reason fair play, to controul those passions; and has delegated authority to say to them, as he said to the waters, "thus far shall ye "go, and no farther." The angry man is his own severest tormentor; his breast knows no peace, while his raging passions are restrained by no sense of either religious or moral duties. What would be his case, if his unforgiving example, if I may use such an expression, were followed by his ALL-MERCIFUL MAKER, whose forgiveness he can only hope for, in proportion as he himself forgives and loves his fellow-creatures!

XLV.

THE WORLD.

THURSDAY, Oct. 7, 1756. N° 197.

IF we give credit to the vulgar opinion, or even to the assertions of some reputable authors, both antient and modern, poor human nature was not originally formed for keeping: every age has degenerated; and, from the fall of the firſt man, my unfortunate anceſtor, our ſpecies has been tumbling on, century by century, from bad to worſe, for about ſix thouſand years.

Conſidering this progreſſive ſtate of deterioration, it is a very great mercy that things are no worſe with us at preſent; ſince, geometrically ſpeaking, the human ought by this time to have ſunk infinitely below the brute and the vegetable ſpecies, which are neither of them ſuppoſed to have dwindled or degenerated conſiderably, except in a very few inſtances: for it muſt be owned that our modern oaks are inferior to thoſe of Dodona, our breed of horſes to that of the Centaurs, and our breed of fowls to that of the Phœnixes.

But is this really the caſe? Certainly not. It is only one of thoſe many errors which are artfully ſcattered by the deſigns of a few, and blindly adopted by the ignorance and folly of the many. The moving exclamations of — *theſe ſad times! this degenerate age!* the affecting lamentations over *declining virtue* and *triumphant vice*, and the tender and final farewell bidden every day to unrewarded and diſcouraged public ſpirit, arts, and ſciences, are the common-place topics of the pride, the envy, and the malignity, of the human heart, that can more eaſily forgive, and even commend, antiquated and remote, than bear cotemporary and contiguous, merit. Men of theſe mean ſentiments have always been the ſatiriſts of their own, and the panegyriſts of former times. They give this tone, which fools, like birds in the dark, catch by ear, and whiſtle all day long.

As

As it has constantly been my endeavor to root out, if I could, or, if I could not, to expose, the vices of the human heart, it shall be the object of this day's paper to examine this strange inverted entail of virtue and merit upwards, according to priority of birth, and seniority of age. I shall prove it to be forged, and consequently null and void to all intents and purposes whatsoever.

If I loved to jingle, I would say that human nature has always been invariably the same, though always varying; that is, the same in substance, but varying in forms and modes, from many concurrent causes, of which perhaps we know but few. Climate, education, accidents, severally contribute to change those modes; but in all climates, and in all ages, we discover through them the same passions, affections, and appetites, and the same degree of virtues and vices.

This being unquestionably the true state of the case, which it would be endless to bring instances to prove, from the histories of all times and of all nations, I shall, by way of warning to the incautious, and of reproof to the designing, proceed to explain the reasons, which I have but just hinted at above, why the human nature of the time being has always been reckoned the worst and most degenerate.

Authors, especially poets, though great men, are, alas! but men; and, like other men, subject to the weaknesses of human nature, though perhaps in a less degree: but it is however certain that their breasts are not absolutely strangers to the passions of jealousy, pride, and envy. Hence it is that they are very apt to meaſure merit by the century, to love dead authors better than living ones, and to love them the better, the longer they have been dead. The Auguſtan age is therefore their favorite æra, being at leaſt ſeventeen hundred years diſtant from the preſent. That emperor was not only a judge of wit, but, for an emperor, a tolerable performer too; and Mæcenas, his firſt miniſter, was both a patron and a poet: he not only encouraged and protected, but fed and fattened men of wit at his own table, as appears from Horace: no ſmall encouragement for panegyric. Thoſe were times indeed for genius to diſplay itſelf! It was honored, taſted, and rewarded. But now —— *O tempora! O mores!* One muſt however do juſtice to the authors, who thus declaim againſt their own times, by acknowledging that they are ſeldom the aggreſſors; their own times have commonly begun with them. It is their reſentment, not their judgment, if thəy have any, that ſpeaks this language. Anger and deſpair make them endeavour to lower that merit, which, till brought very low indeed, they are conſcious they cannot equal.

There is another and more numerous ſet of much greater men, who ſtill more loudly complain of the ignorance, the corruption, and the degeneracy, of the preſent age. Theſe are the conſummate volunteer, but unregarded and unrewarded politicians, who, at a modeſt computation, amount to at leaſt three millions of ſouls in this political country, and who are all of them both able and willing to ſteer the great veſſel of the ſtate, and to take upon themſelves the whole load of buſineſs, and burthen of *employments*, for the
ſervice

ſervice of their dear country. The adminiſtration for the time being is always the worſt, the moſt incapable, the moſt corrupt, that ever was, and negligent of every thing but their own intereſt. *Where are now your Cecils and your Walſinghams?* Thoſe who aſk that queſtion could anſwer it, if they would ſpeak out, *Themſelves:* for they are all that, and more too.

I ſtept the other day, in order only to inquire how my poor country did, into a coffee-houſe, that is without diſpute the ſeat of the ſoundeſt politics in this great metropolis, and ſat myſelf down within ear-ſhot of the principal council-table. Fortunately for me, the preſident, a perſon of age, dignity, and becoming gravity, had juſt begun to ſpeak. He ſtated, with infinite perſpicuity and knowledge, the preſent ſtate of affairs in other countries, and the lamentable ſituation of our own. He traced with his finger upon the table, by the help of ſome coffee which he had ſpilt in the warmth of his exordium, the whole courſe of the Ohio, and the boundaries of the Ruſſian, Pruſſian, Auſtrian, and Saxon dominions; foreſaw a long and bloody war upon the continent, calculated the ſupplies neceſſary for carrying it on, and pointed out the beſt methods of raiſing them, which, for that very reaſon, he intimated, would not be purſued. He wound up his diſcourſe with a moſt pathetic peroration, which he concluded with ſaying, *Things were not carried on in this manner in queen Elizabeth's days; the public was conſidered, and able men were conſulted and employed. Thoſe were days!* "Aye, ſir, "and nights too, I preſume," ſaid a young fellow who ſtood near him, "ſome longer and ſome ſhorter,

"according

"according to the variation of the ſeaſons; pretty "much like ours." Mr. Preſident was a little ſurprized at the ſuddenneſs and pertneſs of this interruption; but, recompoſing himſelf, anſwered with that cool contempt that becomes a great man, "I did "not mean aſtronomical days, but political ones." The young fellow replied, "O then, ſir, I am your "ſervant," and went off in a laugh.

Thus informed and edified, I went off too, but could not help reflecting in my way upon the ſingular ill-luck of this my dear country, which, as long as ever I remember it, and as far back as I have read, has always been governed by the only two or three people, out of two or three millions, totally incapable of governing, and unfit to be truſted. But theſe reflections were ſoon interrupted by numbers of people, whom I obſerved crowding into a public houſe. Among them I diſcovered my worthy friend and taylor, that induſtrious mechanic, Mr. Regnier. I applied to him, to know the meaning of that concourſe; to which, with his uſual humanity, he anſwered, "We "are the maſter-taylors, who are to meet to-night to "conſider what is to be done about our journeymen, "who inſult and impoſe upon us, to the great detri-"ment of trade." I aſked him whether, under his protection, I might ſlip in and hear their deliberations? He ſaid, "Yes, and welcome; for that they ſhould "do nothing to be aſhamed of." I profited of this permiſſion, and, following him into the room, found a conſiderable number of theſe ingenious artiſts aſſembled, and waiting only for the arrival of my friend, who it ſeems was too conſiderable for buſineſs to

begin

begin without him. He accordingly took the lead, opened the meeting with a very handſome ſpeech, in which he gave many inſtances of the inſolence, the unreaſonableneſs, and the exorbitant demands, of the journeymen taylors, and concluded with obſerving, "that, if the government minded any thing now-a-"days but themſelves, ſuch abuſes would not have "been ſuffered; and, had they been but attempted "in queen Elizabeth's days, ſhe would have *worked* "them with a witneſs." Another orator then roſe up to ſpeak; but, as I was ſure that he could ſay nothing better than what had juſt fallen from my worthy friend, I ſtole off unobſerved, and was purſuing my way home, when in the very next ſtreet I diſcovered a much greater number of people, though by their dreſs of ſeemingly inferior note, ruſhing into another public-houſe. As numbers always excite my curioſity, almoſt as much as they do each other's paſſions, I crowded in with them, in order to diſcover the object of this meeting, not without ſome ſuſpicion that this frequent ſenate might be compoſed of the journeymen taylors, and convened in oppoſition to that which I had juſt left. My ſuſpicion was ſoon confirmed by the eloquence of a journeyman, a finiſher I preſume, who expatiated, with equal warmth and dignity, upon the injuſtice and oppreſſion of the maſter taylors, to the utter ruin of thouſands of poor journeymen and their families; and concluded with aſſerting, "it was a ſhame that the government and "the parliament did not take care of ſuch abuſes; "and that, had the maſter taylors done theſe things

"in

" in queen Elizabeth's days, ſhe would have *maſtered* " them with a vengeance, ſo ſhe would."

I confeſs I could not help ſmiling at this ſingular conformity of ſentiments, and almoſt of expreſſions, of the maſter politicians, the maſter taylors, and the journeymen taylors. I am convinced that the two latter really and honeſtly believed what they ſaid; it not being in the leaſt improbable that their underſtandings ſhould be the dupes of their intereſts: but I will not ſo peremptorily anſwer for the interior conviction of the political orator, though at the ſame time I muſt do him the juſtice to ſay, he ſeemed full dull enough to be very much in earneſt.

The ſeveral ſcenes of this day ſuggeſted to me when I got home various reflections, which perhaps I may communicate to my readers in ſome future paper.

XLVI.

SPEECH ON THE *LICENSING BILL.*

THE editor, being deſirous of giving a ſpecimen of lord Cheſterfield's eloquence, has made choice of the three following ſpeeches; the firſt in the ſtrong nervous ſtyle of Demoſthenes; the two latter, in the witty, ironical manner of Tully. That he had ſtudied with attention theſe great models, and endeavoured to imitate them, will not eſcape the notice of thoſe, who will be at the trouble of comparing their orations with his. But his imitation is that of a man of genius and taſte, who improves whatever he he touches, not of that herd of retailers ſo juſtly diſtinguiſhed by the name of *imitatores, ſervile pecus*.

The firſt abſtract of this ſpeech, on the licenſing bill, appeared in Fog's Journal, N° 5. It was incorrect and defective, eſpecially in the part relating to the line of the poet, applied to Pompey. This gave a handle to the authors of the Gazetteer, ever on the watch on theſe occaſions, to fall upon the noble ſpeaker, and to refer him to Tully, to whom we owe the fulleſt account of this occurrence, *Ep. ad Att.* II. 19. Their triumph was ſhort, and the ſpeech was publiſhed in the Magazines the very next month, probably not without the earl's conſent, and thence verbatim in the debates of the houſe of lords, vol. V. p. 210. The following abſtract from theſe will be ſufficient to give an idea of the ſubject of the diſcourſe. "The only re-" markable (occurrence) of this ſeſſion, which re-" mains to be taken notice of, is contained in the pro-" ceedings upon the bill, to explain and amend ſo" much of an act made in the twelfth year of the reign" of queen Anne, entituled, *An act for reducing the*" *laws relating to rogues, vagabonds, ſturdy beggars*" *and vagrants, into one act of parliament*; *and for*" *the more effectual puniſhing ſuch rogues, vagabonds,*" *ſturdy beggars, and vagrants, and ſending them*" *whither they ought to be ſent, as relates to common*" *players of interludes*. The bill, which was paſſed" into a law, and remains ſtill in force, was or-" dered by the houſe of commons to be prepared" and brought-in on Friday the 20th of May, and "was occasioned by a farce called *the golden rump*, "which had been brought to the then master * of "the theatre in Lincoln's-inn-fields, who, upon "perusal, found it was designed as a libel upon "the government, and therefore, instead of having "it acted, he carried it to a gentleman concerned "in the administration; and he having commu-"nicated it to some other members of the house of "commons, it was resolved to move for leave to "bring-in a bill for preventing any such attempt "for the future; and the motion being complied "with by that house upon the 20th of May, 1737, "the bill was brought-in on Tuesday the 24th, "and passed through both houses with such dis-"patch, that it was ready for the royal assent by "Wednesday the 8th of June, and accordingly re-"ceived the royal assent on Tuesday the 21st, "when his majesty put an end to this session of "parliament.

"In both houses there were long debates, and "great opposition to this bill, in every step it "made; and in the house of lords the following "is the substance of what was said by the earl "of Chesterfield against it, viz:

"MY LORDS,

THE bill now before you I apprehend to be of a very extraordinary, a very dangerous, nature. It seems designed not only as a restraint on the licentiousness of the stage; but it will prove a most arbi-

* One Mr. Giffard, who had removed thither with a company of players from Goodman's-fields, where he had a theatre, which was silenced by this very act.

 trary

trary reſtraint on the liberty of the ſtage; and I fear it looks yet further, I fear it tends towards a reſtraint on the liberty of the preſs, which will be a long ſtride towards the deſtruction of liberty itſelf. It is not only a bill, my lords, of a very extraordinary nature, but it has been brought in at a very extraordinary ſeaſon, and puſhed with moſt extraordinary diſpatch. When I conſidered how near it was to the end of the ſeſſion, and how long this ſeſſion had been protracted beyond the uſual time of the year; when I conſidered that this bill paſſed through the other houſe with ſo much precipitancy, as even to get the ſtart of a bill which deſerved all the reſpect, and all the diſpatch, the forms of either houſe of parliament could admit of; it ſet me upon inquiring, what could be the reaſon for introducing this bill at ſo unſeaſonable a time, and preſſing it forward in a manner ſo very ſingular and uncommon. I have made all poſſible inquiry; and as yet, I muſt confeſs, I am at a loſs to find out the great occaſion. I have, it is true, learned from common report without doors, that a moſt ſeditious, a moſt heinous farce had been offered to one of the theatres, a farce for which the authors ought to be puniſhed in the moſt exemplary manner: but what was the conſequence? The maſter of that theatre behaved as he was in duty bound, and as common prudence directed: he not only refuſed to bring it upon the ſtage, but carried it to a certain honorable gentleman in the adminiſtration, as the ſureſt method of having it abſolutely ſuppreſſed. Could this be the occaſion of introducing ſuch an extraordinary bill, at ſuch an extraordinary ſeaſon, and puſhing it in ſo extraordinary

a man-a manner? Surely no:—The dutiful behaviour of the players, the prudent caution they ſhewed upon that occaſion, can never be a reaſon for ſubjecting them to ſuch an arbitrary reſtraint: it is an argument in their favour; and a material one, in my opinion, againſt the bill. Nay farther, if we conſider all circumſtances, it is to me a full proof that the laws now in being are ſufficient for puniſhing thoſe players who ſhall venture to bring any ſeditious libel upon the ſtage, and conſequently ſufficient for deterring all the players from acting any thing that may have the leaſt tendency towards giving a reaſonable offence.

I do not, my lords, pretend to be a lawyer, I do not pretend to know perfectly the power and extent of our laws; but I have converſed with thoſe that do, and by them I have been told, that our laws are ſufficient for puniſhing any perſon that ſhall dare to repreſent upon the ſtage what may appear, either by the words or the repreſentation, to be blaſphemous, ſeditious, or immoral. I muſt own, indeed, I have obſerved of late a remarkable licentiouſneſs in the ſtage. There have but very lately been two plays acted, which one would have thought ſhould have given the greateſt offence; and yet both were ſuffered to be often repreſented without diſturbance, without cenſure. In one *, the author thought fit to repreſent the three great profeſſions, religion, phyſic, and law, as inconſiſtent with common ſenſe: in the other †, a moſt tragical ſtory was brought upon the ſtage, a cataſtrophe too recent, too melancholy, and of too ſolemn a nature, to be heard of any where but from the pulpit.

* *Paſquin, a comedy.* † *King Charles I, a tragedy.*

How these pieces came to pass unpunished, I do not know; if I am rightly informed, it was not for want of law, but for want of prosecution, without which no law can be made effectual: but if there was any neglect in this case, I am convinced it was not with a design to prepare the minds of the people, and to make them think a new law necessary.

Our stage ought certainly, my lords, to be kept within due bounds; but for this, our laws, as they stand at present, are sufficient. If our stage-players at any time exceed those bounds, they ought to be prosecuted, they may be punished: we have precedents, we have examples of persons having been punished for things less criminal than either of the two pieces I have mentioned. A new law must therefore be unnecessary, and in the present case it cannot be unnecessary without being dangerous: every unnecessary restraint on licentiousness is a fetter upon the legs, is a shackle upon the hands, of liberty. One of the greatest blessings we enjoy, one of the greatest blessings a people, my lords, can enjoy, is liberty; but every good in this life has its alloy of evil. Licentiousness is the alloy of liberty: it is an ebullition, an excrescence; it is a speck upon the eye of the political body, which I can never touch but with a gentle, with a trembling hand, lest I destroy the body, lest I injure the eye upon which it is apt to appear. If the stage becomes at any time licentious, if a play appears to be a libel upon the government, or upon any particular man, the king's courts are open, the law is sufficient for punishing the offender; and in this case the person injured has a singular advantage, he can be under no difficulty to prove who is the publisher; the players themselves are the publishers, and there can be no want of evidence to convict them.

But, my lords, suppose it true, that the laws now in being are not sufficient for putting a check to, or preventing, the licentiousness of the stage; suppose it absolutely necessary some new law should be made for that purpose: yet it must be granted, that such a law ought to be maturely considered, and every clause, every sentence, nay every word of it, well-weighed and examined, lest, under some of those methods presumed or pretended to be necessary for restraining licentiousness, a power should lie concealed, which might be afterwards made use of for giving a dangerous wound to liberty. Such a law ought not to be introduced at the close of a session; nor ought we, in the passing of such a law, to depart from any of the forms prescribed by our ancestors for preventing deceit and surprize. There is such a connection between licentiousness and liberty, that it is not easy to correct the one, without dangerously wounding the other; it is extremely hard to distinguish the true limit between them: like a changeable silk, we can easily see there are two different colors, but we cannot easily discover where the one ends, or where the other begins. There can be no great and immediate danger from the licentiousness of the stage: I hope it will not be pretended, that our government may, before next winter, be overturned by such licentiousness, even though our stage were at present under no sort of controul. Why then may we not delay till next session passing any law against the licentiousness of the

the ſtage? Neither our government can be altered, nor our conſtitution overturned, by ſuch a delay; but by paſſing a law raſhly and unadviſedly, our conſtitution may at once be deſtroyed, and our government rendered arbitrary. Can we then put a ſmall, a ſhort-lived inconvenience in the balance with perpetual ſlavery? Can it be ſuppoſed, that a parliament of Great Britain will ſo much as riſk the latter, for the ſake of avoiding the former?

Surely, my lords, this is not to be expected, were the licentiouſneſs of the ſtage much greater than it is, were the inſufficiency of our laws more obvious than can be pretended; but when we complain of the licentiouſneſs of the ſtage, and the inſufficiency of our laws, I fear we have more reaſon to complain of bad meaſures in our polity, and a general decay of virtue and morality among the people. In public as well as private life, the only way to prevent being ridiculed or cenſured, is to avoid all ridiculous or wicked meaſures, and to purſue ſuch only as are virtuous and worthy. The people never endeavour to ridicule thoſe they love and eſteem, nor will they ſuffer them to be ridiculed: if any one attempts it, the ridicule returns upon the author; he makes himſelf only the object of public hatred and contempt. The actions or behaviour of a private man may paſs unobſerved, and conſequently unapplauded, uncenſured; but the actions of thoſe in high ſtations can neither paſs without notice, nor without cenſure or applauſe; and therefore an adminiſtration, without eſteem, without authority among the people, let their power be never ſo great, let their power be never ſo arbitrary,

arbitrary, will be ridiculed: the feverest edicts, the most terrible punishments, cannot prevent it. If any man therefore thinks he has been censured, if any man thinks he has been ridiculed, upon any of our public theatres, let him examine his actions, he will find the cause; let him alter his conduct, he will find a remedy. As no man is perfect, as no man is infallible, the greatest may err, the most circumspect may be guilty of some piece of ridiculous behaviour. It is not licentiousness, it is an useful liberty always indulged the stage in a free country, that some great men may there meet with a just reproof, which none of their friends will be free enough, or rather faithful enough, to give them. Of this we have a famous instance in the Roman history. The great Pompey, after the many victories he had obtained, and the great conquests he had made, had certainly a good title to the esteem of the people of Rome: yet that great man, by some error in his conduct, became an object of general dislike; and therefore in the representation of an old play, when Diphilus, the actor, came to repeat these words, *Nostra miseria tu es Magnus*, the audience immediately applied them to Pompey, who at that time was as well known by the name Magnus, as by the name Pompey, and were so highly pleased with the satire, that, as Cicero says, they made him repeat the words a hundred times over. An account of this was immediately sent to Pompey, who, instead of resenting it as an injury, was so wise as to take it for a just reproof; he examined his conduct, he altered his measures, he regained by degrees the esteem of the people, and therefore neither feared

 the

the wit, nor felt the ſatire, of the ſtage. This is an example which ought to be followed by great men in all countries. Such accidents will often happen in every free country; and many ſuch would probably have afterwards happened at Rome, if they had continued to enjoy their liberty: but this ſort of liberty on the ſtage came ſoon after, I ſuppoſe, to be called licentiouſneſs; for we are told that Auguſtus, after having eſtabliſhed his empire, reſtored order in Rome by reſtraining licentiouſneſs. God forbid! we ſhould in this country have order reſtored, or licentiouſneſs reſtrained, at ſo dear a rate as the people of Rome paid for it to Auguſtus.

In the caſe I have mentioned, my lords, it was not the poet that wrote, for it was an old play; nor the players that acted, for they only repeated the words of the play: it was the people who pointed the ſatire; and the caſe will always be the ſame. When a man has the misfortune to incur the hatred or contempt of the people, when public meaſures are deſpiſed, the audience will apply what never was, what could not be, deſigned as a ſatire on the preſent times; nay, even though the people ſhould not apply, thoſe, who are conſcious of the wickedneſs or weakneſs of their conduct, will take to themſelves what the author never deſigned. A public thief is as apt to take the ſatire, as he is apt to take the money, which was never deſigned for him. We have an inſtance of this in the caſe of a famous comedian of the laſt age; a comedian who was not only a good poet, but an honeſt man, and a quiet and good ſubject. The famous Moliere, when he wrote his Tartuffe, which

is

is certainly an excellent and a good moral comedy, did not design to satyrize any great man of that age; yet a great man in France at that time took it to himself, and fancied the author had taken him as a model for one of the principal, and one of the worst, characters in that comedy: by good luck he was not the licenser, otherwise the kingdom of France had never had the pleasure, the happiness I may say, of seeing that play acted; but, when the players first purposed to act it at Paris, he had interest enough to get it forbid. Moliere, who knew himself innocent of what was laid to his charge, complained to his patron the prince of Conti, that as his play was designed only to expose hypocrisy, and a false pretence to religion, it was very hard it should be forbid being acted; when at the same time they were suffered to expose religion itself every night publicly upon the Italian stage: to which the prince wittily answered, "It is true, Moliere, Harlequin ridicules "heaven, and exposes religion; but you have done "much worse,—you have ridiculed the first minister "of religion."

I am as much for restraining the licentiousness of the stage, and every sort of licentiousness, as any of your lordships can be: but, my lords, I am, I shall always be, extremely cautious and fearful of making the least encroachment upon liberty; and therefore, when a new law is proposed against licentiousness, I shall always be for considering it deliberately and maturely, before I venture to give my consent to its being passed. This is a sufficient reason for my being against passing this bill at so unseasonable a time,

time, and in so extraordinary a manner; but I have many reasons for being against passing the bill itself, some of which I shall beg leave to explain to your lordships.

The bill, my lords, at first view, may seem to be designed only against the stage; but to me it plainly appears to point somewhere else. It is an arrow, that does but glance upon the stage; the mortal wound seems designed against the liberty of the press. By this bill you prevent a play's being acted, but you do not prevent its being printed; therefore, if a licence should be refused for its being acted, we may depend upon it the play will be printed. It will be printed and published, my lords, with the refusal in capital letters on the title page. People are always fond of what is forbidden. *Libri prohibiti* (prohibited books) are in all countries diligently and generally sought after. It will be much easier to procure a refusal, than it ever was to procure a good house, or a good sale; therefore we may expect, that plays will be wrote on purpose to have a refusal; this will certainly procure a good house or a good sale. Thus will satires be spread and dispersed through the whole nation, and thus every man in the kingdom may, and probably will, read for sixpence what a few only could have seen acted, and that not under the expence of half a crown. We shall then be told, What! will you allow an infamous libel to be printed and dispersed, which you would not allow to be acted? You have agreed to a law to prevent its being acted: can you refuse your assent to a law to prevent its being printed and published?

lished? I should really, my lords, be glad to hear, what excuse, what reason one could give for being against the latter, after having agreed to the former; for, I protest, I cannot suggest to myself the least shadow of an excuse. If we agree to the bill now before us, we must, perhaps, next session, agree to a bill for preventing any plays being printed without a licence. Then satires will be wrote by way of novels, secret histories, dialogues, or under some such title; and thereupon we shall be told, What! will you allow an infamous libel to be printed and dispersed, only because it does not bear the title of a play? Thus, my lords, from the precedent now before us, we shall be induced, nay we can find no reason for refusing, to lay the press under a general licence, and then we may bid adieu to the liberties of Great Britain.

But suppose, my lords, it were necessary to make a new law for restraining the licentiousness of the stage, which I am very far from granting; yet I shall never be for establishing such a power as is proposed by this bill. If poets and players are to be restrained, let them be restrained as other subjects are, by the known laws of their country: if they offend, let them be tried, as every Englishman ought to be, by God and their country; do not let us subject them to the arbitrary will and pleasure of any one man. A power lodged in the hands of one single man, to judge and determine, without any limitation, without any controul or appeal, is a sort of power unknown to our laws, inconsistent with our constitution. It is a higher, a more absolute power than we trust even

to

to the king himſelf; and therefore, I muſt think, we ought not to veſt any ſuch power in his majeſty's lord chamberlain. When I ſay this, I am ſure, I do not mean to give the leaſt, the moſt diſtant, offence to the noble duke * who now fills the poſt of lord chamberlain; his natural candor and love of juſtice would not, I know, permit him to exerciſe any power, but with the ſtricteſt regard to the rules of juſtice and humanity. Were we ſure his ſucceſſors in that high office would always be perſons of ſuch diſtinguiſhed merit, even the power eſtabliſhed by this bill could give no further alarm, than leſt it ſhould be made a precedent for introducing other new powers of the ſame nature. This, indeed, is an alarm which cannot be avoided, which cannot be prevented, by any hope, by any conſideration; it is an alarm, which, I think, every man muſt take, who has a due regard to the conſtitution and liberties of his country.

I ſhall admit, my lords, that the ſtage ought not, upon any occaſion, to meddle with politics; and for this very reaſon, among the reſt, I am againſt the bill now before us. This bill will be ſo far from preventing the ſtage's meddling with politics, that, I fear, it will be the occaſion of its meddling with nothing elſe; but then it will be a political ſtage *ex parte*. It will be made ſubſervient to the politics and the ſchemes of the court only; the licentiouſneſs of the ſtage will be encouraged, inſtead of being reſtrained, but, like court-journaliſts, it will be licentious only againſt the patrons of liberty, and the protectors of the people: whatever man, whatever

* The duke of Grafton.

party,

party, opposes the court in any of their most destructive schemes, will, upon the stage, be represented in the most ridiculous light the hirelings of a court can contrive. True patriotism, and love of public good, will be represented as madness, or as a cloak for envy, disappointment, and malice; whilst the most flagitious crimes, the most extravagant vices and follies, if they are fashionable at court, will be disguised and dressed-up in the habit of the most amiable virtues. This has formerly been the case in king Charles the second's days: the playhouse was under a licence, what was the consequence? The playhouse retailed nothing but the politics, the vices, and the follies of the court; not to expose them, no, but to recommend them, though it must be granted their politics were often as bad as their vices, and much more pernicious than their other follies. It is true, the court had at that time a great deal of wit, it was then indeed full of men of true wit and great humor; but it was the more dangerous, for the courtiers did then, as thorough-paced courtiers always will do, they sacrificed their honor by making their wit and their humor subservient to the court only; and, what made it still more dangerous, no man could appear upon the stage against them. We know that Dryden, the poet-laureat of that reign, always represents the cavaliers as honest, brave, merry fellows, and fine gentlemen; indeed his fine gentleman, as he generally draws him, is an atheistical, lewd, abandoned fellow, which was at that time, it seems, the fashionable character at court; on the other hand, he always represents the dissenters as hypocritical, dissembling rogues, or stupid

senseless

senseless boobies.—When the court had a mind to fall out with the Dutch, he wrote his Amboyna *, in which he represents the Dutch as a pack of avaritious, cruel, ungrateful rascals:—and when the exclusion-bill was moved in parliament, he wrote his Duke of Guise †, in which those who were for preserving and securing the religion of their country, were exposed under the character of the duke of Guise and his party, who leagued together for excluding Henry IV. of France from the throne, on the account of his religion.—The city of London too was made to feel the partial and mercenary licentiousness of the stage at that time; for the citizens having at that time, as well as now, a great deal of property, they had a mind to preserve that property, and therefore they opposed some of the arbitrary measures which were then begun, but pursued more openly in the following reign; for which reason they were then always represented upon the stage as a parcel of designing knaves, dissembling hypocrites, griping usurers,—and cuckolds into the bargain.

My lords, the proper business of the stage, and that for which only it is useful, is to expose those vices and follies, which the laws cannot lay hold of; and to recommend those beauties and virtues, which ministers and courtiers seldom either imitate or re-

* This is not quite exact. The Dutch war began in 1672. The play was acted and printed in 1673.

† This was certainly a party-play, though the occasion of it may be doubted. It made its appearance in 1683, and was violently attacked by the Whigs. If lord Chesterfield had implicitly adopted the opinions of his grandfather Hallifax, he would scarcely have spoken, as he does here, of the exclusion-bill.

2 ward.

ward. But by laying it under a licence, and under an arbritrary court-licence too, you will, in my opinion, entirely pervert its uſe: for though I have the greateſt eſteem for that noble duke, in whoſe hands this power is at preſent deſigned to fall, though I have an entire confidence in his judgment and impartiality; yet I may ſuppoſe that a leaning towards the faſhions of a court is ſometimes hard to be avoided. It may be very difficult to make one, who is every day at court, believe that to be a vice or folly, which he ſees daily practiſed by thoſe he loves and eſteems. By cuſtom, even deformity itſelf becomes familiar, and at laſt agreeable. To ſuch a perſon, let his natural impartiality be never ſo great, that may appear to be a libel againſt the court, which is only a moſt juſt and a moſt neceſſary ſatire upon the faſhionable vices and follies of the court. Courtiers, my lords, are too polite to reprove one another; the only place where they can meet with any juſt reproof, is a free though not a licentious ſtage; and as every ſort of vice and folly, generally in all countries, begins at court, and from thence ſpreads through the country, by laying the ſtage under an arbitrary court-licence, inſtead of leaving it what it is, and always ought to be, a gentle ſcourge for the vices of great men and courtiers, you will make it a canal for propagating and conveying their vices and follies through the whole kingdom.

From hence, my lords, I think it muſt appear, that the bill now before us cannot ſo properly be called a bill for reſtraining licentiouſneſs, as it may be called a bill for reſtraining the liberty of the ſtage, and for reſtraining it too in that branch which, in all countries,

countries, has been the most useful; therefore I must look upon this bill as a most dangerous encroachment upon liberty in general. Nay, farther, my lords, it is not only an encroachment upon liberty, but it is likewise an encroachment upon property. Wit, my lords, is a sort of property: it is the property of those who have it, and too often the only property they have to depend on. It is indeed but a precarious dependence. Thank God! we, my lords, have a dependence of another kind; we have a much less precarious support, and therefore cannot feel the inconveniencies of the bill now before us; but it is our duty to encourage and protect wit, whosesoever's property it may be. Those gentlemen who have any such property, are all, I hope, our friends. Do not let us subject them to any unnecessary or arbitrary restraint. I must own, I cannot easily agree to the laying of any tax upon wit; but by this bill it is to be heavily taxed, it is to be excised; for, if this bill passes, it cannot be retailed in a proper way without a permit, and the lord chamberlain is to have the honor of being chief-gauger, supervisor, commissioner, judge, and jury. But what is still more hard, though the poor author, the proprietor I should say, cannot perhaps dine till he has found out and agreed with a purchaser; yet, before he can propose to seek for a purchaser, he must patiently submit to have his goods rummaged at this new excise-office, where they may be detained for fourteen days, and even then he may find them returned as prohibited goods, by which his chief and best market will be for ever shut against him; and that without any cause, without the least shadow of reason, either from the laws of his country, or the laws of the stage.

These hardships, this hazard, which every gentleman will be exposed to, who writes any thing for the stage, must certainly prevent every man of a generous and free spirit from attempting any thing in that way; and, as the stage has always been the proper channel for wit and humour, therefore, my lords, when I speak against this bill, I must think, I plead the cause of wit, I plead the cause of humour, I plead the cause of the British stage, and of every gentleman of taste in the kingdom. But it is not, my lords, for the sake of wit only; even for the sake of his majesty's lord chamberlain, I must be against this bill. The noble duke who has now the honor to execute that office has, I am sure, as little inclination to disoblige as any man; but, if this bill passes, he must disoblige, he may disoblige some of his most intimate friends. It is impossible to write a play, but some of the characters, or some of the satire, may be interpreted so as to point at some person or another, perhaps at some person in an eminent station. When it comes to be acted, the people will make the application; and the person against whom the application is made will think himself injured, and will at least privately resent it: at present this resentment can be directed only against the author; but, when an author's play appears with my lord chamberlain's passport, every such resentment will be turned from the author, and pointed directly against the lord chamberlain, who by his stamp made the piece current. What an unthankful office are we therefore by this bill to put upon his majesty's lord chamberlain! an office which can no way contribute to his honor or profit, and such a one as must necessarily gain him a great deal of ill-will, and create him a number of enemies.

The last reason I shall trouble your lordships with, for my being against the bill, is that, in my opinion, it will in no way answer the end proposed: I mean the end openly proposed; and I am sure the only end which your lordships propose. To prevent the acting of a play which has any tendency to blasphemy, immorality, sedition, or private scandal, can signify nothing, unless you can prevent its being printed and published. On the contrary, if you prevent its being acted, and admit of its being printed, you will propagate the mischief: your prohibition will prove a bellows, which will blow up the fire you intend to extinguish. This bill can therefore be of no use for preventing either the public or the private injury intended by such a play; and consequently can be of no manner of use, unless it be designed as a precedent, as a leading step towards another for subjecting the press likewise to a licenser. For such a wicked purpose it may indeed be of great use; and in that light it may most properly be called a step towards arbitrary power.

Let us consider, my lords, that arbitrary power has seldom or never been introduced into any country at once. It must be introduced by slow degrees, and as it were step by step, lest the people should perceive its approach. The barriers and fences of the people's liberty muſt be plucked up one by one, and ſome plauſible pretences muſt be found for removing or hood-winking, one after another, thoſe ſentries who are poſted by the conſtitution of a free country, for warning the people of their danger. When theſe preparatory ſteps are once made, the people may then, indeed, with regret, ſee ſlavery and arbitrary power making long ſtrides over their land, but it will be too late to think of preventing or avoiding the impending ruin. The ſtage, my lords, and the preſs, are two of our out-ſentries; if we remove them, if we hood-wink them,—if we throw them in fetters, the enemy may ſurprize us. Therefore I muſt look upon the bill now before us as a ſtep, and a moſt neceſſary ſtep too, for introducing arbitrary power into this kingdom: it is a ſtep ſo neceſſary, that if ever any future ambitious king, or guilty miniſter, ſhould form to himſelf ſo wicked a deſign, he will have reaſon to thank us, for having done ſo much of the work to his hand; but ſuch thanks, or thanks from ſuch a man, I am convinced, every one of your lordſhips would bluſh to receive, and ſcorn to deſerve.

XLVII.

LORD CHESTERFIELD's first speech on the Gin act *, Feb. 21, 1743, after the second reading of the Bill.

MY LORDS,

THE bill now under our consideration appears to me to deserve a much closer regard than seems to have been paid to it in the other house, through which it was hurried with the utmost precipitation, and where it passed almost without the formality of a debate; nor can I think that earnestness, with which some lords seem inclined to press it forward here, consistent with the importance of the consequences which may with great reason be expected from it.

It has been urged, that where so great a number have formed expectations of a national benefit from any bill, so much deference, at least, is due to their judgment, as that the bill should be considered in a committee. This, my lords, I admit to be in other cases a just and reasonable demand; and will readily allow that the proposal, not only of a considerable number, but even of any single lord, ought to be fully examined, and regularly debated, according to the usual forms of this house. But in the present case,

* The act of parliament, that had been passed in the 9th year of George II. by which no person was permitted to sell spirituous liquor in less quantity than two gallons, without a licence, for which 50 pounds was to be paid, having proved, from the difficulties in the execution, ineffectual to obstruct the progress of drunkenness among the common people; a new bill was moved and passed in the house of commons, by which a small duty was laid on the spirits *per* gallon at the still-head, and the price of licences reduced to twenty shillings.

case, my lords, and in all cases like the present, this demand is improper, because it is useless; and it is useless, because we can do now all that we can do hereafter in a committee. For the bill before us is a money-bill, which, according to the present opinion of the commons, we have no right to amend, and which therefore we have no need of considering in a committee, since the event of all our deliberations must be, that we are either to reject or pass it in its present state. For I suppose no lord will think this a proper time to enter into a controversy with the commons, for the revival of those privileges to which I believe we have a right; and such a controversy, the least attempt to amend a money-bill will certainly produce.

To desire therefore, my lords, that this bill may be considered in a committee, is only to desire that it may gain one step without opposition; that it may proceed through the forms of the house by stealth, and that the consideration of it may be delayed, till the exigencies of the government shall be so great, as not to allow time for raising the supplies by any other method.

By this artifice, gross as it is, the patrons of this wonderful bill hope to obstruct a plain and open detection of its tendency. They hope, my lords, that the bill shall operate in the same manner with the liquor which it is intended to bring into more general use; and that, as those who drink spirits are drunk before they are well aware that they are drinking, the effects of this law shall be perceived before we know that we have made it. Their intent is, to give us a dram of policy, which is to be swallowed before it is tasted, and which, when once it is swallowed, will turn our heads.

But, my lords, I hope we shall be so cautious as to examine the draught which these state empirics have thought proper to offer us; and I am confident that a very little examination will convince us of the pernicious qualities of their new preparation, and shew that it can have no other effect than that of poisoning the public.

The law before us, my lords, seems to be the effect of that practice of which it is intended likewise to be the cause, and to be dictated by the liquor of which it so effectually promotes the use; for surely it never before was conceived, by any man intrusted with the administration of public affairs, to raise taxes by the destruction of the people.

Nothing, my lords, but the destruction of all the most laborious and useful part of the nation, can be expected from the licence which is now proposed to be given, not only to drunkenness, but to drunkenness of the most detestable and dangerous kind, to the abuse not only of intoxicating, but of poisonous liquors.

Nothing, my lords, is more absurd than to assert, that the use of spirits will be hindered by the bill now before us, or indeed that it will not be in a very great degree promoted by it. For what produces all kind of wickedness, but the prospect of impunity on one part, or the solicitation of opportunity on the other? Either of these have too frequently been sufficient to overpower the sense of morality, and even of religion;

and

and what is not to be feared from them, when they ſhall unite their force, and operate together, when temptations ſhall be increaſed, and terror taken away?

It is allowed, by thoſe who have hitherto diſputed on either ſide of this queſtion, that the people appear obſtinately enamoured of this new liquor; it is allowed on both parts, that this liquor corrupts the mind, and enervates the body, and deſtroys vigor and virtue, at the ſame time that it makes thoſe who drink it too idle and too feeble for work; and, while it impoveriſhes them by the preſent expence, diſables them from retrieving its ill conſequences by ſubſequent induſtry.

It might be imagined, my lords, that thoſe who had thus far agreed would not eaſily find any occaſions of diſpute; nor would any man, unacquainted with the motives by which parliamentary debates are too often influenced, ſuſpect that after the pernicious qualities of this liquor, and the general inclination among the people to the immoderate uſe of it, had been generally admitted, it could be afterwards inquired, whether it ought to be made more common, whether this univerſal thirſt for poiſon ought to be encouraged by the legiſlature, and whether a new ſtatute ought to be made, to ſecure drunkards in the gratification of their appetites.

To pretend, my lords, that the deſign of this bill is to prevent or diminiſh the uſe of ſpirits, is to trample upon common ſenſe, and to violate the rules of decency as well as of reaſon. For when did any man hear, that a commodity was prohibited by licenſing its ſale, or that to offer and refuſe is the ſame action?

It is indeed pleaded, that it will be made dearer by the tax which is proposed, and that the increase of the price will diminish the number of the purchasers; but it is at the same time expected, that this tax shall supply the expence of a war on the continent. It is asserted therefore, that the consumption of spirits will be hindered; and yet that it will be such as may be expected to furnish, from a very small tax, a revenue sufficient for the support of armies, for the re-establishment of the Austrian family, and the repressing of the attempts of France.

Surely, my lords, these expectations are not very consistent; nor can it be imagined that they are both formed in the same head, though they may be expressed by the same mouth. It is however some recommendation of a statesman, when, of his assertions, one can be found reasonable or true; and in this, praise cannot be denied to our present ministers: for though it is undoubtedly false, that this tax will lessen the consumption of spirits, it is certainly true that it will produce a very large revenue, a revenue that will not fail but with the people from whose debaucheries it arises.

Our ministers will therefore have the same honor with their predecessors, of having given rise to a new fund, not indeed for the payment of our debts, but for much more valuable purposes, for the cheering of our hearts under oppression, and for the ready support of those debts which we have lost hopes of paying. They are resolved, my lords, that the nation, which no endeavours can make wise, shall, while they are at its head, at least be merry; and, since public happiness

neſs is the end of government, they ſeem to imagine that they ſhall deſerve applauſe by an expedient, which will enable every man to lay his cares aſleep, to drown ſorrow, and loſe in the delights of drunkenneſs both the public miſeries and his own.

Luxury, my lords, is to be taxed, but vice prohibited, let the difficulties in executing the law be what they will. Would you lay a tax upon a breach of the ten commandments? Would not ſuch a tax be wicked and ſcandalous; becauſe it would imply an indulgence to all thoſe who could pay the tax? Is not this a reproach moſt juſtly thrown by proteſtants upon the church of Rome? Was it not the chief cauſe of the Reformation? And will you follow a precedent which brought reproach and ruin upon thoſe that introduced it? This is the very caſe now before us. You are going to lay a tax, and conſequently to indulge a ſort of drunkenneſs, which almoſt neceſſarily produces a breach of every one of the ten commandments. Can you expect the reverend bench will approve of this? I am convinced they will not, and therefore I wiſh I had ſeen it full upon this occaſion. I am ſure I have ſeen it much fuller upon ſome other occaſions, in which religion had no ſuch deep concern.

We have already, my lords, ſeveral ſorts of funds in this nation, ſo many that a man muſt have a good deal of learning to be maſter of them. Thanks to his majeſty, we have now amongſt us the moſt learned man of the nation in this way. I wiſh he would riſe up and tell us, what name we are to give to this new fund. We have already the civil liſt fund, the ſinking fund,

fund, the aggregate fund, the South-sea fund, and God knows how many others. What name we are to give to this new fund I know not, unless we are to call it the drinking fund. It may perhaps enable the people of a certain foreign territory to drink claret, but it will disable the people of this kingdom from drinking any thing else but gin; for, when a man has, by gin-drinking, rendered himself unfit for labor or business, he can purchase nothing else, and then the best thing he can do is to drink on till he dies.

Surely, my lords, men of such unbounded benevolence, as our present ministers, deserve such honors as were never paid before: they deserve to bestride a butt upon every sign-post in the city, or to have their figures exhibited as tokens where this liquor is to be sold by the licence which they have procured. They must be at least remembered to future ages, as the happy politicians, who, after all expedients for raising taxes had been employed, discovered a new method of draining the last reliques of the public wealth, and added a new revenue to the government: nor will those, who shall hereafter enumerate the several funds now established among us, forget among the benefactors to their country the illustrious authors of the drinking fund.

May I be allowed, my lords, to congratulate my countrymen and fellow-subjects upon the happy times which are now approaching, in which no man will be disqualified from the privilege of being drunk; when all discontent and disloyalty shall be forgotten, and the people, though now considered by the ministry as enemies, shall acknowledge the lenity of that government,

government, under which all reſtraints are taken away?

But, to a bill for ſuch deſirable purpoſes, it would be proper, my lords, to prefix a preamble, in which the kindneſs of our intentions ſhould be more fully explained, that the nation may not miſtake our indulgence for cruelty, nor conſider their benefactors as their perſecutors. If therefore this bill be conſidered and amended (for why elſe ſhould it be conſidered?) in a committee, I ſhall humbly propoſe, that it ſhall be introduced in this manner. "Whereas the deſigns of the preſent miniſtry, whatever they "are, cannot be executed without a great number of "mercenaries, which mercenaries cannot be hired "without money; and whereas the preſent diſpoſition "of this nation to drunkenneſs inclines us to believe, "that they will pay more chearfully for the undiſturbed enjoyment of diſtilled liquors, than for any "other conceſſion that can be made by the govern"ment; be it enacted, by the king's moſt excellent "majeſty, that no man ſhall hereafter be denied the "right of being drunk on the following condi"tions."

This, my lords, to trifle no longer, is the proper preamble to this bill, which contains only the conditions on which the people of this kingdom are to be allowed henceforward to riot in debauchery, in debauchery licenſed by law, and countenanced by the magiſtrates. For there is no doubt but thoſe, on whom the inventors of this tax ſhall confer authority, will be directed to aſſiſt their maſters in their deſign to encourage the conſumption of that liquor, from which

which ſuch large revenues are expected, and to multiply without end thoſe licences which are to pay a yearly tribute to the crown.

By this unbounded licence, my lords, that price will be leſſened, from the increaſe of which the expectations of the efficacy of this law are pretended; for the number of retailers will leſſen the value, as in all other caſes, and leſſen it more than this tax will increaſe it. Beſides, it is to be conſidered, that at preſent the retailer expects to be paid for the danger which he incurs by an unlawful trade, and will not truſt his reputation or his purſe to the mercy of his cuſtomer, without a profit proportioned to the hazard; but, when once the reſtraint ſhall be taken away, he will ſell for common gain, and it can hardly be imagined that, at preſent, he ſubjects himſelf to informations and penalties for leſs than ſix-pence a gallon.

The ſpecious pretence, on which this bill is founded, and indeed the only pretence that deſerves to be termed ſpecious, is the propriety of taxing vice; but this maxim of government has, on this occaſion, been either miſtaken or perverted. Vice, my lords, is not properly to be taxed, but ſuppreſſed; and heavy taxes are ſometimes the only means by which that ſuppreſſion can be attained. Luxury, my lords, or the exceſs of that which is pernicious only by its exceſs, may very properly be taxed, that ſuch exceſs, though not ſtrictly unlawful, may be made more difficult. But the uſe of theſe things which are ſimply hurtful, hurtful in their own nature, and in every degree, is to be prohibited. None, my lords, ever heard in any nation of a tax upon theft or adultery, becauſe a tax implies

implies a licence granted for the use of that which is taxed, to all who shall be willing to pay it.

Drunkenness, my lords, is universally and in all circumstances an evil; and therefore ought not to be taxed, but punished, and the means of it not to be made easy by a slight impost, which none can feel, but to be removed out of the reach of the people, and secured by the heaviest taxes, levied with the utmost rigor. I hope those, to whose care the religion of the nation is particularly consigned, will unanimously join with me in maintaining the necessity, not of taxing vice, but suppressing it, and unite for the rejecting of a bill, by which the future, as well as present, happiness of thousands must be destroyed.

XLVIII.

Lord Chesterfield's second speech on the Gin act, February 24, 1743.

MY LORDS,

THOUGH the noble lord * who has been pleased to excite us to an unanimous concurrence with himself and his associates in the ministry, in passing the excellent and wonder-working bill; this bill which is to lessen the consumption of spirits, without lessening the quantity which is distilled; which is to restrain drunkards from drinking, by setting their favourite liquor always before their eyes; to conquer habits by continuing them; and correct vice by indulging it, according to the lowest

* The duke of Newcastle.

reckoning,

reckoning, for at leaſt another year; ſtill, my lords, ſuch is my obſtinacy, or ſuch my ignorance, that I cannot yet comply with his propoſal, nor can prevail with myſelf either to concur with meaſures ſo apparently oppoſite to the intereſt of the public, or to hear them vindicated, without declaring how little I approve it.

During the courſe of this long debate, I have endeavoured to recapitulate and digeſt the arguments which have been advanced, and have conſidered them both ſeparately and conjointly, but find myſelf at the ſame diſtance from conviction as when I firſt entered the houſe.

In vindication of this bill, my lords, we have been told that the preſent law is ineffectual; that our manufacture is not to be deſtroyed; or not this year; that the ſecurity offered by the preſent bill has induced great numbers to ſubſcribe to the new fund; that it has been approved by the commons; and that, if it be found ineffectual, it may be amended another ſeſſion.

All theſe arguments, my lords, I ſhall endeavour to examine, becauſe I am always deſirous of gratifying thoſe great men to whom the adminiſtration of affairs is intruſted, and have always very cautiouſly avoided the odium of diſaffection, which they will undoubtedly throw, in imitation of their predeceſſors, upon all thoſe whoſe wayward conſciences ſhall oblige them to hinder the execution of their ſchemes.

With a very ſtrong deſire, therefore, though with no great hopes, of finding them in the right, I venture to begin my inquiry, and engage in the examination

nation of their first assertion, that the present law against the abuse of strong liquors is without effect.

I hope, my lords, it portends well to my inquiry, that the first position which I have to examine is true; nor can I forbear to congratulate your lordships upon having heard from the new ministry one assertion not to be contradicted.

It is evident, my lords, from daily observation, and demonstrable from the papers upon the table, that every year, since the enacting of the last law, that vice has increased which it was intended to repress, and that no time has been so favourable to the retailers of spirits as that which has passed since they were prohibited.

It may therefore be expected, my lords, that, having agreed with the ministers in their fundamental proposition, I shall concur with them in the consequence which they draw from it; and, having allowed that the present law is ineffectual, should admit that another is necessary.

But, my lords, in order to discover whether this consequence be necessary, it must first be inquired why the present law is of no force? For, my lords, it will be found, upon reflection, that there are certain degrees of corruption that may hinder the effect of the best laws. The magistrates may be vicious, and forbear to enforce that law by which themselves are condemned; they may be indolent, and inclined rather to connive at wickedness, by which they are not injured themselves, than to repress it by a laborious exertion of their authority; or they may be timorous, and, instead of awing the vicious, may be awed by them.

In any of these cases, my lords, the law is not to be condemned for its inefficacy, since it only fails by the defect of those who are to direct its operations. The best and most important laws will contribute very little to the security or happiness of a people, if no judges of integrity and spirit can be found amongst them. Even the most beneficial and useful bill that ministers can possibly imagine, a bill for laying on our estates a tax of the fifth part of their yearly value, would be wholly without effect, if collectors could not be obtained.

I am therefore, my lords, yet doubtful, whether the inefficacy of the law now subsisting necessarily obliges us to provide another: for those that declared it to be useless, owned at the same time that no man endeavoured to enforce it; so that perhaps its only defect may be, that it will not execute itself.

Nor, though I should allow that the law is at present impeded by difficulties which cannot be broken through, but by men of more spirit and dignity than the ministers may be inclined to trust with commissions of the peace, yet it can only be collected, that another law is necessary, not that the law now proposed will be of any advantage.

Great use has been made of the inefficacy of the present law, to decry the proposal made by the noble lord, for laying a high duty upon these pernicious liquors. High duties have already, as we are informed, been tried without advantage; high duties are at this hour imposed upon those spirits which are retailed, yet we see them every day sold in the streets, without the payment of the tax required; and there-

fore

fore it will be folly to make a ſecond eſſay of means which have been found, by the eſſay of many years, unſucceſsful.

It has been granted on all ſides in this debate, nor was it ever denied on any other occaſion, that the conſumption of any commodity is moſt eaſily hindered by raiſing its price; and its price is to be raiſed by the impoſition of a duty. This, my lords, which is, I ſuppoſe, the opinion of every man, of whatever degree of experience or underſtanding, appears likewiſe to have been thought of by the authors of the preſent law; and therefore they imagined that they had effectually provided againſt the increaſe of drunkenneſs, by laying, upon that liquor which ſhould be retailed in ſmall quantities, a duty which none of the inferior claſſes of drunkards would be able to pay.

Thus, my lords, they conceived that they had reformed the common people, without infringing the pleaſures of others; and applauded the happy contrivance, by which ſpirits were to be made dear only to the poor, while every man who could afford to purchaſe two gallons was at liberty to riot at his eaſe, and, over a full-flowing bumper, look down with contempt upon his former companions, now ruthleſsly condemned to diſconſolate ſobriety.

But, my lords, this intention was fruſtrated, and the project, ingenious as it was, fell to the ground: for, though they had laid a tax, they unhappily forgot this tax would make no addition to the price unleſs it was paid; and that it would not be paid unleſs ſome were empowered to collect it.

Here, my lords, was the difficulty; those who made the law were inclined to lay a tax from which themselves should be exempt, and therefore would not charge the liquor as it issued from the still; and when once it was dispersed in the hands of petty dealers, it was no longer to be found without the assistance of informers; and informers could not carry on the business of prosecution, without the consent of the people.

It is not necessary to dwell any longer upon the law, the repeal of which is proposed, since it appears already that it failed, only from a partiality not easily defended, and from the omission of what is now proposed, the collecting the duty from the still-head.

If this method be followed, there will be no longer any need of informations, or of any rigorous or new measures; the same officers that collect a smaller duty may levy a greater; nor can they be easily deceived with regard to the quantities that are made; the deceits, at least, that can be used, are in use already; they are frequently detected and suppressed, nor will a larger duty enable the distillers to elude the vigilance of the officers with more success.

Against this proposal, therefore, the inefficacy of the present law can be no objection. But it is urged, that such duties would destroy the trade of distilling; and a noble lord has been pleased to express great tenderness for a manufacture so beneficial and extensive.

That a large duty, levied at the still, would destroy, or very much impair, the trade of distilling, is certainly supposed by those who defend it, for they

proposed

proposed it only for that end; and what better method can they propose, when they are called to deliberate upon a bill for the prevention of the excessive use of distilled liquors?

The noble lord has been pleased kindly to inform us, that the trade of distilling is very extensive, that it employs great numbers, and that they have arrived at exquisite skill, and therefore—note well the consequence—the trade of distilling is not to be discouraged.

Once more, my lords, allow me to wonder at the different conceptions of different understandings. It appears to me, that since the spirits, which the distillers produce, are allowed to enfeeble the limbs, and vitiate the blood, to pervert the heart, and obscure the intellects, that the number of distillers should be no argument in their favour! for I never heard that a law against theft was repealed or delayed because thieves were numerous. It appears to me, my lords, that if so formidable a body are confederated against the virtue or the lives of their fellow-citizens, it is time to put an end to the havock, and to interpose, while it is yet in our power to stop the destruction.

So little, my lords, am I affected with the merit of the wonderful skill which the distillers are said to have attained, that it is, in my opinion, no faculty of great use to mankind, to prepare palatable poison; nor shall I ever contribute my interest for the reprieve of a murderer, because he has, by long practice, obtained great dexterity in his trade.

If their liquors are so delicious, that the people are tempted to their own destruction, let us at length, my lords, secure them from these fatal draughts, by bursting the vials that contain them; let us crush at once these artists in slaughter, who have reconciled their countrymen to sickness and to ruin, and spread over the pitfals of debauchery such baits as cannot be resisted.

The noble lord has, indeed, admitted that this bill may not be found sufficiently coercive, but gives us hopes that it may be improved and enforced another year, and persuades us to endeavour a reformation of drunkenness by degrees, and, above all, to beware at present of hurting the *manufacture*.

I am very far, my lords, from thinking that there are, this year, any peculiar reasons for tolerating murder; nor can I conceive why the manufacture should be held sacred now, if it be to be destroyed hereafter. We are, indeed, desired to try how far this law will operate, that we may be more able to proceed with due regard to this valuable manufacture.

With regard to the operation of the law, it appears to me, that it will only enrich the government, without reforming the people; and I believe there are not many of a different opinion. If any diminution of the sale of spirits be expected from it, it is to be considered that this diminution will, or will not, be such as is desired for the reformation of the people. If it be sufficient, the manufacture is at an end, and all the reasons against a higher duty are of equal force against this: but if it is not sufficient, we have, at leaſt, omitted part of our duty, and have neglected the health and virtue of the people.

I cannot, my lords, yet diſcover why a reprieve is deſired for this manufacture; why the preſent year is not equally propitious to the reformation of mankind, as any will be that may ſucceed it. It is true we are at war with two nations, and perhaps with more; but war may be better proſecuted without money than without men; and we but little conſult the military glory of our country, if we raiſe ſupplies for paying our armies, by the deſtruction of thoſe armies that we are contriving to pay.

We have heard the neceſſity of reforming the nation by degrees, urged as an argument for impoſing firſt a lighter duty, and afterwards a heavier. This complaiſance for wickedneſs, my lords, is not ſo defenſible as that it ſhould be battered by arguments in form, and therefore I ſhall only relate a reply made by Webb, the noted walker, upon a parallel occaſion.

This man, who muſt be remembered by many of your lordſhips, was remarkable for vigor, both of mind and body, and lived wholly upon water for his drink, and chiefly upon vegetables for his other ſuſtenance. He was one day recommending his regimen to one of his friends who loved wine, and who perhaps might ſomewhat contribute to the proſperity of this ſpirituous manufacture, and urged him, with great earneſtneſs, to quit a courſe of luxury, by which his health and his intellects would equally be deſtroyed. The gentleman appeared convinced, and told him, "that he would conform to his counſel, "and thought he could not change his courſe of life "at once, but would leave off ſtrong liquors by de-"grees." "By degrees," ſays the other with indignation, "if you ſhould unhappily fall into the fire, "would you caution your ſervants not to pull you "out but by degrees?"

This anſwer, my lords, is applicable to the preſent caſe. The nation is ſunk into the loweſt ſtate of corruption; the people are not only vicious, but inſolent beyond example; they not only break the laws, but defy them, and yet ſome of your lordſhips are for reforming them by degrees.

I am not ſo eaſily perſuaded, my lords, that our miniſters really intend to ſupply the defects that may hereafter be diſcovered in this bill. It will doubtleſs produce money, perhaps much more than they appear to expect from it. I doubt not but the licenſed retailers will be more than fifty thouſand, and the quantity retailed muſt increaſe with the number of retailers. As the bill will, therefore, anſwer all the ends intended by it, I do not expect to ſee it altered; for I have never obſerved miniſters deſirous of amending their own errors, unleſs they are ſuch as have cauſed a deficiency in the revenue.

Beſides, my lords, it is not certain that, when this fund is mortgaged to the public creditors, they can prevail upon the commons to change the ſecurity. They may continue the bill in force, for the reaſons, whatever they are, for which they have paſſed it; and the good intentions of our miniſters, however ſincere, may be defeated, and drunkenneſs, legal drunkenneſs, eſtabliſhed in the nation.

This,

This, my lords, is very reaſonable; and therefore we ought to exert ourſelves for the ſafety of the nation, while the power is yet in our own hands; and, without regard to the opinion or proceedings of the other houſe, ſhew that we are yet the chief guardians of the people.

The ready compliance of the commons, with the meaſures propoſed in this bill, has been mentioned here, with a view, I ſuppoſe, of influencing us; but ſurely by thoſe who had forgotten our independence, or reſigned their own. It is not only the right, but the duty of either houſe, to deliberate, without regard to the determinations of the other: for how ſhould the nation receive any benefit from the diſtinct powers that compoſe the legiſlature, unleſs the determinations are without influence upon each other? If either the example or authority of the commons can divert us from following our own convictions, we are no longer part of the legiſlature; we have given up our honors, and our privileges; and what then is our concurrence but ſlavery, or our ſuffrage but an echo?

The only argument, therefore, that now remains, is the expediency of gratifying thoſe, by whoſe ready ſubſcription the exigencies our new ſtateſmen have brought upon us have been ſupported, and of continuing the ſecurity by which they have been encouraged to ſuch liberal contributions.

Public credit, my lords, is indeed of very great importance; but public credit can never be long ſupported without public virtue; nor indeed, if the government could mortgage the morals and health of the people, would it be juſt and rational to confirm the bargain. If the miniſtry can raiſe money only by the deſtruction of their fellow-ſubjects, they ought to abandon thoſe ſchemes for which the money is neceſſary; for what calamity can be equal to unbounded wickedneſs?

But, my lords, there is no neceſſity for a choice which may coſt us or our miniſters ſo much regret; for the ſame ſubſcriptions may be procured by an offer of the ſame advantages to a fund of any other kind; and the ſinking fund will eaſily ſupply any deficiency that might be ſuſpected in another ſcheme.

To confeſs the truth, I ſhould feel very little pain from an account that the nation was for ſome time determined to be leſs liberal of their contributions; and that money was withheld, till it was known in what expeditions it was to be employed, to what princes ſubſidies were to be paid, and what advantages were to be purchaſed by it for our country. I ſhould rejoice, my lords, to hear that the lottery, by which the deficiencies of this duty are to be ſupplied, was not filled; and that the people were grown, at laſt, wiſe enough to diſcern the fraud, and to prefer honeſt commerce, by which all may be gainers, to a game by which the greateſt number muſt certainly be loſers.

The lotteries, my lords, which former miniſters have propoſed, have always been cenſured by thoſe that ſaw their nature and their tendency; they have been conſidered as legal cheats, by which the ignorant and the raſh are defrauded, and the ſubtle and avaricious often enriched; they have been allowed to divert the people from trade, and to alienate them from

useful

useful induſtry. A man who is uneaſy in his circumſtances, and idle in his diſpoſition, collects the remains of his fortune, and buys tickets in a lottery; retires from buſineſs, indulges himſelf in lazineſs, and waits, in ſome obſcure place, the event of his adventure. Another, inſtead of employing his ſtock in trade, rents a garret, and makes it his buſineſs, by falſe intelligence and chimerical alarms, to raiſe and ſink the price of tickets alternately, and takes advantage of the lies which he has himſelf invented.

Such, my lords, is the traffick that is produced by this ſcheme of getting money; nor were theſe inconveniencies unknown to the preſent miniſters in the time of their predeceſſors, whom they never ceaſed to purſue with the loudeſt clamors, whenever the exigencies of the government reduced them to a lottery.

If I, my lords, might preſume to recommend to our miniſters the moſt probable method of raiſing a large ſum, for the payment of the troops of the electorate, I ſhould, inſtead of the tax and lottery now propoſed, adviſe them to eſtabliſh a certain number of licenſed wheel-barrows, on which the laudable trade of thimble and button might be carried on for the ſupport of the war, and ſhoe-boys might contribute to the defence of the houſe of *Auſtria* by raffling for apples.

Having now, my lords, examined, with the utmoſt candor, all the reaſons which have been offered in defence of the bill, I cannot conceal the reſult of my inquiry. The arguments have had ſo little effect upon my underſtanding, that, as every man judges of others by himſelf, I cannot believe that they have

any

any influence, even upon those that offer them; and therefore I am convinced that this bill must be the result of considerations which have been hitherto concealed, and is intended to promote designs which are never to be discovered by the authors before their execution.

With regard to these motives and designs, however artfully concealed, every lord in this house is at liberty to offer his conjectures.

When I consider, my lords, the tendency of this bill, I find it calculated only for the propagation of diseases, the suppression of industry, and the destruction of mankind. I find it the most fatal engine that ever was pointed at a people; an engine by which those who are not killed will be disabled, and those who preserve their limbs will be deprived of their senses.

This bill therefore appears to be designed only to thin the ranks of mankind, and to disburden the world of the multitudes that inhabit it, and is perhaps the strongest proof of political sagacity that our new ministers have yet exhibited. They well know, my lords, that they are universally detested, and that, whenever a Briton is destroyed, they are freed from an enemy; they have therefore opened the floodgates of gin upon the nation, that, when it is less numerous, it may be more easily governed.

Other ministers, my lords, who had not attained to so great a knowledge in the art of making war upon their country, when they found their enemies clamorous and bold, used to awe them with prosecutions and penalties, or destroy them like burglars with prisons and with gibbets. But every age, my lords, produces some improvement; and every nation, however degenerate, gives birth, at some happy period of time, to men of great and enterprizing genius. It is our fortune to be witnesses of a new discovery in politics; we may congratulate ourselves upon being cotemporaries with those men, who have shewed that hangmen and halters are unnecessary in a state, and that ministers may escape the reproach of destroying their enemies, by inciting them to destroy themselves.

This new method may, indeed, have upon different constitutions a different operation; it may destroy the lives of some, and the senses of others; but either of these effects will answer the purposes of the ministry, to whom it is indifferent, provided the nation becomes insensible, whether pestilence or lunacy prevails among them. Either mad or dead the greatest part of the people must quickly be, or there is no hope of the continuance of the present ministry.

For this purpose, my lords, what could have been invented more efficacious than an establishment of a certain number of shops, at which poison may be vended; poison so prepared as to please the palate, while it wastes the strength, and only kills by intoxication? From the first instant that any of the enemies of the ministry shall grow clamorous and turbulent, a crafty hireling may lead him to the ministerial slaughter-house, and ply him with their wonder-working liquor, till he is no longer able to speak or think; and, my lords, no man can be more agree-

able

able to our miniſters, than he that can neither ſpeak nor think, except thoſe who ſpeak without thinking.

But, my lords, the miniſters ought to reflect, that though all the people of the preſent age are their enemies, yet they have made no trial of the temper and inclinations of poſterity. Our ſucceſſors may be of opinions very different from ours; they may perhaps approve of wars on the continent, while our plantations are inſulted and our trade obſtructed; they may think the ſupport of the houſe of Auſtria of more importance to us than our own defence; and may perhaps ſo far differ from their fathers, as to imagine the treaſures of Britain very properly employed in ſupporting the troops, and increaſing the ſplendor, of a foreign electorate.

Whatever, my lords, be the true reaſon for which this bill is ſo warmly promoted, I think they ought, at leaſt, to be deliberately examined; and therefore cannot think it conſiſtent with our regard for the nation, to ſuffer it to be precipitated into a law. The year, my lords, is not ſo far advanced but that ſupplies may be raiſed by ſome other method, if this ſhould be rejected; nor do I think that we ought to conſent to this, even though our refuſal ſhould hinder the ſupplies, ſince we have no right, for the ſake of any advantage, however certain or great, to violate all the laws of heaven and earth, and to fill the exchequer with the price of the lives of our fellow-ſubjects.

Let us therefore, my lords, not ſuffer ourſelves to be driven forward with ſuch haſte, as may hinder us from obſerving whither we are going. Let us not be perſuaded to precipitate our counſels, by thoſe who know that all delays are detrimental to their deſigns, becauſe delays may produce new information; and they are conſcious that the bill will be the leſs approved, the more it is underſtood.

But every reaſon which they can offer againſt the motion is, in my opinion, a reaſon for it; and therefore I ſhall readily agree to poſtpone the clauſe, and no leſs readily to reject the bill.

If, at laſt, reaſon and evidence are vain, if neither juſtice nor compaſſion can prevail, but the nation muſt be deſtroyed for the ſupport of the government; let us at leaſt, my lords, confine our aſſertions, in the preamble, to truth. Let us not affirm that drunkenneſs is eſtabliſhed by the advice or conſent of the lords ſpiritual, ſince I am confident not one of them will ſo far contradict his own doctrine, as to vote for a bill which gives a ſanction to one vice, and miniſters opportunities and temptations to all others, and which, if it be not ſpeedily repealed, will overflow the whole nation with a deluge of wickedneſs.

XLIX.

His excellency the earl of CHESTERFIELD's letter to their high mightineſſes, the ſtates general of the united provinces, on taking leave, Feb. 26, N. S. 1732.

HIGH AND MIGHTY LORDS,

THE king, my maſter, who recalls me to attend the duties of my poſt about his royal perſon, has commanded me to repeat to you, on this occaſion, the ſtrongeſt aſſurances of his inviolable friendſhip for this illuſtrious republic.

It was by theſe aſſurances that I opened my commiſſion to your high mightineſſes: I am happy to cloſe it in the ſame manner; and I rejoice in the reflection that, throughout its whole duration, which has not been a ſhort one, every thing has viſibly concurred to evince the ſentiments of a monarch, who is incapable of expreſſing any but ſuch as are real.

His majeſty is truly ſenſible of the advantages that accrue to both nations from the alliance by which they are ſo ſtrictly connected. Ever attentive to the welfare of his ſubjects, and to that of his allies, he is determined to maintain, and, if poſſible, more cloſely to cement, an union formed by the common intereſt of the people, the balance of Europe, and the intereſt of the proteſtant religion, and which a happy preſcription ſeems to make unalterable for the future. Such is the ſyſtem which has never been departed from, but when the true intereſts of either the one or the other have been miſtaken or ſacrificed.

The

XLIX.

Lettre de ſon excellence mylord CHESTERFIELD aux états généraux des provinces-unies, pour prendre congé, le 26 Février, N. S. 1732.

HAUTS ET PUISSANS SEIGNEURS,

LE roi, mon maître, qui me rappelle pour remplir les fonctions de ma charge auprès de ſa perſonne, m'a ordonné de vous réitérer en cette occaſion les plus fortes aſſurances de ſon inviolable amitié pour cette illuſtre république.

C'eſt par-là que je commençai ma commiſſion auprès de vos hautes puiſſances; il m'eſt doux de la terminer de même, et je me félicite de ce que, pendant un aſſez long-tems qu'elle a duré, tout a viſiblement concouru à vérifier les ſentimens d'un monarque incapable d'en témoigner qui ne ſoient réels.

Le roi ſent vivement les avantages que les deux nations retirent de l'alliance qui les unit ſi étroitement. Toujours attentif au bonheur de ſes ſujets, et à celui de ſes alliés, il eſt réſolu d'entretenir, et s'il eſt poſſible, de ſerrer de plus en plus les nœuds d'une union que le bien commun des peuples, l'équilibre de l'Europe, l'intérêt de la religion proteſtante ont formée, et qu'une heureuſe preſcription ſemble rendre deſormais inaltérable. Tel eſt le ſyſtême dont on ne s'eſt jamais éloigné, que quand les véritables intérêts de l'une ou de l'autre nation ont été ignorés ou ſacrifiés.

Les

The light in which I repreſent to your high mightineſſes the diſpoſition of the king my maſter, is the ſame in which I ſhall give his majeſty an account of yours. The re-eſtabliſhment of the tranquillity of Europe is a ſtriking and recent proof of the good effects ariſing from this mutual confidence. Providence, which had united our intereſts, ſeems likewiſe to have united our counſels. Harmony, the object of my moſt ardent wiſhes, has invariably ſubſiſted as a thing of courſe. It has ſuperſeded my endeavours, and has left me, if I may ſo ſay, but the pleaſing regret of having been rather a ſpectator than a promoter of it.

If it were not cuſtomary, on theſe occaſions, to laviſh thoſe terms which are moſt expreſſive of the feelings of the heart, and which too often mean no more than mere ceremony, I ſhould make uſe of the moſt emphatical language, high and mighty lords, to expreſs my gratitude for the reception you have honored me with, during the execution of my commiſſion; nor ſhould I be afraid of ſaying too much.

But let my wiſhes be accepted in lieu of a ſpeech.

May the great diſpoſer of all events grant that your high mightineſſes may long and abundantly enjoy the proſperity, procured to your country by the wiſdom of your counſels! may he ſuſpend the courſe of human infirmities, and protract the period of life, in favour of thoſe whoſe experience, abilities, and labours, may contribute to the ſafety and glory of this republic! and may each moment of its exiſtence be

ſignalized

Les traits que j'employe pour repréſenter à vos hautes puiſſances les diſpoſitions du roi mon maître, ſont les mêmes dont je me ſervirai pour lui rendre compte des vôtres. Le rétabliſſement de la tranquillité de l'Europe eſt une preuve ſenſible et récente des bons effets qu'a produit cette confiance mutuelle. La providence, qui avoit uni nos intérêts, ſembloit auſſi avoir uni nos conſeils. L'harmonie, l'objet de mes deſirs les plus ardens, s'eſt entretenue comme d'elle-même. Elle a prévenu mes ſoins, et ne m'a laiſſé, ſi je puis parler ainſi, que le doux regret de n'y avoir contribué en rien, et de n'en avoir été que le ſpectateur.

Si dans des circonſtances pareilles à celles où je me trouve aujourd'hui, on n'eût pas prodigué tous les termes les plus capables d'exprimer les mouvemens du cœur, pendant qu'on ne fait ſouvent que s'acquitter d'un ſimple devoir de cérémonie, j'employerois, hauts et puiſſans ſeigneurs, ſans craindre d'en dire trop, les expreſſions les plus énergiques, pour vous marquer la vive reconnoiſſance, que m'inſpire l'accueil que vous m'avez témoigné durant le cours de ma commiſſion.

Mes vœux me tiendront lieu de diſcours.

Faſſe le grand arbitre des événemens, que vos hautes puiſſances participent longtems et abondamment à la proſpérité, que la ſageſſe de vos conſeils procure à votre patrie! Daigne-t il ſuſpendre le cours des infirmités humaines, et étendre les bornes de la vie, en faveur de ceux dont l'expérience, les talens et les travaux peuvent contribuer à la ſûreté et à la gloire de cette république! et daigne-t-il marquer

ſignalized by ſome ſucceſs, worthy of thoſe virtues and that courage, which firſt laid the foundation of it, and have ſupported it in ſo high a degree of ſplendor to this day!

(Signed,)

CHESTERFIELD.

L.

The earl of CHESTERFIELD's ſpeech to the ſtates general, on his taking leave of their high mightineſſes at the Hague, May 18, N. S. 1745.

HIGH AND MIGHTY LORDS,

THE king my maſter, on permitting me to return to England, has given me expreſs orders to renew to your high mightineſſes the ſtrongeſt aſſurances of his eſteem and friendſhip.

It is happy for me that ſo honorable a commiſſion lays on me ſo eaſy a duty.

As a faithful interpreter of the ſentiments of a ſincere friendſhip, I am far from borrowing the flattering expreſſions which a feigned friendſhip ſtands in need of.

Let crafty policy employ the moſt ſeducing artifices to cover its ambitious deſigns; let it put every ſpring in motion to gain your confidence, or at leaſt to lull you into a fatal ſecurity. True friendſhip, ſuch as that which unites the king my maſter with your high mightineſſes, deſpiſes thoſe artifices, and

chaque moment de ſa durée par quelque ſuccès di ne des vertus et du courage, qui en ont jetté les fondemens, et qui l'ont fait ſubſiſter avec tant d'éclat juſqu'à ce jour!

(*Etoit ſigné*,)

CHESTERFIELD.

L.

Diſcours de ſon excellence, le comte de CHESTERFIELD, aux états généraux, en prenant congé de leurs hautes puiſſances: à la Haye, le 18 Mai, N. S. 1745.

HAUTS ET PUISSANS SEIGNEURS,

LE roi mon maître, en me permettant de retourner en Angleterre, m'a expreſſément ordonné de renouveller à vos hautes puiſſances les aſſurances les plus fortes de ſon eſtime et de ſon amitié.

Il eſt heureux pour moi qu'une commiſſion ſi honorable m'impoſe un devoir ſi facile.

Interprète des ſentimens d'une amitié ſincère, je n'ai garde d'emprunter les expreſſions flatteuſes, dont une amitié ſimulée a beſoin de ſe parer.

Qu'une politique ruſée employe, pour couvrir ſes deſſeins ambitieux, tout ce que l'art a de plus ſéduiſant. Qu'elle mette tout en œuvre pour ſurprendre votre confiance, ou du moins pour vous endormir dans une funeſte ſécurité; la vraie amitié, telle que celle qui unit le roi mon maître avec vos hautes puiſſances, mépriſe ces artifices, et déteſte ces

 détours.

abhors those indirect means. It is simple, and its language is the same.

The close union of the two nations is neither the effect of some transient views, nor the fruit of accidental conjunctures, but the just consequence of our reciprocal and invariable interests. Nature pointed it out to us, in placing us as she has done; and the uninterrupted experience of almost a century must convince us that our mutual prosperity depends on our union. This truth is so indisputable, that all those who presume to call it in question may justly be considered as our common enemies.

Vicinity is to most nations but a fatal source of jealousy and discord; whereas we have the singular happiness of being neighbours in a manner fit to procure us infinite advantages, without a possibility of any distrust or umbrage arising therefrom, if we do not forget our grand interests.

Such are the king's notions; and, from my own observation, I will take upon me to assure his majesty that your high mightinesses are in the same way of thinking. Who can be ignorant of it? Our allies know it, our enemies feel it. Europe has already often reaped the precious fruits of our harmony. What may she not further expect from it?

The love of liberty, which first laid the foundation of this republic, and has since so often signalized her, this so noble and generous love still unites your strength and your councils to those of the king my master. Actuated by the same spirit, and pursuing the same end, the sole object of your endeavours is to restore and secure public liberty and tranquillity.

What

détours. Elle eſt ſimple, et ſon langage lui reſſemble.

L'étroite union des deux nations n'eſt ni l'effet de quelques vues paſſagères, ni le fruit de quelque ſituation accidentelle; mais une ſuite réfléchie de nos intérêts réciproques et invariables. La nature nous l'a marquée, en nous plaçant comme elle a fait, et une expérience non interrompue de près d'un ſiècle, ne nous permet pas d'ignorer que notre proſpérité mutuelle dépend de notre union. Cette vérité eſt ſi inconteſtable, que nous devons regarder comme nos ennemis communs tous ceux qui prétendent la révoquer en doute.

Le voiſinage n'eſt pour la plûpart des peuples qu'une ſource funeſte de jalouſie ou de diſcorde; au lieu que nous avons le bonheur ſingulier d'être voiſins, d'une manière propre à nous procurer des avantages infinis, ſans qu'il en puiſſe naître ni défiance ni ombrage, ſi nous n'oublions pas nos grands intérêts.

Telles ſont les idées du roi, et ſur ce que j'ai vu de près, j'oſerai l'aſſurer que vos hautes puiſſances penſent de même. Qui peut l'ignorer? Nos alliés le ſavent; nos ennemis le ſentent. L'Europe a déja ſouvent recueilli des fruits précieux de notre harmonie. Que n'en doit-elle pas eſpérer encore?

L'amour de la liberté, qui fonda cette république, et qui l'a déja ſi ſouvent ſignalée depuis; cet amour ſi noble et ſi généreux, unit encore aujourd'hui vos forces et vos conſeils à ceux du roi mon maître. Animés d'un même eſprit, et tendant au même but, vos efforts n'ont pour objet que de rétablir et d'aſſurer la liberté et la tranquillité publique. Quel

 deſſein

What design can be more laudable? What work more worthy of a just and magnanimous zeal?

Pursue, high and mighty lords, that design, with your wonted steadiness and wisdom; continue those efforts, without suffering yourselves to be dismayed; and may heaven crown your undertakings with the success they deserve!

As for what relates to myself, high and mighty lords, nothing could be more pleasing to me than to be charged a second time with the king's orders at this court, especially on an occasion where the business was to concert measures for fulfilling those very engagements which I contributed to form some years ago.

I shall never forget the kind reception I met with, both times, from your high mightinesses; and my gratitude will end but with my days. But if your high mightinesses will condescend to remember me; view me, high and mighty lords, only on the side of my sincere zeal for the common welfare of both nations, my respectful veneration for your government, and, if I may presume to use the expression, my tender attachment to this republic.

CHESTERFIELD.

deſſein plus louable? Quel ouvrage plus digne d'un zèle juſte et magnanime?

Pourſuivez, hauts et puiſſans ſeigneurs, ce deſſein, avec votre fermeté et votre ſageſſe ordinaire! continuez ces efforts, ſans vous laiſſer décourager; et veuille le ciel couronner vos entrepriſes du ſuccès qu'elles méritent!

Pour ce qui me regarde, hauts et puiſſans ſeigneurs, rien ne pouvoit m'arriver de plus flatteur que d'être chargé, pour la ſeconde fois, des ordres du roi auprès de vos hautes puiſſances, ſur-tout dans une occaſion où il s'agiſſoit de concerter les moyens de ſatisfaire aux engagemens que je contribuai à former il y a quelques années.

Je n'oublierai jamais le gracieux accueil dont vos hautes puiſſances m'ont honoré alors et à-préſent; et ma reconnoiſſance ne finira qu'avec mes jours. Mais ſi vos hautes puiſſances daignent ſe ſouvenir de moi, ne m'enviſagez, hauts et puiſſans ſeigneurs, que du côté de mon zéle ſincère pour le bien commun des deux nations; de ma vénération reſpectueuſe pour votre gouvernement, et, ſi j'oſe me ſervir de cette expreſſion, de mon tendre attachement pour cette république.

CHESTERFIELD.

LI.

The ſpeech of his excellency, PHILIP earl of CHESTERFIELD, lord lieutenant-general and general governor of Ireland, to both houſes of parliament, at Dublin, on Tueſday the 8th day of October, 1745.

MY LORDS, AND GENTLEMEN,

I AM honored with the king's commands to meet you here in parliament, and to co-operate with you in whatever may tend to eſtabliſh, or promote, the true intereſt of this kingdom. His majeſty's tender concern for all his ſubjects, and your zeal and duty for him, have mutually been too long experienced for me now to repreſent the one, or recommend the other.

Your own reflections will beſt ſuggeſt to you the advantages you have enjoyed under a ſucceſſion of proteſtant princes, by nature inclined, and by legal authority enabled, to preſerve and protect you; as your own hiſtory, and even the experience of ſome ſtill alive among you, will beſt paint the miſeries and calamities of a people ſcourged, rather than governed, by blind zeal, and lawleſs power.

Theſe conſiderations muſt neceſſarily excite your higheſt indignation at the attempt now carrying on in Scotland, to diſturb his majeſty's government, by a pretender to his crown: one nurſed up in civil and religious error; formed to perſecution and oppreſſion, in the ſeat of ſuperſtition and tyranny; whoſe groundleſs

groundless claim is as contrary to the natural rights of mankind, as to the particular laws and constitutions of these kingdoms; whose only hopes of support are placed in the enemies of the liberties of Europe in general; and whose success would consequently destroy your liberty, your property, and your religion.

But this success is little to be feared, his majesty's subjects giving daily and distinguished proofs of their zeal for the support of his government, and the defence of his person; and a considerable number of national troops, together with six thousand Dutch chearfully furnished to his majesty by his good allies the states general, being now upon their march to Scotland, a force more than sufficient to check the progress, and chastise the insolence, of a rebellious and undisciplined multitude.

The measures that have hitherto been taken, to prevent the growth of popery, have, I hope, had some, and will still have a greater, effect; however, I leave it to your consideration, whether nothing farther can be done, either by new laws, or by the more effectual execution of those in being, to secure this nation against the great number of papists, whose speculative errors would only deserve pity, if their pernicious influence upon civil society did not both require and authorize restraint.

GENTLEMEN OF THE HOUSE OF COMMONS,

I have ordered the proper officers to lay before you the several accounts and estimates; and I have the pleasure to acquaint you, that I have nothing to

ask

ask but the usual and necessary supplies for the support of the establishment.

The king, having thought it necessary, at this time, to send for two battalions more from hence, has ordered that, immediately upon their landing in England, they should be put upon the British establishment: and that the supplemental increase of regular forces, for your defence here, shall be made in the least expensive manner, by additional companies only; after which augmentation, the number of troops will still be within the usual military establishment.

MY LORDS, AND GENTLEMEN,

It is with the greatest satisfaction that I hear of the present flourishing state of the linen manufacture; and I most earnestly recommend to you the care and improvement of so valuable a branch of your trade. Let not its prosperity produce negligence; and let it never be supposed to be brought to its utmost extent and perfection. Trade has always been the support of all nations, and the principal care of the wisest.

I persuade myself that the business of this session will be carried on with that temper and unanimity, which a true and unbiassed regard for the public naturally produces, and which the present state of affairs more particularly demands. For my own part, I make no professions; you will, you ought to judge of me only by my actions.

LII.

His excellency the earl of CHESTERFIELD's ſpeech to both houſes of parliament at Dublin, on Friday April 11, 1746.

MY LORDS, AND GENTLEMEN,

THE buſineſs of the ſeſſion being now concluded, I believe you cannot be unwilling to return to your reſpective counties, as you muſt be ſenſible that the many good laws which you have paſſed will receive additional weight by your authority in executing, and by your example in obſerving, them.

The almoſt unprecedented temper and unanimity with which you have carried on the public buſineſs, your unſhaken fidelity to the king, your inviolable attachment to the preſent happy conſtitution, and your juſt indignation at the attempts lately made to ſubvert it, will advantageouſly diſtinguiſh this ſeſſion in the journals of parliament; and the concurrent zeal and active loyalty of all his majeſty's proteſtant ſubjects, of all denominations, throughout this kingdom, prove at once how ſenſible and how deſerving they are of his care and protection. Even thoſe deluded people, who ſcarcely acknowledge his government, ſeem, by their conduct, tacitly to have confeſſed the advantages they enjoy under it. At my return to his majeſty's preſence, I ſhall not fail moſt faithfully to report theſe truths, ſince the moſt faith-

ful

ful will be, at the same time, the most favourable representation.

The rebellion, which rather disturbed than endangered the king's government, has been defeated, though not yet totally suppressed; but as those flagitious parricides who were abandoned enough to avow, and desperate enough to engage in, the cause of popery and tyranny, have already been repulsed and pursued, by the valour and activity of his royal highness the duke, there is the strongest reason to believe that he will soon complete the work which he has so gloriously begun, and restore the tranquillity of the kingdom. This attempt, therefore, to shake his majesty's throne, will serve to establish it the more firmly, since all Europe must know the unanimous zeal and affection of his subjects for the defence and support of his person and government; and those hopes are at last extinguished, with which the pretender has so long flattered, and, as it now appears, deceived himself. Even the manner in which he has been assisted by those powers who encouraged him to the attempt, must convince him that he has now been, what he ever will be, only the occasional tool of their politics, not the real object of their care.

GENTLEMEN OF THE HOUSE OF COMMONS,

I have the king's commands to thank you, in his name, for the unanimity and dispatch with which you have granted the necessary supplies for the support of the establishment; you may depend upon their being applied with the utmost exactness and frugality.

I must

I must not omit my own acknowledgments for the particular confidence you have placed in me, by leaving to my care and management the great sum that you voluntarily voted for national arms, and for the fortifying the harbour of Corke. The considerable saving which will appear upon those, as well in the interest upon the loan, as in the application of the principal, will, I hope, prove that I have been truly sensible of the trust reposed in me.

The assistance which you have given to the protestant charter schools, is a most prudent, as well as a most compassionate, charity; and I do very earnestly recommend to your constant protection and encouragement that excellent institution, by which such a considerable number of unhappy children are annually rescued from the misery that always, and the guilt that commonly accompanies, uninstructed poverty and idleness.

MY LORDS, AND GENTLEMEN,

Though Great Britain has, in the course of this century, been often molested by insurrections at home, and invasions from abroad, this kingdom has happily, and deservedly, enjoyed that uninterrupted tranquillity, which trade and manufactures, arts and sciences, require for their improvement and perfection. Nature too has been peculiarly favourable to this country, whose temperate climate and fruitful soil do invite, and would reward, care and industry. Let me, therefore, most seriously recommend to you, in your private as well as in your public capacities, the utmost attention to those important objects, which at once enrich, ſtrengthen, and adorn, a nation. They will flouriſh wherever they are cultivated; and they are always beſt cultivated by the indulgence, the encouragement, and above all by the example, of perſons of ſuperior rank.

I cannot conclude, without repeating my heartieſt thanks to you for your kind addreſſes, in which you expreſs your approbation of my conduct. My duty to the king, who wiſhes the intereſt and happineſs of all his ſubjects, called for my utmoſt endeavours to promote yours; and my inclinations conſpired with my duty. Theſe ſentiments ſhall, I aſſure you, be the only motives of all my actions, of which your intereſt muſt conſequently be the only object.

LIII.

LIII.

A short character of the president de MONTESQUIEU, by lord CHESTERFIELD *.

ON the tenth of this month (February 1755), died at Paris, universally and sincerely regretted, Charles Secondat, baron de Montesquieu, and *president à mortier* of the parliament at Bourdeaux. His virtues did honor to human nature; his writings, justice. A friend to mankind, he asserted their undoubted and inalienable rights with freedom, even in his own country, whose prejudices in matters of religion and government he had long lamented, and endeavoured, not without some success, to remove. He well knew, and justly admired, the happy constitution of this country, where fixed and known laws equally restrain monarchy from tyranny, and liberty from licentiousness. His works will illustrate his name, and survive him as long as right reason, moral obligation, and the true spirit of laws, shall be understood, respected, and maintained †.

* This was sent from Bath by lord Chesterfield, on hearing of the death of his friend. It was inserted in the London Evening-Post, but without the name of the author. See *Memoirs*, Sect. VI.

† On the death of the celebrated Mr. de Fontenelle next year, lord Chesterfield likewise sent from Bath the following short account, to be inserted in the same paper. The two nations were then at war with each other. "Letters by this day's Flanders mail bring advice, that, on the 9th instant, died at Paris, aged 99 years, 11 months, and 12 days, Mr. Bernard le Bowier de Fontenelle, dean [*doyen* in French means the oldest member] of the French academy, and of the royal academies of *belles-lettres* and of sciences, a member of the royal society of London, and of the royal academy at Berlin. The high reputation he has justly acquired by his writings renders any encomium superfluous."

LIV.

A letter from the earl of CHESTERFIELD to Mr. de BOUGAINVILLE *, read in the academy of inſcriptions and belles lettres, on Tueſday, June 17, 1755.

SIR,

I WAS both aſtoniſhed and flattered when your brother told me I might, if I choſe it, be admitted into the moſt reſpectable and moſt reſpected ſociety in Europe. Dazzled at firſt ſight with ſo flattering an object, and led away by the deluſions of ſelf-love, I gave myſelf up to the pleaſing idea. I already aſpired after the honor, without once conſidering whether I was qualified for it. Reflection followed; and modeſty reſtrained me. I carefully examined myſelf, in hopes of finding ſome ſpecious claims, or at leaſt ſome pretence, that might in ſome meaſure juſtify your good opinion of me; but alas! Sir, that inquiry has been very mortifying to me. I found that my younger years had been waſted in diſſipation and pleaſure, which ſcarce allowed me time ſo much as to think of the ſciences; and that, my riper years having been wholly devoted to buſineſs, I had never been at leiſure to cultivate them. The ſtudy of the ſciences would require the whole, and more than the whole, of a man's life; would it then be conſiſtent with decency to enter upon it at threeſcore? eſpecially at this diſtance, where I can have no opportunity of

* Secretary to the academy, and brother to the gentleman who has made himſelf ſo conſpicuous by ſeveral navigations, and eſpecially his voyage about the world.

improving

LIV.

Lettre de mylord C[illegible]STERFIELD à Mr. de BOUGAINVILLE *, lue à l'académie des inscriptions et belles-lettres, le mardi 17 Juin, 1755.

MONSIEUR,

JE fus également étonné et flatté quand monsieur votre frère me dit de votre part qu'il ne tiendroit qu'à moi d'être aggrégé au corps le plus respectable et le plus respecté de l'Europe. Ebloui d'abord par l'éclat d'un objet si flatteur, et séduit par les illusions de l'amour-propre, je me livrai à une si douce idée : j'aspirois déjà à cet honneur, sans songer seulement si j'en étois digne. Mais la réflexion suivit, et la pudeur me retint. Je m'examinai soigneusement, dans l'espérance de trouver quelques droits un peu spécieux, ou du moins quelques prétentions, qui pussent en quelque façon justifier votre prévention en ma faveur ; mais hélas ! monsieur, cette recherche m'a été bien humiliante ; j'ai trouvé que ma jeunesse, prodiguée dans la dissipation et les plaisirs, m'avoit à peine permis de penser seulement aux sciences, et que mon âge plus avancé, occupé entiérement par les affaires, ne m'avoit pas accordé le loisir de les cultiver. Les sciences demandent non-seulement toute la vie, mais encore bien plus que toute la vie de l'homme. La bienséance souffrira-t-elle donc qu'un sexagenaire se présente pour y commencer son noviciat ? sur-tout privé comme il l'est par l'éloignement des occasions de

improving by the instructions and example of the learned members of that illustrious body. So circumstanced, I am at a loss what to do. I think I ought not to sollicit an honor for which I am so unqualified; and yet, I must confess, I cannot help ardently wishing for it. I leave it entirely to you. The interests of the society must be dear to you, who have been so eminently distinguished by it. I am not to suppose you would betray them, in return for the regard and esteem with which I have the honor to be, &c.

(Signed,)

CHESTERFIELD.

LV.

A letter of thanks from the earl of CHESTERFIELD, on his being admitted a free foreign member of the academy; read at the meeting, on Friday, August 8, 1755.

GENTLEMEN,

THE mind is naturally prepared for honors or mortifications, from a consciousness of its own deserts; but when a man is undeservedly or unexpectedly raised to the one, or exposed to the other, the effect is a confused sensation, not to be expressed, which at once stuns the soul, and takes away all power of utterance, whether of gratitude or complaint.

This sensation, gentlemen, is what I now experience. The honor of being associated to one of the most illustrious

profiter des instructions, et de se former sur les modèles des illustres membres d'un si illustre corps. Que dois-je donc faire dans ces circonstances? Il ne me paroît pas permis de postuler un honneur que je mérite si peu, mais en même tems j'avoue qu'il m'est impossible de ne le pas ardemment desirer. Je m'en remets à vous entiérement; les intérêts de l'académie doivent vous être chers; elle a reconnu et distingué votre mérite; je ne dois pas supposer que vous vouliez les trahir en considération du zèle et de l'estime avec lesquels j'ai l'honneur d'être, &c.

(*Signé*,)

CHESTERFIELD.

LV.

Lettre de remerciment de mylord CHESTERFIELD, reçu au nombre des académiciens libres étrangers, lue dans la séance du vendredi 8 Août 1755.

MESSIEURS,

ON se trouve naturellement préparé aux honneurs et aux disgraces, lorsqu'on sent qu'on en est digne; mais lorsque, sans les mériter, ou sans avoir pû les attendre, on se voit élevé aux uns, ou exposé aux autres, leur effet est un sentiment confus qui ne peut s'exprimer; il étourdit l'ame, et étouffe également la voix de la reconnoissance ou de la plainte.

Ce sentiment, messieurs, vous me le faites éprouver. L'association que m'accorde une des plus illustres

lustrious academies in Europe, amazes and confounds me. I am equally at a loss to account for the motives of your choice, and to find expressions adequate to my gratitude.

In vain have I recourse to the deceits of self-love. They can never make me forget the degree of merit which might justify your preference, nor prevent my fears that this may be thought to be the first error you have ever been guilty of. To what principle is it reducible, that you should confer such an honor on a foreigner, who is separated from you, not only by the sea, but still more so by the want of those talents that so eminently distinguish you? Is it owing to the natural politeness of your nation, which manifests itself to, or rather diffuses itself over, all others? No, gentlemen; distance of place has been favourable to me. Fame, that messenger, who never keeps within the bounds of strict truth, who magnifies every object, and seems to gather strength in proportion to the space she measures, has doubtless transformed my love of literature into actual knowledge, and your propensity to indulgence has inclined you to believe her.

Our taste is formed in the early years of our life. I owed mine to the tincture I then received of those pleasing attainments, which adorn every station, and embellish every period of life. From my heart I both loved and honored them, but it was my misfortune to want opportunities for making a sufficient progress in them. Too much addicted to pleasure in my younger years, and hurried away, in riper age, by the torrent of public affairs, that time has glided away too swiftly, which would have been better employed

académies de l'Europe, m'étonne et me confond. Quels furent les motifs de votre choix? Je les cherche, et les trouve aussi peu que des expressions proportionnées à ma reconnoissance.

L'amour-propre me prête-t-il ses illusions? Elles ne sauroient me faire oublier le degré de mérite qui pourroit justifier votre préférence, ni m'empêcher de craindre que ce choix ne paroisse votre premiere erreur. A quel principe un étranger que la mer, moins encore que les talens qui vous distinguent, a séparé de vous, pourroit-il devoir un tel honneur? Seroit-ce à cette politesse si naturelle à votre nation, qui se manifeste, ou plûtôt qui se répand sur toutes les autres? Non, messieurs, l'éloignement m'a été favorable. La renommée, cette messagère qui toujours manque d'exactitude, et souvent de fidélité, qui grossit également tous les objets, et qui semble acquérir des forces à proportion du chemin qu'elle parcourt, aura transformé en connoissance, mon amour pour les belles-lettres, et disposés comme vous l'êtes à l'indulgence, sans doute vous l'en avez trop crue.

Les premières années de la vie décident de nos goûts. J'ai dû les miens à la teinture que je reçus alors de ces connoissances aimables qui relèvent tous les états, et qui embellissent tous les âges. Mon cœur les chérit et les respecta, mais j'eus le malheur de ne pouvoir suffisamment les cultiver. Trop dissipé dans ma jeunesse, entrainé, dans l'âge mûr, par le torrent des affaires publiques, j'ai vu s'écouler, avec trop de rapidité, un tems que les lettres auroient mieux rempli.

 Mon

ployed in literary improvements. All I could do was to be a well-wisher to them, and I have been a warm one. Why am I compelled to confess that the altars I have raised to literature were, in some measure, like that of Athens, dedicated *to the unknown God!*

Restored to myself, though late, I seek in these studies a resource for old age, and a rational amusement for retirement. These I find in your memoirs, which afford me both instruction and pleasure. There the genius and the works of antiquity are rescued from oblivion, explained, and brought within my reach, and, I will venture to add, emulated by your own.

The brightest days of literary societies are preceded by a faint dawn; but your infancy was that of a body that feels what it is one day to be. It was the infancy of Hercules. At a time when the academy seemed wholly intent upon conferring immortality on the great monarch who had given it being, she was extending her views, and preparing her labors. She took a retrospective survey of past ages, and stood forth to future ages as a repository for great actions, and a model of taste. So successful was this institution in promoting genius and talents, that, in a very few years, it was more difficult to limit the number of places than to fill them properly.

But now that my name is to appear in your list, have we not room to be apprehensive of an unfavourable revolution? and, by admitting me into your society, do you not authorize the complaints that are made concerning the degeneracy of the times? These complaints, gentlemen, are the common-place of pride,

Mon zèle fut tout ce que je pus leur donner, et ce zèle fut vif. Pourquoi me vois-je obligé de reconnoître que les autels qu'il lui éleva furent, peut-être, à l'exemple de celui d'Athènes, consacré *à la divinité inconnue ?*

Revenu, quoique trop tard, à moi-même, je cherche dans les lettres des ressources pour l'âge, des agrémens pour la retraite. Vos mémoires me les fournissent; j'y puise des instructions et des plaisirs; j'y trouve le génie et les ouvrages de la belle antiquité arrachés de l'oubli, développés, mis à ma portée, et je ne crains point d'ajouter, égalés par les vôtres.

Les jours les plus brillans des sociétés littéraries sont ordinairement dévancés par une foible aurore; mais votre enfance fut celle d'un corps qui sent ce qu'il doit être un jour. C'étoit l'enfance d'Hercule. Dans le tems que l'académie sembloit ne s'occuper que du soin de donner l'immortalité au grand monarque qui lui donnoit l'existence, elle étendoit toujours ses vues, et préparoit ses travaux. Elle jettoit ses regards sur les siècles passés, et s'annonçoit aux siècles futurs, comme chargée du dépôt des grandes actions, et des modèles du goût. Une heureuse fécondité multiplia en si peu d'années les génies et les talens, que bientôt il devint plus difficile de limiter le nombre des places que de les bien remplir.

Mais à présent que mon nom va paroître sur votre liste, n'y a-t-il pas lieu de craindre une révolution peu avantageuse; et n'autorisez-vous pas, en me faisant entrer dans votre corps, les plaintes qu'on fait que notre siècle dégénere ? Ces plaintes, messieurs, sont le

pride, envy, and ill-nature; the human heart indulges them with a secret complacency. It is easier to forgive a past and remote superiority, than to endure cotemporary, and, if I may be allowed the expression, contiguous merit. Your choice may be blamed, but will never be imputed to necessity. Such a suspicion would be contradicted by too many eminent men, formed upon your model in your own country. It will only be said that, as you can receive no additional lustre, you have condescended to reflect some part of yours upon me.

I have the honor to be, &c.

(Signed,)

CHESTERFIELD.

London, July 31, 1755.

lieu commun de l'orgueil, de l'envie, et de la malignité ; le cœur humain s'y livre avec complaisance ; il est plus facile pour lui de pardonner une supériorité passée, et perdue dans l'éloignement, que de souffrir un mérite contemporain, et si j'ose hasarder ce mot, contigu. On pourra blâmer votre choix, mais on ne l'attribuera jamais à la nécessité. Trop de savans illustres, formés à votre modèle dans votre propre patrie, démentiroient un tel soupçon. On dira simplement que, ne pouvant recevoir un nouveau lustre, vous avez daigné me communiquer une partie du vôtre.

J'ai l'honneur d'être, &c.

(Signé,)

CHESTERFIELD.

A Londres, ce 31 Juillet, 1755.

LVI.

LVI.

Preface to Love Elegies, by WILLIAM HAMMOND Esquire, published in 1742 *.

THE following elegies were wrote by a young gentleman lately dead, and justly lamented.

As he had never declared his intentions concerning their publication, a friend of his, into whose hands they fell, determined to publish them, in the persuasion that they would neither be unwelcome to the public, nor injurious to the memory of their author. The reader must decide, whether this determination was the result of just judgment or partial friendship; for the editor feels, and avows so much of the latter, that he gives up all pretensions to the former.

The author composed them ten years ago, before he was two-and-twenty years old; an age, when fancy and imagination commonly riot, at the expence of judgment and correctness, neither of which seem wanting here. But, sincere in his love as in his friendship, he wrote to his mistresses, as he spoke to his friends, nothing but the true genuine sentiments of his heart; he sate down to write what he thought, not to think what he should write; it was nature and sentiment only that dictated to a real mistress, not

* See Memoirs of lord Chesterfield under that year. This preface, which fell from his pen, is a noble monument of his feelings, his taste, and the love which he bore to his country; a sentiment as distant from modern patriotism, as those that usurp that qualification are from the noble author.

youthful

youthful and poetic fancy, to an imaginary one. Elegy therefore ſpeaks here her own, proper, native language, the unaffected plaintive language of the tender paſſions; the true elegiac dignity and ſimplicity are preſerved, and united; the one without pride, the other without meanneſs. Tibullus ſeems to have been the model our author judiciouſly preferred to Ovid; the former writing directly from the heart, to the heart; the latter too often yielding and addreſſing himſelf to the imagination.

The undiſſipated youth of the author allowed him time to apply himſelf to the beſt maſters, the antients, and his parts enabled him to make the beſt uſe of them; for, upon thoſe great models of ſolid ſenſe and virtue, he formed not only his genius, but his heart, both well prepared by nature to adopt, and adorn the reſemblance. He admired that juſtneſs, that noble ſimplicity of thought, and expreſſion, which have diſtinguiſhed and preſerved their writings to this day; but he revered that love of their country, that contempt of riches, that ſacredneſs of friendſhip, and all thoſe heroic and ſocial virtues, which marked them out as the objects of the veneration, though not the imitation, of ſucceeding ages; and he looked back with a kind of religious awe and delight, upon thoſe glorious and happy times of Greece and Rome, when wiſdom, virtue, and liberty, formed the only triumvirates, ere luxury invited corruption to taint, or corruption introduced ſlavery to deſtroy, all public and private virtues. In theſe ſentiments he lived, and would have lived even in theſe times: in theſe ſentiments he died — but in

theſe

these times too — *Ut non erepta à diis immortalibus vita, sed donata mors esse videatur.*

LVII.

The Character of RICHARD, Earl of Scarborough, August 29, 1759 *.

IN drawing the character of lord Scarborough, I will be strictly upon my guard against the partiality of that intimate and unreserved friendship, in which we lived for more than twenty years; to which friendship, as well as to the public notoriety of it, I owe much more than my pride will let my gratitude own. If this may be suspected to have biassed my judgment, it must, at the same time, be allowed to have informed it; for the most secret movements of his soul were, without disguise, communicated to me only. However, I will rather lower than heighten the colouring; I will mark the shades, and draw a credible rather than an exact likeness.

He had a very good person, rather above the middle size; a handsome face, and, when he was chearful, the most engaging countenance imaginable; when grave, which he was oftenest, the most respectable one. He had in the highest degree the air,

* I received this piece from lady Chesterfield. Indeed it wants no marks of authenticity. The noble author's mind and heart are painted in it in the liveliest manner; and he who can read it without sharing his feelings must have a soul very different from his.

manners

manners and addreſs of a man of quality, politeneſs with eaſe, and dignity without pride.

Bred in camps and courts, it cannot be ſuppoſed that he was untainted with the faſhionable vices of theſe warm climates; but (if I may be allowed the expreſſion) he dignified them, inſtead of their degrading him into any mean or indecent action. He had a good degree of claſſical, and a great one of modern, knowledge; with a juſt, and, at the ſame time, a delicate taſte.

In his common expences he was liberal within bounds; but in his charities and bounties he had none. I have known them put him to ſome preſent inconveniencies.

He was a ſtrong, but not an eloquent or florid ſpeaker in parliament. He ſpoke ſo unaffectedly the honeſt dictates of his heart, that truth and virtue, which never want, and ſeldom wear, ornaments, ſeemed only to borrow his voice. This gave ſuch an aſtoniſhing weight to all he ſaid, that he more than once carried an unwilling majority after him. Such is the authority of unſuſpected virtue, that it will ſometimes ſhame vice into decency at leaſt.

He was not only offered, but preſſed to accept, the poſt of ſecretary of ſtate; but he conſtantly refuſed it. I once tried to perſuade him to accept it; but he told me, that both the natural warmth and melancholy of his temper made him unfit for it; and that moreover he knew very well that, in thoſe miniſterial employments, the courſe of buſineſs made it neceſſary to do many hard things, and ſome unjuſt ones, which could only be authoriſed by the jeſuitical

ſuitical caſuiſtry of the direction of the intention; a doctrine which he ſaid he could not poſſibly adopt. Whether he was the firſt that ever made that objection, I cannot affirm; but I ſuſpect that he will be the laſt.

He was a true conſtitutional, and yet practicable patriot; a ſincere lover and a zealous aſſerter of the natural, the civil, and the religious rights of his country. But he would not quarrel with the crown, for ſome ſlight ſtretches of the prerogative; nor with the people, for ſome unwary ebullitions of liberty; nor with any one, for a difference of opinion in ſpeculative points. He conſidered the conſtitution in the aggregate, and only watched that no one part of it ſhould preponderate too much.

His moral character was ſo pure, that if one may ſay of that imperfect creature man, what a celebrated hiſtorian ſays of Scipio, *nil non laudandum aut dixit, aut fecit, aut ſenſit*; I ſincerely think, (I had almoſt ſaid I know) one might ſay it with great truth of him, one ſingle inſtance excepted, which ſhall be mentioned.

He joined to the nobleſt and ſtricteſt principles of honor and generoſity the tendereſt ſentiments of benevolence and compaſſion; and as he was naturally warm, he could not even hear of an injuſtice or a baſeneſs, without a ſudden indignation, nor of the misfortunes or miſeries of a fellow creature, without melting into ſoftneſs, and endeavouring to relieve them. This part of his character was ſo univerſally known, that our beſt and moſt ſatyrical Engliſh poet ſays;

When

When I confeſs, there is who feels for fame,
And melts to goodneſs, Scarb'rough need I name?

He had not the leaſt pride of birth and rank, that common narrow notion of little minds, that wretched miſtaken ſuccedaneum of merit; but he was jealous to anxiety of his character, as all men are who deſerve a good one. And ſuch was his diffidence upon that ſubject, that he never could be perſuaded that mankind really thought of him as they did. For ſurely never man had a higher reputation, and never man enjoyed a more univerſal eſteem. Even knaves reſpected him; and fools thought they loved him. If he had any enemies (for I proteſt I never knew one), they could only be ſuch as were weary of always hearing of Ariſtides the Juſt.

He was too ſubject to ſudden guſts of paſſion, but they never hurried him into any illiberal or indecent expreſſion or action; ſo invincibly habitual to him were good-nature and good-manners. But, if ever any word happened to fall from him in warmth, which upon ſubſequent reflection he himſelf thought too ſtrong, he was never eaſy till he had made more than a ſufficient atonement for it.

He had a moſt unfortunate, I will call it a moſt fatal kind of melancholy in his nature, which often made him both abſent and ſilent in company, but never moroſe or ſour. At other times he was a chearful and agreeable companion; but, conſcious that he was not always ſo, he avoided company too much, and was too often alone, giving way to a train of gloomy reflexions.

His

His conſtitution, which was never robuſt, broke rapidly at the latter end of his life. He had two ſevere ſtrokes of apoplexy or palſy, which conſiderably affected his body and his mind.

I deſire that this may not be looked upon as a full and finiſhed character, writ for the ſake of writing it; but as my ſolemn depoſit of the truth to the beſt of my knowledge. I owed this ſmall tribute of juſtice, ſuch as it is, to the memory of the beſt man I ever knew, and of the deareſt friend I ever had.

END OF THE SECOND VOLUME.

INDEX

TO THE

MISCELLANEOUS PIECES.

A.

B.

C.

the connections between England and Hanover, 146—151. His miſcellanies in a periodical paper called Old England, or The Conſtitutional Journal, 152—166. His cenſures of the miniſtry, 152—160. His account of the method of conducting the paper, 160—166. His writings in a periodical paper called The World, 166—319. His account of a country gentleman going to Paris with his family, 166—177. His remarks on noſtrums and ſpecifics, 177—180. His account of a ſingular method of ſhort writing, 181—185. Expoſes the danger of reading romances, 186—191. His remarks on the little benefit accruing to Engliſhmen from their travels, 191—198. His ironical commendation of the preſent times, 198—205. His account of the members of a club, 206—213. His deſcription of a club-dinner, 213—219. His reflection on his entertainment there, 220—226. His eſſay on the Italian opera, 226—232. His remarks on the neceſſity of an Engliſh dictionary, and his recommendation of doctor Johnſon's, 232—238. His humorous obſervations on the Engliſh language, 238—244. His remarks on the prevailing cuſtom among ladies of painting, 244—250. His account of the reception of the paper, 251—256. His remarks on the utility of prejudices, 257—261. His paper on duelling, 261—268. His paper on the pride of birth, 268—273. His paper on affectation, 274—278. His advice to the ladies on their return into the country, 279—284. His eſſay on civility and good-breeding, 284—289. His account of people of faſhion, 289—299. His

D.

F.

G.

H.

H.

I.

L.

M.

N.

O.

P.

S.

S.

T.

W.

END OF THE SECOND VOLUME.

www.ingramcontent.com/pod-product-compliance
Lightning Source LLC
Chambersburg PA
CBHW032313280326
41932CB00009B/802

* 9 7 8 3 7 4 4 7 1 5 7 0 6 *